MEASURING
THE MASTER RACE

Measuring the Master Race

Physical Anthropology in Norway
1890-1945

Jon Røyne Kyllingstad

OpenBook Publishers

ISBN Paperback: 978-1-909254-54-1
ISBN Hardback: 978-1-909254-55-8
ISBN Digital (PDF): 978-1-909254-56-5
ISBN Digital ebook (epub): 978-1-909254-57-2
ISBN Digital ebook (mobi): 978-1-909254-58-9
DOI: 10.11647/OBP.0051

Cover image: Measurement of upper arm length as demonstrated in Rudolf Martin, *Lehrbuch der Anthropologie*, p. 163. Image in the public domain.

All paper used by Open Book Publishers is SFI (Sustainable Forestry Initiative) and PEFC (Programme for the Endorsement of Forest Certification Schemes) Certified.

Printed in the United Kingdom and United States by Lightning Source for Open Book Publishers (Cambridge, UK).

Contents

List of Illustrations

Foreword

The work that resulted in this book began with a master's thesis submitted to the Department of History at the University of Oslo in the spring of 2001. This was later rewritten into the book *Kortskaller og langskaller* (*Short Skulls and Long Skulls*), published in Norwegian in 2004 and now reworked and expanded into this English edition.

While working with the first version of the book I was affiliated to the Centre for Technology, Innovation and Culture (the TIK centre), the Department of Archaeology, Conservation and History and the Forum for University History at the University of Oslo. I also spent some brief, but important periods of time in the Department of Anatomy at the University of Oslo, where Anatomy Professor Per Holck gave me access to the anthropological book collection and database.

The writing and publication of *Kortskaller og langskaller* received financial support from the Norwegian Non-Fiction Writers and Translators Organisation, the TIK Centre, the Forum for University History, the Norwegian Historical Association and the Fritt Ord Foundation. The translation and publication of the English edition is financially supported by NORLA (the Norwegian Literature Abroad Foundation) and by Norsk Teknisk Museum, Norway's national museum for science, technology and medicine.

It was Erika Hagelberg who first came up with the idea of an English version. She also helped me approach potential publishers and has given invaluable advice, help and criticism during the process of rewriting the book for a non-Norwegian audience.

This book is not an English translation of the original Norwegian work. Most of it has been thoroughly rewritten for a new audience and to incorporate new material and new perspectives. Since the publication of *Kortskaller og langskaller*, I have done more research on topics related to the history of Norwegian physical anthropology and racial science. My doctoral thesis *Menneskeåndens universalitet* (*The Psychological Unity of Humanity*) dealt with the political context and institutional framework of Norwegian physical anthropology and adjacent disciplines, such as archaeology. After receiving my doctoral degree, I was involved in writing a multi-volume work on the history of the University of Oslo. This gave me new insight into the institutions under whose auspices physical anthropological research was undertaken. Insights from both the doctoral work and the university history project are incorporated into this book.

A number of people over the years have contributed their ideas, constructive criticism, professional and psychological support, among them Trond Haug, Christine Myrvang, Kjartan Soltvedt, Tore Tennøe, Jorunn Sem Fure, Knut Kjeldstadli, John Peter Collett, Ole Anders Røberg, Per Haave, Hege Roll-Hansen, Ketil Gjølme Andersen, Anne Vaalund, Nils Roll-Hansen, Ingvild Kyllingstad, Ageliki Lefkaditou and Ottar Dahl. I am also very grateful to Tim Challmann for his invaluable linguistic help with this English-language edition. I am particularly indebted to Robert Marc Friedman at the IAKH (UiO), who was my supervisor for many years; to Torben Hviid Nielsen, Arve Monsen and Fredrik Thue who, through critical reading and thoughtful feedback, have contributed immensely to my work; and last but not least to Erika Hagelberg, without whom this book would never have seen the light of day.

Finally, I am greatly indebted to Ragne, Tora and Ingvild, who have had the demanding task of sharing a family life with the author during all these years.

Jon Røyne Kyllingstad
Oslo, 6 November 2014

Introduction

The notion of a Germanic or Nordic race was a linchpin of Nazi ideology. The Nazis believed that this 'superior race' had the right to extend their *Lebensraum* (living space) at the expense of others, and they put this idea into practice with brutal efficiency. It was not the Nazis, however, who invented the concept of a superior Nordic-Germanic race. In the early twentieth century, it was common practice to rank humanity into inferior and superior races, and many saw the Nordic-Germanic race as the pinnacle of humankind. This belief was particularly widespread in nations that were considered to be of Germanic origin, such as the U.S., England, Germany and the Scandinavian countries. In all these countries there were racial ideologues who held that humankind's progress would come to a halt unless the presumed master race was protected from racial mixing and allowed to expand at the expense of 'inferior' races.

One important reason why these ideas were taken seriously by so many was that they claimed foundation in scientific fact. For centuries, European scholars believed that the Germanic-speaking nations of northern Europe could trace their roots back to the Germanic tribes described in ancient Roman sources. During the nineteenth century this historical notion of a Germanic people was transformed into a scientific concept of race. In numerous scientific publications, the Germanics were defined as a distinct type of human being, one characterised by a specific set of inheritable bodily traits such as blond hair, blue eyes, a tall stature and an elongated head shape. While this race was commonly referred to as 'Germanic' throughout the nineteenth century, after the turn of the twentieth the label 'Nordic' was usually favoured.

Scandinavia was generally seen as the heartland and cradle of the Nordic race. In contrast to the region's peripheral geographical and political position, therefore, Scandinavia was of primary importance in the

http://dx.doi.org/10.11647/OBP.0051.11

worldview of those advocating Nordic racial supremacy, especially German nationalists including the Nazis, who proved to be deeply fascinated by all things Scandinavian. Among Scandinavians themselves, the idea of Nordic racial superiority had a significant impact upon notions of national identity, and in the nineteenth and early twentieth centuries Scandinavian scholars played an important role in creating and perpetuating the concept of a Nordic race. By imbuing the idea of the Nordic race with scientific legitimacy, these scholars also advanced its international recognition and acceptance.

Measuring the Master Race focuses on the involvement of Norwegian academics in the development of a scientific concept of the Nordic race. The book charts the emergence of this idea and its scientific credibility in Norway during the nineteenth century. Individual chapters explore the shifting theories and preconceptions upon which the concept was based, how it affected national narratives and notions of national identity, and how it finally lost academic credibility in Norway during the years leading up to World War II.

From the late nineteenth century and into the interwar years, Norwegian scientists undertook numerous studies of the racial composition and biological history of Norwegians. They conducted extensive surveys of the living national population, gathering data on bodily traits such as arm span, height and head shape, and comparing these measurements with similar data obtained from anatomical studies of human bones from ancient graves. Working with these comparisons, scientists developed theories about prehistoric migrations, the mixing and settlement of various primordial races, and the eventual rise of the Norwegian people. Although these researchers voiced different ideas concerning the origin and racial composition of the national population, they all agreed on the 'fact' that the Norwegian people belonged to the ancient blue-eyed, long-skulled and tall Nordic race.

In retrospect, as the notion of racial superiority has lost scientific and political credibility, and the very concept of race itself has become highly controversial, these research activities may seem perplexing and preposterous. No present-day scientists claim credibility for pre-war traditions of racial science, and racial classifications based on skull measurements appear to be a flawed, racist, pseudo-scientific relic of the past. Nevertheless, the Norwegian scholars who set out to explore the racial roots of the nation with the help of calipers and rulers were actually mainstream scientists operating within the established scientific discipline of physical anthropology and working alongside colleagues from all over the Western world. Driven by the aim of charting human biological diversity and evolutionary history, physical anthropologists observed, measured and compared the exterior features of human bodies, and then used this data to classify humans into races in much the same way as zoologists classified animals into families, genera and species.

At the peak of physical anthropology's popularity, academics working in this discipline were considered to be the leading experts on race. If one wished to speak authoritatively about race, it was a great advantage to be an anthropologist or at least to be able to invoke the support of anthropological expertise. In order to understand how the concept of a superior Nordic race gained and lost scientific credibility, therefore, it is necessary to explore how physical anthropology became a discipline of recognised authority on racial issues. Moreover, it is important to study the changing ways that anthropologists have drawn the boundaries between science and non-science in their field of research, and to attempt to understand how this has affected the scientific legitimacy of the concept of a Nordic race. How can we explain that for a long period the Nordic race was considered to be a real entity that physical anthropologists could delineate, identify and describe scientifically? How and why did that same concept subsequently come to be perceived as a dubious ideological notion based on weak evidence and pseudo-scientific reasoning? This book helps to shed light on these questions by examining the activities of Norwegian anthropologists in their national and international historical contexts.

The history of physical anthropology was characterised by processes that took place both within nations and across borders. Anthropologists in Western Europe operated on the international stage: they were connected with each other through personal and professional networks, and they presented their research findings in anthropological journals, textbooks and conferences aimed at international academic audiences. The actual research, however, was usually carried out within a national context, was often financed by national funding bodies and conducted by national research institutions, and had the principal aim of studying the racial composition and history of the national or colonial population. Thus, although the history of physical anthropology was affected by the interplay of national, transnational and international processes and contexts, the scope, subject matter and societal role of physical anthropology varied between nations. Hence the discipline's development in one country was related, but not necessarily identical, to its development in other national contexts. Facts and viewpoints that were considered scientifically valid among anthropologists in one country, for example, might elsewhere be deemed controversial or unacceptable. In the case of Norway, the rise and eventual fall of the concept of the Nordic master race was affected but not determined by shifts in its status within the international scientific world.

In order to understand these processes it is important to bear in mind the unique character of academic life in a small country like Norway. The Norwegian 'community' of professional anthropologists never amounted to more than three or four people, and these individuals had to go abroad to undertake training, obtain research materials, publish their research, attend conferences and participate in scientific debates. Simply because they came from a small country, Norwegian anthropologists had a particularly strong international orientation, and therefore the history of Norwegian physical anthropology and its engagement with the idea of a Nordic race must be understood in an international context. This book is not, however, a systematic comparative study, nor is it a general account of the international history of physical anthropology. Instead, *Measuring the Master Race* limits itself to exploring important historical connections between physical anthropology, racial science and the concept of a Nordic race in Norway and in other countries with links to the Norwegian academic community.

Since there were so few Norwegian anthropologists, they worked closely with Norwegian colleagues in related disciplines. The anthropological exploration of the nation's racial identity and origin was strongly interconnected with research being carried out in other disciplines relating to Norway's history and culture (e.g. archaeology, philology, history). And all this research was entwined with ongoing academic, political and cultural tugs-of-war over Norwegian national identity. *Measuring the Master Race* traces some of these interconnections. The book examines how physical anthropological race theories, and the idea of a Nordic master race in particular, shaped the national narratives advocated by Norwegian philologists, historians, archaeologists and public intellectuals; it offers an analysis of the influence wielded by these academic debates and ideological struggles over national identity on Norwegian anthropology.

Physical anthropology was also closely related to eugenics, which emerged as a significant international movement in the early twentieth century. Eugenicists feared that the biological evolution of humankind had been arrested by anti-selective forces in modern society, and they called for an interventionist population policy in order to protect superior elements from being outnumbered by inferior ones. Eugenicists generally turned their attention towards individuals and families carrying those genetic traits assumed to be inferior. Some eugenicists, however, maintained that the primary goal of eugenics was to protect the superior races—first and foremost the Nordic race—against miscegenation and to help them expand at the expense of supposedly inferior races. According to these eugenicists, physical anthropology was highly relevant to eugenics, since the anthropological mapping of inferior and superior racial elements in a population was regarded as a way of assessing its genetic quality. This book elucidates the relationship in Norway between eugenics, anthropology and the concept of a superior Nordic race.

Measuring the Master Race is the first broad and contextualised account of the history of Norwegian physical anthropology to be published in English. In addition to the Norwegian edition of this book, *Kortskaller og langskaller,*[1] a descriptive overview of the history of Norwegian physical anthropology was published in Norwegian in 1990 by the anatomist Per Holck.[2] Holck's account was an important starting point for this book. In addition to Holck various scholars have addressed specific issues in the history of Norwegian physical anthropology. Of particular importance has been the history of early twentieth-century physical anthropological research on the Sami, the indigenous people of northern Scandinavia. This research included the excavation of a substantial number of human skulls from Sami graves in northern Norway, skulls still stored in the anthropological collection at the University of Oslo. The Sami grave excavations are today generally perceived as a racist undertaking characterised by a lack of respect for the affected Sami communities; there is an ongoing debate about the future of the skulls, some of which were reburied in 2011. The topical relevance of this issue has led to a number of historical inquiries into the physical anthropological research carried out in this period. This includes work by the archaeologist Audhild Schanche addressing the controversial Sami grave excavations both in relation to her own research on prehistoric Sami

---

1   Jon Røyne Kyllingstad, *Kortskaller og langskaller: Fysisk antropologi i Norge og striden om det Nordiske herremenneske* (Oslo: Spartacus, 2004).

2   Per Holck, *Den fysiske antropologi i Norge. Fra anatomisk institutts historie 1815-1990* (Oslo: Anatomisk institutt, University of Oslo, 1990).

burial costumes and as part of her involvement in the official assessment of the University's collection of ancient Sami bones.[3] The historian Bjørg Evjen has also explored late-nineteenth-century and early-twentieth-century anthropological research in northern Norway, with a specific focus on the Sami and on how anthropologists classified groups in northern Scandinavian into races.[4]

The history of Norwegian physical anthropology is also touched upon by philologist Torgeir Skorgen in his general introduction to the history of racism,[5] and in a number of works on the history of eugenics in Norway. The most comprehensive of these works are those written by Per Haave and Nils Roll-Hansen, and my account of Norwegian eugenics is greatly indebted to them. However, neither Haave nor Roll-Hansen have specifically turned their attention to the relationship between physical anthropology and eugenics, which is one of the focuses of my research.[6]

---

3   Audhild Schanche, 'Saami Skulls, Anthropological Race Research and the Repatriation Question in Norway', in Cressida Fforde, Jane Hubert and Paul Tumbull (eds.), *The Dead and their Possessions. The Repatriation in Principle, Policy and Practice* (London: Routledge, 2002), pp. 47-58; *Graver i ur og berg. Samisk gravskikk og religion 1000 f.kr. til 1700 e. Kr.* (Ph.D. thesis, University of Tromsø, 1997); 'Samiske hodeskaller og den antropologiske raseforskningen i Norge', appendix to I. Lønnig, M. Guttor, J. Holme, et al. (eds.), *Innstilling fra Utvalg for vurdering av retningslinjer for bruk og forvalting av skjelettmateriale ved Anatomisk institutt* (Oslo: University of Oslo, 1998); 'Rase, etnisitet og samisk forhistorie: et forskningshistorisk tilbakeblikk', in Jan Eivind Myhre (ed.), *Historie, etnisitet og politikk* (Tromsø: Institutt for historie, University of Tromsø, 2000), pp. 3-18.

4   Bjørg Evjen, 'Measuring Heads: Physical Anthropological Research in North Norway', *Acta Borealia*, Vol. 14, no. 2 (1997); 'Kort- og langskaller: fysisk-antropologisk forskning på samer, kvener og nordmenn', *Heimen*, Vol. 37, no. 4 (2000), pp. 273-292.

5   Torgeir Skorgen, *Rasenes oppfinnelse: rasetenkningens historie* (Spartacus: Oslo, 2002).

6   Per Haave, *Sterilisering av tatere 1934-1977: En historisk undersøkelse av lov og praksis* (Oslo: The Norwegian Research Council, 2000); 'Zwangssterilisierung in Norwegen—eine wohlfahrtsstaatliche Politik in sozialdemokratischer Regie?', *NORDEUROPAforum, Zeitschrift für Politik, Wirtschaft und Kultur*, Vol. 11 no. 2 (2001), pp. 55-78; 'Sterilization Under the Swastika: The Case of Norway', *International Journal of Mental Health*, Vol. 36, no. 1 (2007). Nils Roll-Hansen, 'Norwegian Eugenics: Sterilization as Social Reform', in Gunnar Broberg and Nils Roll-Hansen (eds.), *Eugenics and the Welfare State: Norway, Sweden, Denmark, and Finland* (Ann Arbor, MI: Michigan State University Press, 1995); 'Den norske debatten om rasehygiene', *Historisk tidsskrift*, Vol. 59 (1980), pp. 259-83; 'Geneticists and the Eugenics Movement in Scandinavia', *The British Journal for the History of Science*, Vol. 22, no. 3 (1989), pp. 335-46; 'Eugenics Before World

The significance of physical anthropology's relationship with other disciplines, particularly eugenics, emerges as I chart the development of the concept of the Nordic master race. The book begins with a short account of some key events in the rise of the scientific concept of a Germanic race. In the 1830s and 1840s, Scandinavian anatomists, archaeologists, linguists, historians and ethnographers put forward a grand theory claiming that a succession of different races had migrated to Europe in prehistoric times and had given rise to the various European nations. According to this theory, a Germanic race existed that could be scientifically delineated and identified. This race was tall, blond, blue-eyed and had an elongated head shape. It was assumed to have settled in Europe during the Iron Age, established itself as a ruling caste over the previously settled populations and ushered in the development of an advanced European civilisation. This theory achieved great international acclaim and went on to have long-lasting effects on academic debates about history and national origin in Europe.

Chapter 2 argues that Norwegian historians writing in the 1830s and 1840s were inspired by the idea of the superior Germanic race. These historians traced the roots of the nation back to the invasion of a Germanic Iron Age tribe and praised Norwegians for being the principal bearers of Germanic virtues. This national myth of origin was widely believed and endorsed by Norwegian historians, philologists and archaeologists in the mid-nineteenth century, but beginning in the late 1860s it was overthrown by the views of a new generation of scholars. These scholars dismissed the theory of a Germanic invasion and refused to see the nation's history as the unfolding of psychological characteristics inherited from a Germanic race.

Chapter 3 describes the establishment of a Norwegian tradition of physical anthropological research from the late 1880s onwards, and argues that the first generation of Norwegian physical anthropologists was influenced by a German and French school of research—anthroposociology—which embraced the idea of a superior Nordic race and saw the struggles between inferior and superior races as the key to interpreting history and society. This led to a revival of Norwegian ideas of nationhood based on racial determinism and Germanic racial superiority, and in chapter 4 I argue

<hr/>

War II: The Case of Norway', *History and Philosophy of the Life Sciences*, Vol. 2, no. 2 (1980), pp. 269-98; 'Eugenics in Scandinavia after 1945: Change of Values and Growth in Knowledge', *Scandinavian Journal of History*, Vol. 24, no. 2 (1999), pp. 199-213.

that such ideas had a significant, but not pervasive, impact on the prevailing concepts of nationhood among the Norwegian academic elite. Around the turn of the century it was conventional to think that Norwegians had their prehistoric roots in a Germanic race; however, it was not commonplace to explain Norwegian culture and history as predominantly determined by inherited Germanic virtues.

Chapter 5 deals with the rise of eugenics during World War I and shows that leading Swedish and Norwegian eugenicists were strongly inspired by the notion of a Nordic master race, holding that one of the principal goals of eugenics was the purification and propagation of this race. Chapters 6 and 7 present the leading Norwegian anthropologists of the 1920s and 1930s, and argue that they all supported eugenics but had different views on the relationship between eugenics and anthropology. Halfdan Bryn, the foremost Norwegian anthropologist of the 1920s, saw eugenics as a tool for the protection and expansion of the superior Nordic race, and claimed that anthropology was highly relevant to eugenics since it could help identify inferior and superior (Nordic) racial elements in the national population. His colleagues, the married couple Alette and Kristian Emil Schreiner, favoured a style of eugenics that focused on the propagation of healthy individuals rather than on protecting the purity of the Nordic race. In line with this aim, their anthropological research was not primarily legitimated as part of a eugenic enterprise, but was instead linked to archaeology, ethnography and the investigation of the prehistory of the Norwegians and the Sami.

In spite of their different ideas on eugenics, Bryn and the Schreiners cooperated closely in the early interwar years, and chapter 8 is a detailed study of the huge collaborative project they launched just after World War I—an anthropological survey of a total cohort of Norwegian military conscripts, meant to provide deep insight into the racial composition of the Norwegian people. After many years of work, the project ended in an irresolvable quarrel over the interpretation of the data collected on arm length, eye colour, height and other physical characteristics. This disagreement over seemingly petty details was, however, connected to a deep ideological controversy over the Nordic master race. While chapter 8 deals with the scientific content of the controversy and elucidates how the scientists involved strove to justify their differing views with the help of empirical evidence and scientific reasoning, chapter 9 turns towards the political and social context of the conflict between Bryn and the Schreiners.

From the mid-1920s onwards, Halfdan Bryn became increasingly involved in a network of German right-wing nationalists and physical anthropologists who favoured the protection and expansion of the Nordic race and who, in the late 1920s, won growing support within German physical anthropology for their ideas. These scholars became even more influential during the Nazi period, when their academic careers flourished along with the political success of the concept of the Nordic race. Halfdan Bryn died in 1933, the year of the Nazi takeover in Germany, but by that point his scientific reputation was already on the rise in Germany. In contrast to his academic success in Germany, however, Bryn's prestige in Norway declined significantly during the last years of his life due to his advocacy of the Nordic race. Although the notion of a superior Nordic race had been acknowledged as a scientifically sound idea since the 1890s by the Norwegian academic community, by the time Bryn died in 1933, the idea had lost much of its scientific credibility and was about to be cast aside as a pseudo-scientific concept.

The relationship between science and racism is a recurrent theme in *Measuring the Master Race*, and throughout the book I have used the term 'racism' to denote a specific set of attitudes, ideas and actions. I have mainly used the term to denote the basic idea that humankind can be divided into biologically distinct races, and that these can then be ranked in a hierarchy and assigned unequal moral worth due to perceived differences in intellectual abilities. This idea was commonly held in the Western world at the end of the nineteenth and beginning of the twentieth centuries, and it was often assumed to be scientifically sound. The term 'racism', however, is also used in a more restricted sense, namely to characterise explicitly formulated ideologies which turned belief in racial inequality into the basic building block of a comprehensive worldview.

Even though I use the word 'racism' to denote two partly overlapping notions, I have tried to distinguish throughout the text between their meanings. The distinction is important, since many of the participants in the academic and public debates who were staunchly opposed to specific racist doctrines—such as the idea of Nordic superiority—nevertheless based their scientific reasoning and their worldview on the (often implicit) notion of a hierarchy of races. I am fully aware that the use of the term 'racism' in a historical study is problematic. It is a politically-charged word with an ambiguous meaning, and it may seem anachronistic to use it to denote ideas and actions that were current prior to the 1930s, when the term was first introduced into public and academic debates.[7] However, the aim of this book is not only to study ideas and actions, but also to make past events comprehensible and relevant to present-day readers. To this end, it is necessary to take into account the concept of 'racism', which is probably the most important point of reference for the present-day reader when he or she deals with issues of race.

The fact that 'racism' is a normative concept should not prevent us from using it as a conceptual tool in our study of the past or the present. Racism is the negation of human equality and universal human rights. It is a threat to these basic values upon which any society should be founded. There is no better cause, then, for trying to understand what racism is and has been. One of the reasons racist ideas have been able to thrive and influence is the fact that they were once considered to be scientifically sound. This book is a contribution to the growing literature on the history of racial science, and it is my hope that it will also be a small contribution to a more nuanced understanding of the phenomenon we call 'racism'.

---

7   According to George M. Fredrickson (in his *Racism: A Short History* [Princeton, NJ: Princeton University Press, 2002], pp. 151-61), the term emerged for the first time in the early 1920s but started to be used more widely only in the 1930s.

1. The Origin of the Long-Skulled Germanic Race

The early 1840s were a decisive period in the rise of the concept of a Germanic race. During that decade, Swedish anatomist Anders Retzius launched the cephalic index, a new method for identifying races. On the basis of differences in head measurements, he split humankind into two basic categories: the short-skulled brachycephalics and the long-skulled dolichocephalics. By combining these two categories with a set of anatomical and geographical criteria, he developed a system of racial classification that made it possible to divide Europeans into a number of racial types and to establish the scientific concept of a long-skulled, blond Germanic race. Retzius' system became an important starting point for decades of research and debate on the racial divisions of Europe. However, Retzius' work was based on already existing scholarly traditions; he was not the first person in the history of science to create a racial classification system, and he invented neither the idea of the Germanics nor the concept of race itself. Thus, in order to understand the background to Retzius' innovations, we first need to take a brief look at the rise of racial science in the eighteenth century.

The rise of racial science

Scientific notions of race arose in parallel with European colonial expansion, encounters with non-European peoples and the emergence of the transatlantic slave trade. These encounters with other peoples and other continents provoked Enlightenment scholars' interest in the

http://dx.doi.org/10.11647/OBP.0051.01

origins and causes of human variation, and sparked the drive to classify humankind into different racial groups. This scientific enterprise was woven into ongoing controversies regarding the legitimacy of slavery and into theological debates over the creation of man.

One of the most influential works from this period was *De generis humani varietate native*, published in the late eighteenth century by the German anatomist and natural historian Johan Friedrich Blumenbach, who believed that racial differences had arisen through adaptation to different environments. Blumenbach argued that the human species had originated in the Caucasus region and was perfectly adapted to the Caucasian climate. Accordingly, the so-called Caucasian race (which included people from Europe, the Middle East and North Africa) was the original, and therefore superior, type of man. The inferior races—the American, Mongolian, Malayan and Ethiopian—had emerged through adaptation to less favourable environments.[1] By asserting humanity's common origin, Blumenbach's scientific view accorded with traditional interpretations of the biblical account of creation and the descent of all humankind from Adam and Eve. The idea that all races belong to one species has been labelled 'monogenism', and has its counterpart in 'polygenism', the idea that God created a number of fixed human species. Monogenists and polygenists agreed that the Europeans were more civilised and had a greater moral worth than other races, but disagreed on the significance of the differences between the various races. Polygenists argued that Africans were inherently inferior, a view that often led to the conclusion that they were natural-born slaves. Monogenists, on the other hand, maintained that racial inferiority was caused by poor cultural or environmental conditions, climate or food, and often claimed this effect could be reversed if Africans were exposed to a more stimulating environment. Educate the slaves and set them free, argued the abolitionists, and their descendants will become like us.[2]

---

1   See, for example, Timothy Lenoir, 'Kant, Blumenbach, and Vital Materialism in German Biology', *Isis*, Vol. 71, no. 1 (1980), pp. 77-108. Blumenbach's book was published in a number of different editions between 1775 and 1795. This account refers to the last edition.

2   See, for example, Nicholas Hudson, 'From "Nation" to "Race": The Origin of Racial Classification in Eighteenth-Century Thought', *Eighteenth-Century Studies*, Vol. 29, no. 3 (1996), pp. 247-64; Snait B. Gissis, 'Visualizing "Race" in the Eighteenth Century', *Historical Studies in the Natural Sciences*, Vol. 41, no. 1 (2011), pp. 41-103; Ann Thomsen, 'Issues at Stake in Eighteenth-Century Racial Classification', *Cromohs*, no. 8 (2003), pp. 1-20, http://www.cromohs.unifi.it

Racial ethnology

Debates over monogenism and polygenism continued into the nineteenth century. However, while monogenism had been the dominant theory in the eighteenth century, by the 1840s the idea of fixed, unchangeable racial differences was gaining currency. Furthermore, while the Enlightenment discourse on race had been intertwined with controversies around slavery and colonialism, and had focused on the racial distinctions between Europeans and the rest of mankind, it was now increasingly being argued that race was relevant to national differences within Europe. The rising interest in the racial classification of Europeans was fuelled by an upsurge of nationalism in the 1830s and 1840s. Following the Napoleonic Wars, Europe was comprised of a number of multi-ethnic states (e.g. Russia, Austria and the Ottoman Empire) and various ethnic groups divided into small states (e.g. what would later become Italy and Germany). All over Europe, there was a growing political impetus to adjust state borders in accordance with national boundaries and the demands of national minorities. States competed for power and national honour, and there was a great deal of interest in cultural identity and roots. This in turn led to rising scientific interest in the origins and ancient history of the European nations.

From the early decades of the nineteenth century, linguists took the lead in exploring these issues. Around 1800, they recognised the existence of a historical connection between Sanskrit and modern European languages, and they developed the theory of an extinct Indo-European language. This led to the evolution of comparative Indo-European linguistics as a prestigious scientific discipline that aimed to trace the lineages of the European languages back to their common origin. It was commonly assumed that the various Indo-European languages had spread through human migration and that successive waves of migration to Europe had given rise to the European peoples. By the 1840s, the new linguistic theories were complemented by anatomically-based concepts of race, resulting in a new type of racial science and in attempts to establish a new academic discipline under the name of ethnology.

In 1843 the Ethnological Society of London was founded under the leadership of physician and linguist James Cowles Prichard, a Christian humanist and monogenist, who based his research on the biblical account of creation. Employing linguistic methods, and, to a lesser degree, anatomical comparison, Prichard classified humans into groups, mapped their relatedness and tried to trace them back to a common origin. He ranked people according to a hierarchy of intellectual and moral progress, but believed these differences were the product of variations in culture, environment and way of life. He rejected the existence of insurmountable barriers to the improvement of the so-called inferior races and used this as an argument against slavery. Prichard advocated a humanist and paternalist colonial policy aimed at spreading 'civilisation' and the Christian gospel to the world. Internationally recognised, Prichard's school of ethnology was widely supported in Britain but met with challenges from advocates of polygenism, both in his home country and abroad.[3] One major challenge came from the U.S., where physician Samuel J. Morton pioneered a polygenic strand of ethnology in the 1830s. Morton collected a huge number of crania which he subjected to anatomical comparison in order to classify races, explore the history of humankind and study correlations between brain size and racial superiority. He subsequently founded an American school of ethnology, which his followers developed into a tool for the legitimisation of slavery and racial segregation.[4]

The founder of the *Société Ethnologique de Paris* (1839), British-French physiologist William Edwards, was also opposed to monogenism. Edwards believed that the main aim of ethnology was to explore the origin and identity of the European nations. He proposed that humankind consisted of a number of largely immutable racial types, each equipped with certain innate mental properties, and that the uneven distribution of these racial types could explain national and regional differences in traditions, behaviour and levels of civilisation. Edwards was mainly interested in the origin and history of the French. Many historians saw the French as a mix of ethnic elements with different historical and social roles. While the French commoners were thought to have their roots in an indigenous Celtic population, the aristocracy stemmed from Frankish warriors who had established themselves as a ruling caste during the Migration Period. Edwards set out to prove that these different ethnic and social groups were in fact biologically distinct races with inborn psychological and intellectual differences.[5]

---

3   H. F. Augstein, 'Aspects of Philology and Racial Theory in Nineteenth-Century Celticism: The Case of James Cowles Prichard', *Journal of European Studies*, Vol. 28, no. 4 (1998), pp. 355-71; James Cowles Prichard, *Researches into the Physical History of Mankind*, Vol. 2 (London: Sherwood, Gilbert, and Piper, 1837).

4   C. Loring Brace, *Race Is a Four-Letter Word: The Genesis of the Concept* (New York: Oxford University Press, 2005), pp. 85ff; Ann Fabian, *The Skull Collectors. Race, Science and America's Unburied Dead* (Chicago, IL: University of Chicago Press, 2010).

5   Claude Blanckaert, 'On the Origins of French Ethnology: William Edwards and the Doctrine of Race', in George W. Stocking, Jr., ed., *Bones, Bodies, Behavior: Essays on Biological Anthropology* (Madison, WI: University of Wisconsin Press, 1988), pp. 18-50.

Craniology and the three-age system

The most influential individual involved in the division of Europeans into races was the Swedish anatomist Anders Retzius. Around 1840, he put forward a method of racial classification that divided humans into two basic categories: the dolichocephalics, with long skulls, as measured from the forehead to the occiput, and the brachycephalics, who had shorter, rounder skulls (see Fig. 1). By combining these two categories with other anatomic and geographic criteria, Retzius created a system of racial types that coincided with linguistically defined peoples, such as the Celts, the Slavs and the Germanics, which he then ranked in terms of superiority with the Germanics at the top. The key idea in Retzius' system was the cephalic index, which referred to the ratio of the breadth to the length of the skull and would become a widely used criterion for racial classification in the decades that followed.

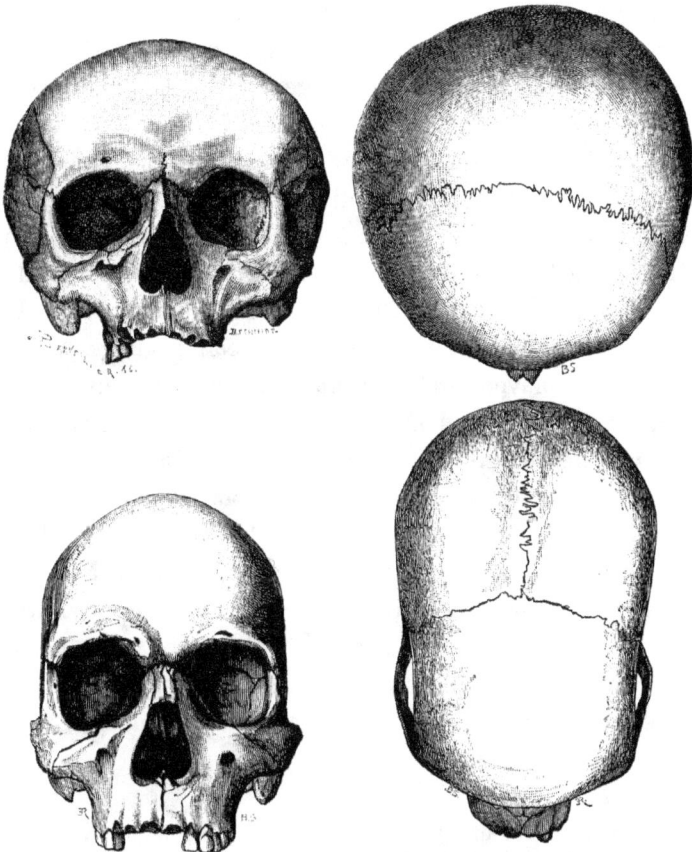

Fig. 1 Brachycephalic or short skull (top), dolichocephalic or long skull (bottom).

Although Retzius was a comparative anatomist, his research questions came from archaeology and comparative linguistics, and the method he launched became an important tool for combining archaeological and linguistic knowledge. By comparing skulls from present-day populations with skulls found at archaeological excavation sites, Retzius claimed he could demonstrate racial continuity or discontinuity between past and present populations. Moreover, he hypothesised that he could clarify the ethnic identity of the inhabitants of the prehistoric settlements and link archaeological evidence to linguistic theories about past migrations and settlements of ethnic groups. It is no coincidence that it was a Scandinavian scholar who devised this technique. Retzius developed his method in order to solve archaeological and linguistic questions about Scandinavian prehistory, and at that time Scandinavian scholars were at the forefront of research in both archaeology and linguistics.

The Dane Rasmus Rask was one of the most influential linguists of his time. Along with his German colleague Jacob Grimm, he helped to establish what later came to be known as 'sound laws': fixed 'rules' that regulate the historical transformation of a language's sound system. The discovery of such law-like regularities made it possible to study the development of languages in times pre-dating all written sources, which was to prove important for the rise of comparative Indo-European linguistics. An important breakthrough in this context was 'Grimm's Law'—also called 'Rask's Rule' or the 'First Germanic Sound Shift'—which described a series of consonant changes that in the distant past had helped to split the proto-Germanic language from the other Indo-European languages.[6]

Scandinavians played an even more crucial role in the field of archaeology. Indeed, it was Danish archaeologist Christian Jürgensen Thomsen who developed the ground-breaking three-age system that divided prehistory into the Stone Age, the Bronze Age and the Iron Age. Prior to this other scholars had proposed that prehistoric cultures had advanced from an age of stone tools to ages of bronze and iron tools. However, when Thomsen began organising the display of antiquities at the new National Museum of Denmark in the early 1820s, no methods existed for dating artefacts according to such a scheme. Thomsen began to group all artefacts that were found together at the same excavation site

---

6   Even Hovdhaugen et al., *The History of Linguistics in the Nordic Countries* (Helsinki: Societas Scientiarum Fennica, 2000), pp. 159-72.

and which could be assumed to stem from the same period. On the basis of this, he developed a comparative typology that made it possible to also date artefacts that were not part of such closed finds. This new method opened up opportunities for exploring the time period that lay beyond the advent of writing—an important prerequisite for the rise of a concept of 'prehistory' and of archaeology as an autonomous scientific discipline.[7]

Even if the three-age system implies that all human societies evolved along a common trajectory, Danish archaeologists did not believe that the development from the Stone Age to the Iron Age had taken place within one and the same Scandinavian population. Instead, they assumed that each 'age' was introduced through the immigration of a new group of people and sought to prove this by making their interpretations of the archaeological evidence fit already-existing linguistic and historical accounts of the settling of Scandinavia. One such account had already been put forward in the eighteenth century by Peter Fredrik Suhm and Gerhard Schøning, who were, respectively, the leading historians in Denmark and Norway. Their account was based on the then commonly-held view that the main human groupings stemmed from Noah's sons Shem, Ham and Japheth, each of whose descendants had peopled their own continents, and that the linguistic division of humankind had arisen when God confused the languages in order to prevent the completion of the Tower of Babel. Basing themselves on the Bible, logical reasoning, linguistic arguments and interpretations of classical literature and Norse mythology, Suhm and Schøning tried to reconstruct the route that the forefathers of the Scandinavians and Germans had followed into Scandinavia from their assumed place of origin somewhere north of the Black Sea.[8]

In 1818, this theory was further elaborated by Rasmus Rask, who dismissed its biblical underpinning but claimed to have detected a series of Scandinavian-related languages along the route that the Scandinavian and German forefathers were assumed to have followed. From the Black Sea region, these groups were thought to have wandered northwards

---

7   Peter Rowley-Conwy, *From Genesis to Prehistory: The Archaeological Three Age System and its Contested Reception in Denmark, Britain, and Ireland* (Oxford: Oxford University Press, 2007); Bruce Trigger, *A History of Archaeological Thought* (Cambridge: Cambridge University Press, 2006), pp. 73-87.

8   Stian Larsen, *Med dragning mot nord. Gerhard Schøning som historiker* (Master's thesis, University of Tromsø, 1999); Rowley-Conwy, *From Genesis to Prehistory*, pp. 22-29.

into present-day Russia. There, the Scandinavians had split off from the Germans before moving further north of the Gulf of Bothnia and into the Scandinavian Peninsula, where they encountered an indigenous population of Finno-Ugrians, the forefathers of the Sami, the indigenous people of northern Scandinavia. The three-age theory was initially invented in an attempt to fit Danish archaeological findings into this account, the idea being that the three archaeological ages corresponded to the periods in which three linguistically different peoples settled in Scandinavia.[9]

Rask, Schöning and Suhm's migration theory met with increasing criticism in the 1830s, and the subsequent debate provided an important background for the introduction of craniology as a method for determining the ethnic identity of the peoples that had inhabited Stone Age, Bronze Age and Iron Age settlements. The publication in 1838-1843 of a two-volume work by Swedish zoologist and ethnographer Sven Nilsson was a seminal event. Nilsson compared finds from the Scandinavian Stone Age and Bronze Age with ethnographic observations on the tools and habits of contemporary 'savages' and 'nomads', and pointed out that the culture of the 'primitive' inhabitants of ancient Scandinavia resembled the culture of contemporary 'primitive' tribes. He proposed that the cultural and social development of all peoples pass through the same three stages of savages, nomads and agriculturalists, and that these stages concurred with the three archaeological ages. Somewhat paradoxically, however, Nilsson also argued that cultural progress in Scandinavian prehistory had been driven by the successive immigrations of increasingly more civilised peoples: Finno-Ugrian savages in the Stone Age, Celtic nomads in the Bronze Age and Germanic farmers in the Iron Age.[10] As evidence for this interconnection between human migrations, the advent of archaeological ages and stages of socio-economic development, Nilsson pointed to anatomical similarities and differences between human skulls. He compared skulls from three Danish Stone Age finds with the skulls of two recently deceased Sami and argued that they all had a typically round shape. To assign the Bronze Age

---

9   Rowley-Conwy, *From Genesis to Prehistory*, pp. 37-42.

10 Sven Nilsson, *Skandinaviska Nordens Ur-Invånare. Ett försök i komparativa Ethnografien och ett Bidrag til Menniskoslägtets utvecklings historia* (Lund: Berlingska Boktryckeriet, 1838-1843). Nilsson had a forerunner. In 1837, Danish physiologist Daniel Esricht published the work *Om Hovedskallerne. Beenradene i vore gamle Gravhöie* (Copenhagen: [n. pub.], 1837), in which he argued that skulls from three Stone Age finds belonged to 'a noble tribe of the Caucasian race'.

to the Celts, Nilsson compared a drawing of a Danish Bronze Age skull with a drawing of the skull of a Scottish Highlander and a plaster cast of a supposedly Celtic skull kept at St. Thomas' Hospital in London. He concluded that both the Sami and the Celtic skulls were different from the typical Iron Age Germanic skull.[11]

To explore the racial connection between the assumed Germanic Iron Age population and the contemporary Swedish population, Nilsson asked his friend Anders Retzius for help. At that time Retzius held a leading position at the *Carolinska Institutet* in Stockholm, a key institution for medical education and research, and he was able to compare 200-300 skulls of recently deceased Swedes. After submitting these to several rounds of examinations and selection, he selected the five crania that he deemed most representative, and, based on this sample, provided a detailed description of the typical Swedish skull, concluding that it was identical to Nilsson's Iron Age skull.[12]

Craniology and the brain

Retzius and fellow ethnologists such as Edwards and Morton took it as their task not only to identify races but also to rank these races in a hierarchy of intellectual ability and moral worth. They did so mainly by comparing skulls, as they believed that intellectual capacity was correlated to the size and shape of the skull. This assumption was based on contemporary theories of brain anatomy, and can partly be attributed to the theories of the mind and the brain that the Austrian physician and comparative anatomist Franz Joseph Gall put forward around 1800. Gall proposed that all animal species could be ranked in a hierarchy according to the complexity of their nervous systems. At the bottom of the hierarchy were the simplest animals (like jellyfish) that were only equipped with scattered nerves. In more advanced animals, all nerves were linked through the spinal cord, and among the most advanced animals, the end of the spinal cord was converted into a brain. Gall therefore saw the

---

11 Nilsson, *Skandinaviska Nordens Ur-Invånare, ett forsök i komparativa Ethnografien och ett bidrag til menniskoslägtets utvecklings historia*, Vol. 1 (Stockholm: P. A. Norstedt & Söner, 1866), pp. 100-06.

12 Anders Retzius, *Om formen af nordboernes cranier. Aftryckt ur Förhandl. vid Naturforskarnes Möte i Stockholm år 1842* (Stockholm: P. A. Norstedt, 1843).

spinal cord as the core element of the nervous system, from which the brain had emerged.[13]

These observations provided the basis for a theory of the brain as a set of mental faculties. From the simplest organisms up to man, there is a steady increase in the number of mental faculties, from the most basic functions that are common to all species (such as the sex drive) up to the highest faculties (such as wisdom and compassion), which man alone possessed. According to Gall, each mental function was localised in a certain organ in the brain. Therefore, the relative strength of different mental faculties was related to the shape of the brain, and indirectly to the shape of the skull.[14] From this starting point, Gall and his followers developed a science of the relationship between psychological characteristics and the shape of the skull which eventually became relatively well-known to the educated public as phrenology.

At the same time as phrenology evolved into a popular movement, particularly in England and the U.S., it also met with increasing opposition from scientists. By the 1840s it was to a large extent scientifically discredited, but, despite this, Gall's basic approach to brain anatomy had a lasting scientific impact. Both the notion of a hierarchy of cerebral development and the idea that the shapes of the brain and the skull are correlated with intellectual ability proved fundamental to the rise of a craniological approach to race typology.

In an 1848 lecture, Retzius praised Gall's basic approach to brain anatomy and hailed him as the first to ascertain that the brain was a transformed part of the spinal cord. However, Retzius also criticised Gall for having misunderstood how this transformation took place. Gall had proposed that the frontal lobes were the final stage in the development of the central nervous system and thus the seat of the higher mental faculties.

---

13 Christian Heinrich Ernst Bischoff and Christoph Wilhelm Hufeland, *Some Account of Dr. Gall's New Theory of Physiognomy Founded upon the Anatomy and Physiology of the Brain* (London: Longman, Hurst, Rees, and Orme, 1807), pp. 15-16, http://bit.ly/1HSosvI; S. Zola-Morgan, 'Localization of Brain Function: The Legacy of Franz Joseph Gall (1758-1828)', *Annual Review of Neuroscience*, Vol. 18, no. 1 (1995), pp. 359-83 (pp. 376ff.); Donald Simpson, 'Phrenology and the Neurosciences: Contributions of F. J. Gall and J. G. Spurzheim', *ANZ Journal of Surgery*, Vol. 75, no. 6 (2005), pp. 475-82.

14 Bischoff and Hufeland, *Some Account of Dr Gall's New Theory*, pp. 1-16; Simpson, 'Phrenology and the Neurosciences'; Zola-Morgan, 'Localization of Brain Function', pp. 376ff.

According to Retzius, the situation was the other way around: during the growth of the human embryo, the frontal brain lobes developed first, then came the parietal lobes and finally the occipital. This matched the hierarchy of the nervous system in vertebrates, from the simplest to the most complex forms: fishes, birds and amphibians only have frontal lobes, whereas mammals have both frontal and parietal lobes, and only human beings and a few other mammals have frontal, parietal and occipital lobes. The posterior part of the brain should therefore be considered the final stage in the development of the brain, the seat of the superior mental faculties.[15]

According to Retzius, not only the different mammal species but also the various human races represented different levels of cerebral development and could be ranked according to the relative development of the posterior part of their brains. When launching his racial classification system in 1843, Retzius proposed that the typically long-skulled Swedish brain was characterised by a significant elongation of the occipital lobe of the cerebrum, which extended well beyond the cerebellum. This was in contrast to the more round-headed Slavic peoples and particularly the even more round-headed Lapps, whose occipital lobes were so small that they could hardly cover the cerebellum. It goes without saying that while Retzius located the most superior intellectual faculties in the occipital lobe, he saw the cerebellum as the seat of most basic mental functions.[16] According to Retzius, it was a 'universally acknowledged fact' that Celtic and Germanic peoples possess the strongest intellectual faculties. This corresponded to their low, narrow and long skulls, with their strongly protruding occipital, and was in contrast to the inferior Slavs and Lapps with their broad skulls and weakly developed occiput.[17]

Retzius' hierarchical classification was based on the assumption that there was a correlation between race, language, intellectual ability, brain anatomy and cultural development. He claimed that his comparative-anatomical theory of the development of the central nervous system was confirmed by the distribution of skull shapes between ethnic groups. Short-skulled peoples had more primitive brains and more primitive

15 Anders Retzius, *Phrénologien bedömd från en anatomisk ståndpunkt. Föredrag hållet vid Skandinaviska Naturforskare-Sällskapets möte i Köpenhamn i Juli 1847* (Copenhagen: Trier, 1848), p. 187.

16 Anders Retzius, *Om formen af nordboernes cranier*, p. 2.

17 Retzius, *Phrénologien*, p. 187ff. Idem, *Om formen af nordboernes cranier*, p. 2.

cultures than long-skulled peoples. This notion fit Nilsson's theory of cultural development from savage via nomad to farmer. It also fit the archaeological theory of the three ages and the linguistic theory of Finno-Ugrian Stone Age aborigines being replaced by more advanced Indo-European invaders.

The success of the Germanic dolichocephalics

The Scandinavian migration theories were not developed in a vacuum, and it is important to understand the interconnections and patterns of influence between the Scandinavian theories and those developed abroad. Suhm, Schøning, Rask, Nilsson and Retzius participated in transnational debates and tried to gain acceptance for their theories from the international scholarly community. Their ideas on the origins of the Scandinavian nations formed part of more general accounts of the origin and development of humankind and the history of the European nations.

Retzius and Nilsson's migration theory was not only an account of the origin of the Swedes, it was also a grand theory about the rise of European civilisation. They proposed that the Sami and the Basques were the descendants of inferior Stone Age peoples that had originally inhabited all of Europe. These short-skulled autochthones had later been overrun by successive waves of Indo-European invaders who brought increased levels of civilisation to Europe: the Celts introduced the Bronze Age, and the Germanics the Iron Age. Thus, the growth of European civilisation was explained by the successive invasion of races with increasingly advanced brains.[18] Retzius' views were extraordinarily influential (see Fig. 2). The racial-succession scheme shaped linguistic, archaeological and ethnological debates on European prehistory from the 1840s to the 1860s,[19] and the system of classifying skulls and human races into dolichocephalics and brachycephalics had an even greater and more long-lasting impact. Indeed, the cephalic index became a key factor in most of the numerous racial typologies that were put forward by European scientists over the next 100 years.

---

18 Anders Retzius, *Ethnologische Schriften von Anders Retzius. Nach dem Tode des Verfassers gesammelt* (Stockholm: P. A. Norstedt & Soner, 1864).
19 See, for example, Richard McMahon, *The Races of Europe: Anthropological Race Classification of Europeans 1839-1939* (Ph.D. thesis, European University Institute, 2007).

European Racial Types.

	Head.	Face.	Hair.	Eyes.	Stature.	Nose.	Synonyms.	Used by.
1 TEUTONIC.	Long.	Long.	Very light.	Blue.	Tall.	Narrow ; aquiline.	Dolicho-lepto. Reihen-gräber. Germanic. Kymric. Nordic. Homo-Europæus.	Koll-mann. Ger-mans. English. French. Deniker. Lapouge
2 ALPINE (Celtic).	Round.	Broad.	Light chest-nut.	Hazel-gray.	Medium, stocky.	Variable ; rather broad ; heavy.	Celto-Slavic. Sarmatian Dissentis. Arvernian. Occidental Homo-Alpinus. Lappanoid	French. Von Hölder. Germans Beddoe. Deniker. Lapouge Pruner Bey.
3 MEDITER-RANEAN.	Long.	Long.	Dark brown or bl'k	Dark.	Medium, slender.	Rather broad.	Iberian. Ligurian. Ibero-Insular Atlanto-Med. }	English. Italians. Deniker.

Fig. 2 William Z. Ripley's racial classification scheme in *The Races of Europe* (1899). Ripley was influenced by Retzius' work; his blue-eyed, blond and tall 'Teutonic race' mirrors Retzius' notion of the Germanic race.

There are many explanations for this success. Retzius' simple craniological method was an easy and convenient way of comparing skulls and classifying races, and his settlement theory fit neatly into already established narratives of national origin. Various nations claimed Celtic, Slavic and Germanic origins, and Retzius' method seemed to be a highly applicable scientific tool for exploring these racial roots. Furthermore, Retzius' racial-succession scheme assigned the European races different roles in the rise of European civilisation and arranged them in a hierarchy that mirrored the existing power relations and differences in technological and economic development in Europe. Historian Richard McMahon has proposed that nineteenth-century racial classifications of Europeans were shaped by the continuous competition between scholars who wanted to demonstrate the racial superiority and historical virtues of their own national groups. Since the northern European countries were ahead of the rest of Europe in terms of industrial progress and colonial expansion, their narratives of Germanic superiority achieved a dominant international currency.[20]

Notions of Germanic national roots had been around since at least the sixteenth and seventeenth centuries and were initially based on the descriptions of ancient peoples in classical literature. *Germania* by the Roman historian Tacitus was a principal source of these ideas. In this text, the virtuous, free and unspoiled 'Germans' were held up in contrast to the decadent Romans. Tacitus' descriptions influenced national narratives in Scandinavia, the Netherlands, Germany and England, where the birth of the nation became associated with the Germanic past and the idea of 'freedom' as a specifically Germanic virtue.

The birth of German nationhood was often seen as the outcome of the epic Germanic victory over the Romans in the Teutoburger Forest in 9 AD that put an end to Roman expansion into Germanic lands. This narrative became a key element in the rising German nationalism after the end of the Napoleonic Wars: the idea of a common 'Germanic' past helped legitimise efforts to unify Germany and, following unification in 1871, highlighted the German Empire at the expense of its neighbouring rivals, 'Celtic' France and the 'Slavic' Russian Empire. The idea of the Germanic race even legitimised Pan-Germanism, which arose in response to its ideological twin sister Pan-Slavism and aimed to unify all of German-speaking Europe. The valorisation of a Germanic past often went hand in hand with a condescending attitude towards the Slavic and Celtic races.

An English penchant for the Germanics dates back to the sixteenth and early seventeenth centuries. English national roots were sought in the Anglo-Saxons, a group of Germanic tribes that settled in England when the Roman Empire collapsed and established a kingdom characterised by 'free' governmental institutions. American colonists also inherited the myth of a golden Anglo-Saxon past, and the notion of a Germanic sense of freedom was even used to justify the American War of Independence. According to the historian Reginald Horsman, however, the 1840s saw the breakthrough of a new type of Anglo-Saxon ideology, combining those well-established ideas of Anglo-Saxon freedom with new concepts of racial superiority. The Anglo-Saxons were now portrayed as a particularly superior branch of the

---

20 Richard McMahon, 'Anthropological Race Psychology 1820-1945: A Common European System of Ethnic Identity Narratives', *Nations and Nationalism*, Vol. 15, no. 4 (2009), pp. 575-96.

Germanic race and were often contrasted with their inferior counterparts, the Celts, and especially the Irish Celts.[21]

Even in France, the Germanic peoples played an important role in traditional accounts of national origin, as the roots of royal dynasties were traced back to the invasion of Germanic warriors in the Age of Migration. In French historiography, it was conventional to describe French commoners as descendants of an indigenous Gallic (Celtic) population, while the aristocracy were seen as descendants of the Frankish (i.e. Germanic) warriors who had invaded the country in the fifth century. In the 1820s and 1830s, the influential historians Amédée and Augustin Thierry transformed this idea into a theory of two hostile nations, of which one (the descendants of Frankish conquerors) exerted an illegitimate dominance over the other (the Celtic Gauls). The Thierry brothers, however, viewed the Celtic race, not the Germanic Franks, as the true core of the French people. This idea became dominant from the 1830s onwards, leading to a tradition of veneration of the Celts among the French and providing an important vantage point for William Edwards' attempts to establish a scientific 'ethnology' in the 1840s. Edwards' theory of stable and unchanging races offered a biological explanation for the Thierry brothers' doctrine: the Celtic people and the Frankish aristocracy belonged to different races with different inborn characteristics undiluted by centuries of cohabitation.[22]

According to McMahon, scholars from non-Germanic nations tended not to question the prevailing account of Germanic virtues, nor did they develop completely alternative narratives. Instead, the Slavic, Celtic or Latin races were defined in opposition to the Germanics, and the disparaging stereotypes of these races were given new interpretations. Rather than heroic, freedom-loving and aristocratic warriors, the Germanics could be portrayed as brutal tyrants and oppressors. Polish scholars, for instance, preferred to portray the Slavs as a peace-loving, hard-working and rooted people who had survived Germanic plunder and violence. Similar stereotypes of peaceful, artistic, humble and oppressed Celts existed in Ireland and France, and were contrasted with the image of brutal warrior-like Germanics.[23]

---

21 Reginald Horsman, 'Origins of Racial Anglo-Saxonism in Great Britain before 1850', *Journal of the History of Ideas*, Vol. 37, no. 3 (1976), pp. 387-410. See also idem, *Race and Manifest Destiny: The Origins of American Racial Anglo-Saxonism* (Cambridge, MA: Harvard University Press, 1981), p. 81.
22 Blanckaert, 'On the Origins of French Ethnology', pp. 21-22.
23 McMahon, 'Anthropological Race Psychology', p. 587.

We have thus seen that the 1830s and 1840s witnessed the breakthrough of a scientific concept of 'the Germanic race', and that the idea of Germanic racial superiority was intertwined with a number of national ideologies, including those of the most powerful nations in the world. But what of Norway, we might ask, one of the smallest and least powerful of the Germanic-speaking nations? What impact did the idea of a superior Germanic race have on the national identity of Norwegians? We will now turn our attention to Norway and attempt to answer these questions.

2. The Germanic Race and Norwegian Nationalism

The 1830s and 1840s are often referred to as the period of national breakthrough in Norwegian intellectual history. In these decades, the nation was explored by folklorists, poets, artists, historians and philologists who, inspired by romantic nationalism, collected fairy tales, songs and myths; studied the language, literature and history of the ancient Norsemen; and sought to unearth their communal roots. Their efforts came at a time when the academic communities of Scandinavia were closely connected to each other, and when Swedish and Danish scholars were establishing their theories of a long-skulled Germanic race. The question, then, is what impact the idea of a superior Germanic race had on the Norwegian scholars who were in search of the roots of the nation.

The national breakthrough

Norway's history and geography influenced the development of national identity, as did the ethnic composition of its population and its relation to other Scandinavian countries. With a population of fewer than two million inhabitants for most of the nineteenth century, Norway stood at the northern periphery of Europe. In the nineteenth century the population was dominated by ethnic Norwegians with a common Norwegian language, but also included minority groups such as Roma travellers, small communities of Finnish-speaking farmers in the southeast, and Finnish-speaking Kvens in the north, as well as the largest minority, the Sami, the indigenous people of northern Scandinavia, Finland and Russia. Until the mid-twentieth century, the Sami were usually referred to as Lapps or Finns

http://dx.doi.org/10.11647/OBP.0051.02

by the ethnic majority population, but these are now considered derogatory terms. The Sami subsisted traditionally as fishermen, hunters and farmers along the coast, and inland as nomadic reindeer herders.

For about 400 years, Norway was under Danish rule. It gained independence in 1814, when a Norwegian Parliament was established and a constitution adopted, but soon afterwards Norway was forced into a union with Sweden which lasted until 1905. Norway's small size and its lack of an unbroken political history had lasting effects on national identity. While Swedes and Danes were able to look back on glorious pasts as important regional powers, Norway was a young state with few historical buildings and monuments and no indigenous high culture of its own. In the nineteenth century, Norwegian nationalism was characterised by a wish to signal Norway's equal status with its more powerful Swedish partner and by the need for symbolic liberation from joint Danish-Norwegian historical and cultural traditions. Instead of studying the royal dynasties, wars and high culture of the previous centuries, Norwegian historians and philologists began to turn their attention to a perceived Norwegian golden age in the Iron Age and Middle Ages. Scholars focused on the language and customs of Norwegian peasants and on the history of the common people in order to establish a historical connection between the independent, medieval Norwegian kingdom that had existed prior to Danish rule and the modern nation-state.[1]

The Norwegian School of History

A professional, academic tradition of researching, teaching and writing about Norway's national history was established for the first time in the 1830s and 1840s at the University of Kristiania (Oslo). A leading figure there was Rudolf Keyser, who became Professor of History in 1837 and developed a national narrative based on the idea of Germanic origins. Later referred to as the Norwegian School of History, this narrative was also embraced by Keyser's student Peter Andreas Munch, who in 1841 attained the second history professorship in Norway. Munch was a high-profile public figure and became the foremost public spokesman for the Norwegian School of History.[2]

---

1   Kåre Lunden, 'History and Society', in William Hubbard et al. (eds.), *Making a Historical Culture: Historiography in Norway* (Oslo: Scandinavian University Press, 1995), pp. 15-51 (pp. 27-45).

2   Ottar Dahl, *Norsk historieforskning i det 19. og 20. århundre* (Oslo: Universitetsforlaget,

A key element in Keyser and Munch's narrative was their account of the prehistoric settlement of the country, which was generally in agreement with the theories presented by the Swedes Anders Retzius and Sven Nilsson (see chapter 1). The ancestors of the Sami were seen as the original Stone Age inhabitants, who had been displaced first by Celts in the Bronze Age and finally by Germanic tribes who established the farming settlements in the Iron Age that gave rise to the Scandinavian nations.[3] Keyser's theory, however, diverged from those of his Swedish and Danish counterparts in one important way: he argued that Scandinavia had been settled not by one, but by two waves of Germanic tribes. Denmark and southwestern Sweden had been settled by South Germanic Goths, who were closely related to the Germans; later, Norway and northeastern Sweden were invaded by North Germanic tribes who ventured north of the Gulf of Bothnia into Scandinavia. Keyser argued that these North Germanics had called themselves Norwegians (*Nordmenn*) and that they eventually spread from Norway to southern Scandinavia, where they conquered the South Germanic (Goth) population and introduced Scandinavian culture to Denmark.[4]

Keyser's theory implied that, despite the weak state of present-day Norway, the forefathers of the Norwegians had once dominated Scandinavia and were the true originators of the ancient Norse culture. Keyser and his disciple Munch assumed that, more than any other Germanic people, the Norwegians had kept the original Germanic social institutions alive, and that this explained the particularly democratic character of Norwegian society as compared to feudal Sweden and Denmark. According to Keyser, Danish feudalism was established when North Germanic (Norwegian) tribes invaded Denmark and subjugated the existing South Germanic population. In Norway, however, the Germanic invaders had not encountered an earlier farming community, since the existing population consisted of the nomadic ancestors of the Sami. This meant that the Norwegians had to cultivate the land themselves instead of becoming a ruling caste. As a result, they had maintained their ancient Germanic institutions and virtues.

Keyser believed that patriarchal households had been the core social institution of the ancient Germanic society. After the invasion of Norway,

---

1990), pp. 43-64.

3   Rudolf Keyser, *Samlede afhandlinger* (Kristiania: P. T. Malling, 1868), pp. 232-46.

4   Rudolf Keyser, *Norges Historie*, Vol. 1 (Kristiania: P. T. Malling, 1866-1870), pp. 19-52.

these households acquired an unrestricted, hereditary title to a piece of conquered land. This gave rise to the allodial right (*Odelsretten*), which was considered both a proto-Germanic invention and the basic building block of Norwegian society. Allodial freeholders (*odelsbøndene*) were federated under the leadership of the heads of the most prestigious families, but the freeholders themselves had absolute authority in their regular meetings, the *ting*. This 'patriarchal-democratic' social order was retained to some extent even after the establishment of a unified Norwegian medieval kingdom. The allodial freeholders and their leaders kept their freedom and obtained a significant political role in the new state. The Norwegian kingdom lost its political autonomy in the late Middle Ages as a consequence of the king undermining his own power base by stripping the peasants of their political role.[5]

Keyser's narrative implied that the present-day Norwegian state embodied both the reawakening of ancient Germanic traditions and modern ideas of liberty and democracy. According to this account, the peasants had been the unifying force in the nation's history, and Norway thereby emerged as distinct from the predominantly aristocratic Sweden and Denmark. Independence from Danish rule and the claims for national autonomy within the Swedish-Norwegian union could be seen both as a struggle for freedom against the aristocracy and the Crown and as a revival of ancient Germanic traditions.

Norwegian versus Danish national narratives

In the 1840s, Norwegian philologists and historians competed with their more established Copenhagen colleagues in an effort to make Kristiania the leading centre for the study of ancient Norse language, culture and history.[6] In such a context, it is scarcely surprising that the Danes were less than accepting of claims that the Norwegians were the true heirs of Norse culture. Even more problematic for the Danes was the Norwegian theory of the ancient South Germanic settlement of Denmark. Close as it was to Prussia and the German Confederation, Denmark had a large

5   Keyser, *Samlede afhandlinger*, pp. 403-51.
6   Trond Werner Pettersen, *Fra dannelse til forskning: filologien ved Det kgl. Fredriks Universitet 1811-1864* (Master's thesis, University of Oslo, 2007), pp. 49, 115; Per Sveaas Andersen, *Rudolf Keyser: embetsmann og historiker* (Oslo: Universitetsforlaget, 1960).

German-speaking minority and was affected by rising German nationalism and Pan-Germanism. Consequently, the Danes had good reason to emphasise their historical ties with Scandinavia, appeal for Scandinavian solidarity against the Germans and fear the political consequences of the Norwegian theory of a German epoch in Danish prehistory.[7]

In 1848 the German linguist and fairytale collector Jacob Grimm published his *History of the German Language*, which lent support to the Norwegian theory. Grimm, however, drew the political conclusion that Jutland, like Alsace, Lorraine, Switzerland, Belgium and the Netherlands, belonged within a Pan-German union, and that Denmark should cease to exist. He argued that Jutland should be united with its German neighbours, and that the rest of the country should be incorporated into the Swedish-Norwegian union. At the time these views attracted keen interest, as a large proportion of the German-speaking minority in Schleswig, in southern Denmark, wanted to join the German Confederation.[8] In 1848, the same year that Grimm's book was published, Danish troops advanced into Schleswig to subdue a pro-German revolt and this, in turn, provoked a Prussian invasion. The Danes appealed to Scandinavian solidarity, but only a small group of Swedish and Norwegian volunteers joined the Danish side. Denmark regained control of its southernmost territory in 1851, only to lose it again in a new war fourteen years later.

During the 1848-51 war, the leading Danish archaeologist Jens Jacob Asmussen Worsaae launched a powerful attack on the Norwegian School of History. Worsaae accepted the view that Scandinavia had been settled in two separate waves, but argued that there was no evidence to prove that the first Gothic settlers were of 'German' origin, or that there had been a subsequent 'Norwegian' invasion of Denmark. While rejecting Grimm's use of the past to bolster the Pan-Germanic cause, Worsaae himself used prehistory to legitimise Danish territorial claims and to enlist Scandinavian

---

7   C. Stephen Briggs, 'C.C. Rafn, J.J.A, Worsaae, Archaeology, History and Danish National Identity in the Schleswig-Holstein Question', *Bulletin of the History of Archaeology*, Vol. 15, no. 2 (2005), pp. 4-25.

8   Inge Adriansen, '"Jyllands formodede tyskhed i oldtiden"—den dansk—tyske strid om Sønderjyllands urbefolkning', in E. Roesdahl, S. P. Meulengracht and P. M. Sørensen (eds.), *The Waking of Angantyr: The Scandinavian Past in European Culture*. ACTA Jutlandica (Aarhus: Aarhus University Press, 1996), pp. 120-46; Peter Rowley-Conwy, 'The Concept of Prehistory and the Invention of the Terms "Prehistoric" and "Prehistorian": The Scandinavian Origin, 1833-1850', *European Journal of Archaeology*, Vol. 9, no. 1 (2006), pp. 103-30 (pp. 112-20).

support for the Danish cause. Worsaae had previously led the excavation of *Danevirke*, a line of Viking fortifications on the southern boundary of Schleswig, and claimed that this had been an ancient Scandinavian line of defence against the Germans.[9] Worsaae was an advocate of Scandinavism, a movement that idealised the common cultural, historical and linguistic heritage of the Scandinavian countries and aspired towards the establishment of Scandinavia as a unified region or even a single nation. Peter Munch, on the other hand, opposed Scandinavism but embraced Pan-Germanism. While criticising the German invasion, he accused the Danish Scandinavists of seeking Swedish and Norwegian support to cleanse Schleswig-Holstein of 'alien' elements with the aim of creating a purified Nordic nationality. This, according to Munch, had led to a split between Scandinavia and the German states, thereby weakening the defence of all Germanic nations against the threat from Russia and Pan-Slavism.[10]

Race and Norwegian nationhood

As we have seen, the notion of Germanic origin was a key feature of the Norwegian School of History. Munch even combined this idea with Pan-Germanism and used it as a rhetorical weapon against Scandinavism. But what was the nature of the 'Germanic-ness' of the Norwegian people? Did Norwegian national virtues coincide with Germanic virtues? And were they seen as biologically given?

According to Munch, the Norwegian School of History's settlement theory was based on something he called 'historical-ethnographic science', which studied the migrations and actions of ancient peoples by means of historical sources, comparative linguistics, archaeology, geography, anatomy and natural history. Munch argued for the inclusion of the latter two disciplines on the grounds that they could yield information concerning the difference between human races and their relations to each other.[11] Munch and Keyser worked in almost every area of this

---

9   J. J. A. Worsaae, *Om en forhistorisk, saakaldet 'tydsk' Befolkning i Danmark: med Hensyn til Nutidens politiske Bevægelser* (Kjøbenhavn: Reitzel, 1849).

10 P. A. Munch, *Skandinavismen nærmere undersøgt med Hensyn til Nordens Ældre national og litteraire Forhold* (Kristiania: Johan Dahls, 1849), pp. 5-10.

11 P. A. Munch, *Om den saakaldte nyere historiske Skole i Norge* (Kristiania: Tønsberg, 1853), p. 6.

historical-ethnographic science. Munch was involved in the geographical charting of Norway, and Keyser was in charge of the National Antiquities Collection at the University of Kristiania. They were, however, first and foremost linguists, philologists and historians; so the Norwegian migration theory was mainly based on comparative linguistics, the interpretation of runic inscriptions and geographic reasoning, as well as on archaeological finds. Neither Munch nor Keyser were involved in racial science, but there were strong links between their research and that being conducted in Norway's neighbouring countries. Keyser's linguistically-based account of the origin of the Norwegians was developed in tandem with Sven Nilsson's racial theory of the settlement of Scandinavia. The two men corresponded frequently, exchanged linguistic and anatomical arguments and evidence, and referred to each other's works in ways that suggest they both assumed linguistically-defined 'peoples' were identical with anatomically-defined 'races'.[12] There are clear points of correspondence and reference between the research work produced by Nilsson, Retzius, Munch and Keyser. From their writings, it is evident that all four men advocated the same racial typology.[13]

In his textbook *The Major Events in World History*, Munch proposed that humankind had originally arisen as a single species in Central Asia, and had later split into four separate races: Iranians, Turanians, Malays and Negroes. The Iranians and the Turanians were roughly equivalent to the so-called Indo-European and Mongolian races of Eurasia, both of which had played a leading role in world history. But while Munch admitted that the Turanians (Mongolians) had created advanced civilisations, such as that of China, he argued that they were less receptive to cultural development than the Iranians (Indo-Europeans) and that the great upheavals in world history could be explained by the struggles between these two races. Munch believed that these struggles would eventually end with the most gifted race, the Iranians, as rulers of the world. He placed both the Sami and the Finns within the inferior Turanian race, seeing the Sami (the 'polar race')

---

12 Andersen, *Rudolf Keyser*, pp. 232-46.
13 Anders Retzius, *Ethnologische Schriften von Anders Retzius. Nach dem Tode des Verfassers gesammelt* (Stockholm: P. A. Norstedt & Søner, 1864), pp. 103-05; Rudolf Keyser, *Samlede afhandlinger* (Kristiania: P. T. Malling, 1868), pp. 3-246; P. A. Munch, *Verdenshistoriens vigtigste Begivenheder: fra de ældste Tider indtil den franske Revolution i kortfattet Fremstilling* (Kristiania: Cappelen, 1840), pp. 1-17.

as a particularly primitive sub-race within the Turanian, characterised by their adaptation to the harsh Arctic climate.[14]

Munch and Keyser believed in a correspondence between anatomical differences (small, weak 'Lapps' and strong Germanics) and degrees of civilisation (inferior Stone Age hunters versus superior Iron Age farmers). These notions of racial inferiority and superiority were a basic prerequisite for their account of national origins. According to this account, the 'Lapps' were driven into the Scandinavian peripheries because their primitiveness left them unable to defend themselves against the invading Germanics. Neither Munch nor Keyser clearly distinguished between the concepts of 'race' and 'folk', and although 'race' more often referred to biology and 'folk' to language and culture in their writings, they generally regarded terms such as 'folk' and *folkeætt* (a people's lineage) as referring to subcategories within a 'race'.

According to Munch, the Germanic people had developed their characteristic features on their march from Central Asia to Europe. Exposure to a challenging environment and conflicts with other peoples had made them strong and warrior-like, and had given them their sense of freedom and their 'aristocratic-democratic' social structure. Therefore, in Munch's view, the mental and physical attributes of the Germanic 'folk' were the product of environmental adaptation. The important point, however, is that when the Germanics entered into the historical era, their psychological characteristics were already fully formed, so the historian could handle them as a given and stable entity. Keyser compared nations to human individuals, and claimed that a nation's psychological character, its pace of cultural development and its role in world history were determined by its family lineage and kinship with other peoples.[15] In short, even though both men advocated monogenism, the practical implications of their notion of a Germanic 'folk' were largely equivalent to a polygenist notion of 'race': Keyser and Munch explained Norwegian history as the unfolding of a set of innate Germanic features. Within this account, the nation was seen not as a product of history, but rather as the product of an inherent national character.

---

14 P. A. Munch, *Verdenshistoriens vigtigste Begivenheder*, pp. 1-4.
15 John Sanness, *Patrioter, Intelligens og Skandinaver* (Oslo: Universitetsforlaget, 1959), pp. 55-58.

Evolution and race

The Norwegian School of History was well known and widely accepted among the educated Norwegian elite during the 1840s and 1850s. However, by the time Munch and Keyser died, in 1863 and in 1864 respectively, their theory had already begun to lose favour: its empirical grounding was undermined by an increasing amount of philological and historical research, and its theoretical foundation was shaken by the advent of new evolutionary approaches to the study of history.

Darwinism had an ambiguous impact on racial science. Darwin's theory implied that the human species had evolved through environmental adaptation—an idea that was hailed by some as a new version of monogenism. In English academia an alliance was formed between the supporters of Darwinism and the ethnologists working in the tradition of James Prichard. On the other hand, owing to the enormous time-span of human evolution, it could also be argued that the rate of change was so slow that, within a normal human time-scale, races could be regarded as essentially immutable. Such a notion of race could be combined with Darwin's theory of selection-driven evolution and turned into a conception of human evolution as driven by the survival of the superior race in the struggle for existence. Therefore, ideas that resembled polygenism could also be maintained within an evolutionary framework, and previous debates between the immutability and adaptability of races could continue.[16]

During the final decades of the nineteenth century, evolutionary theory became a key framework for social and ideological debates in which the question of the immutability or adaptability of human races had huge implications. Some took Darwin's theory to mean that human progress was driven by the struggle for survival between nations, races, social groups and individuals, and that social differences mirror inborn racial qualities. However, the pre-Darwinian evolutionary theory of Jean-Baptiste Lamarck was also maintained alongside the theory of natural selection. According to Lamarckian theory, acquired abilities are passed down between generations, and species can be transformed through the accumulation of useful traits. Lamarckism could be taken to support the

---

16   See, for example, George W. Stocking Jr., 'What's in a Name? The Origins of the Royal Anthropological Institute (1837-71)', *Man*, New Series, Vol. 6, no. 3 (1971), pp. 369-90.

idea that education and the learning of skills create better brains, and that human progress is driven by the interaction between cultural development and increasingly complex brains. This viewpoint could then be combined with theories of social evolution which argued that all societies are destined to pass through the same stages of cultural and social evolution towards ever-increasing complexity.[17]

The Norwegian scholars who turned their back on the Norwegian School of History in the 1860s and 1870s were less inspired by the theory of the survival of the fittest than by various notions of socio-cultural evolution. This was particularly true of Ludvig Kristensen Daa, who became Professor of History at the University of Kristiania in 1864 and soon after launched a successful attack on the views of his predecessors, Keyser and Munch. Over the years, evidence from philology, linguistics, geography and history had gradually undermined Keyser and Munch's settlement theory.[18] Daa summed up these empirical developments and added some of his own, but his critique was also political, ideological and theoretical. It aimed at undermining the basic assumptions upon which Munch and Keyser's theory was founded, and it heralded a new evolutionary approach to Norwegian history. Daa rejected the idea that the Norwegians had their origins in an invasion by a specific North Germanic tribe, suggesting instead that they were the mixed product of several waves of peoples that had settled in Norway over a long time-span.[19] Daa also dismissed the very notions of race and nationhood that underpinned the Norwegian School of History, arguing that peoples were not static entities but the product of historical processes, and that they could arise or vanish but tended to follow an evolutionary trajectory leading to increasingly larger national units. In Daa's view, individual human beings live their lives regardless of the rise and fall of nations; they are adaptable and able to learn new languages and new ways of thinking. Daa pointed to the U.S. as an example, a place where so many diverse peoples from all parts of the world had melted together and given rise to a new nation adapted to the environmental conditions of the New World.[20]

---

17 See, for example, Thomas Gondermann, 'Progression and Retrogression: Herbert Spencer's Explanations of Social Inequality', *History of Human Sciences*, Vol. 20, no. 3 (2007), pp. 21-40.

18 Dahl, *Norsk Historieforskning*, pp. 86-112.

19 Ludvig Kristensen Daa, 'Have germanerne invandret til Skandinavien fra nord eller fra syd?', *Særtrykk av Forhandlinger ved de Skandinaviske Naturforskeres Møde* (Kristiania: [n. pub.], 1869).

20 Ludvig Kristensen Daa, *Nationaliternes udvikling* (Kristiania: J. Chr. Abelsteds,

Daa was one of the first Norwegians to read Darwin, but he was also a religious man who embraced a monogenetic view of human history, which he claimed was in accord with both the Bible and Darwin. Daa was inspired by the aforementioned English ethnographer James Cowles Prichard, as well as by Robert Latham, who became the leading figure of the Ethnological Society of London following Prichard's death in 1848. Latham had visited Norway for an extended period of time during his youth and was a personal friend of Daa.[21] Like Prichard and Latham, Daa rejected polygenism not only on scientific but also on moral grounds, believing that it undermined justice and human society. He noted as a terrifying example how the American tradition of ethnology established by Samuel Morton had been used to justify slavery and to deny civil rights to people of African descent.[22]

Daa also voiced views on the Sami that were based on monogenism and appeared to resemble the paternalist, philanthropic attitude towards colonial subjects that was typical of Prichard and the Ethnological Society of London. But even though he maintained that the Sami had an inferior culture and believed that they were racially different, he did not think that their inferiority was racially determined and argued that they should be assimilated into the more civilised Norwegian nation. Daa clearly warned of the dangers of racial arrogance, hatred and oppression, making him one of a minority to oppose the hard-line assimilation policy that was on the rise in the latter part of the nineteenth century.[23] Daa's attack on the Norwegian School of History was partly motivated by his support for Scandinavism, with his arguments for the assimilation of minorities resembling those he put forward for Scandinavian integration. These views accorded with his general outlook on the development of human civilisation, which entailed peoples and nations merging into ever-larger units.

1869); Ottar Dahl, 'Noen etnografisk synspunkter hos Ludv. Kr. Daa', *Norsk geografisk tidsskrift*, Vol. 16, nos. 1-8 (1957), pp. 46-58.

21 Ludvig Kr. Daa, *Udsigt over Ethnologien: Indbydelseskrift til den offentlige Examen i Christiania Kathedralskole* (Kristiania: Steenske bogtrykkeri, 1855); Yngvar Nielsen, *Universitetets ethnografiske samlinger* (Kristiania: W. C. Fabritius og sønner, 1907), pp. 3-7; Robert G. Latham, *Norway and the Norwegians* (London: Bentley, 1840); George W. Stocking, Jr., 'What's in a Name The Origins of the Royal Anthropological Institute (1837-71)', *Man*, New Series, Vol. 6, no. 3 (1971), pp. 369-90 (p. 373).

22 Daa, *Nationaliternes udvikling*, pp. 36-51.

23 Tor Ivar Hansen, *Et skandinavistisk nasjonsbyggingsprosjekt: Skandinavisk selskab (1864-1971)* (Master's thesis, University of Oslo, 2008), pp. 55-58.

The fall of the Norwegian School of History

Daa may be seen as a transitional figure, representing a new type of evolutionary thought that was to have a significant impact on public debate and Norwegian historical scholarship during the last decades of the nineteenth century. In the 1870s and 1880s, Norway went through a period of significant political and cultural tension leading to the downfall of the established political order. In this politically polarised period, social, cultural and political controversies were interwoven with struggles over evolutionism.[24]

For most of the nineteenth century, Norwegian political life was dominated by a bureaucratic regime staffed by an educated elite of senior civil servants with lifetime positions who, owing to the absence of an aristocracy and a strong capitalist class, had a particularly influential role in Norwegian society. Although farmers gained voting rights in 1814, the civil servants dominated both Parliament and government. However, from around 1870, the civil servants' preeminent position met with growing opposition from a democratic and liberal alliance of peasants and certain segments of the educated urban elite. In the 1880s, this alliance achieved a majority in the Parliament, and a constitutional struggle arose. The conflict ended with the introduction in 1884 of a parliamentary system which redefined the government, previously the leadership of a state bureaucracy, as a political body with a mandate from the Parliament. Political parties were established for the first time. The conservative party *Høyre* (the Right) had its roots in the old regime, while the opposition formed *Venstre* (the Left), which was an alliance of nationalist, democratic and liberal forces within the urban intelligentsia and among the peasants.

The upheaval had implications for issues of national autonomy and national identity since the struggle for democratisation was also a battle for greater national independence within the Swedish-Norwegian union. The opposition wanted the government to be answerable not to the Swedish king but to the Norwegian Parliament. This democratic and national issue also had cultural and social implications. The *embetsmenn* (government functionaries) had traditionally been drawn from a largely

---

24 Gro Hagemann, *Aschehougs Norgeshistorie*, Vol. 9 (Oslo: Aschehoug, 1997), pp. 46-48.

self-recruiting social class dominated by intermarrying families with ancestral roots in Denmark and a common Danish-Norwegian language. The emergence of an opposition to the bureaucratic regime was linked to the rise of a popular-democratic, counter-cultural movement. Its proponents intended to replace the Danish-Norwegian written language with a new language based on Norwegian dialects and to develop a modern, democratic national culture based on rural culture. A key motif was the notion of a cultural and linguistic continuity between present-day rural Norway and the national golden age of the Middle Ages. In contrast, the Danish-Norwegian language, the traditional academic culture and the old powerful families were viewed as undemocratic, non-national elements of society. This style of counter-cultural nationalism had a particularly marked impact on rural communities in the western part of southern Norway, especially on peasants and the educated sons of peasants who were ascending the social ladder.

Academic education was important for the social authority of the *embetsmenn* class. At Norway's only university, they were socialised into an academic culture that set them apart from the populace. When the authority of this academic class began to be challenged in the 1870s and 1880s, old academic ideals were depicted as relics of the past, while new ideas were championed as instances of the universal evolutionary progress of mankind. Arguments were taken from Darwin's theory of biological evolution, from Herbert Spencer's theory of social and cultural evolution, and, importantly, from Auguste Comte's positivism. The latter claimed that modern man was about to leave the metaphysical era and step into a scientific epoch in which scientific method and experience should form the basis for understanding society and exercising political power.[25]

The struggles of the 1880s ushered in a period during which the heterogeneous and somewhat contradictory *Venstre* movement had a clear impact on Norwegian politics and society. Historian Knut Kjeldstadli has argued that *Venstre*'s heyday (lasting roughly from the 1880s until World War II) coincided with the rise of biological thinking in Norway. Professions based on biological knowledge—chiefly medicine—expanded their fields of action and their societal influence, while biological ideas and metaphors had an increasing impact on public debate and political life.

25 Ibid., pp. 46-48.

These would prove particularly relevant to the cultural nationalism that shaped Norwegian public discourse in the decades before the dissolution of the Norwegian-Swedish union in 1905.[26]

The turbulent 1870s and 1880s also saw a change of generations in the small Norwegian community of historians, with a group of young, urban advocates of positivism and evolutionism assuming academic positions. Like Daa, these young intellectuals generally dismissed the notion of the nation as a static and ancient entity, and were inclined to see it as a social organism undergoing slow, incremental evolution. This generation saw no point in searching for the birth of the nation in a prehistoric Germanic invasion; instead, they set themselves the task of exploring the preconditions for the historical continuity and growth of the nation. The young historians were particularly interested in explaining how Norwegian national identity had been preserved throughout the four centuries of Danish rule, and in studying the preconditions for the rebirth of the nation in 1814.[27] Despite the existence of this basic consensus among the new generation of scholars, however, a controversy arose in the 1870s over the interpretation of the Danish period. In parallel with the increasingly polarised public debate, two competing national narratives crystallised: a *Høyre* narrative and a *Venstre* narrative. Conservative historians argued that the decline of the medieval Norwegian state had been due to weakness and poverty. It was only during the period of Danish rule that a real state apparatus was established in Norway, and they claimed that this had been a precondition for the economic and social growth that finally made possible the establishment of the new Norwegian state.[28]

Historian Ernst Sars was the leading architect of the *Venstre* narrative, which had a particularly notable influence on notions of national identity in the decades around the turn of the century. Sars argued for a strong national continuity between the medieval state and the new Norwegian state, and, like Munch and Keyser before him, he saw the free Norwegian peasants as the unifying element that had ensured the continued existence of Norwegian culture through the years of Danish domination. The new Danish-Norwegian

---

26 Knut Kjeldstadli, 'Biologiens tid. Randbemerkninger om viten og venstrestat', in Erik Rudeng, ed., *Kunnskapsregimer* (Oslo: Pax, 1999), pp. 145-51.

27 Narve Fulsås, *Historie og nasjon. Ernst Sars og striden om norsk kultur* (Oslo: Universitetsforlaget, 1999), pp. 138-39.

28 Øystein Rian, 'Norway in Union with Denmark', in William H. Hubbard et al. (eds.), *Making a Historical Culture: Historiography in Norway* (Oslo: Scandinavian University Press, 1995), pp. 132-55 (pp. 132-35).

upper class had imported a foreign culture and lived in isolation from the rest of Norwegian society. During the Enlightenment, however, they were inspired by the peculiarly free societal position of the Norwegian peasants and began to define themselves as Norwegians. This prepared the ground for the democratic constitution of 1814 and the subsequent developments leading towards an increasing integration of folk and elite. Thus, the historical growth of the nation followed a trajectory that led towards the *Venstre* alliance of peasants and the urban elite.

Sars' interpretation of the national history bore many similarities to the Norwegian School of History and its conception of the modern Norwegian constitution as an embodiment of ancient Germanic virtues. However, Sars explicitly distanced himself from what he described as the 'racial principle' in Munch and Keyser's historiography—the idea that the history of the nation could be understood mainly as the unfolding of a set of innate and immutable Germanic characteristics. In contrast, Sars saw the rise of the nation as the preliminary end product of an ongoing historical process.[29]

Archaeology, Vikings and the birth of the nation

Waning interest in theories about prehistoric migrations was due not only to a new 'evolutionary' view of history, but also to the fact that since the heyday of Munch and Keyser, history had become a more specialised discipline that concentrated on the study of written sources. This meant that prehistory now lay outside the historian's field of interest and had instead become the domain of archaeology, which arose as an autonomous discipline in Norway in the 1860s and 1870s. From 1859, the semi-official Society for the Preservation of Norwegian Monuments (*Foreningen til Norske fortidsminnesmerkers bevaring*) began systematic and publicly-funded archaeological excavations in Norway. Most of the excavated artefacts were deposited in the University's Antiquities Collection (*Oldsaksamlingen*), which quadrupled in size between 1870 and 1900. In 1875, the head of the Antiquities Collection, Oluf Rygh, was appointed to the first Norwegian professorship in archaeology and became instrumental in establishing archaeology as an autonomous discipline.[30]

---

29 Fulsås, *Historie og nasjon*, pp. 138-39.
30 Jon Røyne Kyllingstad and Thor Inge Rørvik, *1870-1911: Vitenskapenes universitet*, Universitetet i Oslo 1811-2011, Vol. 2 (Oslo: Unipub, 2011), pp. 384-88.

The main task of Norwegian archaeology was to explore the prehistory of the Norwegians. Excavations focused mainly on Iron Age sites, particularly burial mounds, with more than 1,000 barrows being excavated in a fifty-year period. The most spectacular finds were the Viking ships: the Tune-ship in 1867, the Gokstad-ship in 1880, and—the jewel in the crown—the huge Oseberg-ship in 1904. The Viking ships received great national and international attention and are still regarded as being among the nation's most important cultural treasures. Archaeologist Jørgen Haavardsholm has argued that the Viking ships and the rest of the artefacts from Iron Age burial mounds gave rise to the notion of the 'Viking Age' as a clearly defined historical epoch, which became clearly associated with the birth of the Norwegian nation both in public discourse and in scholarly literature.[31]

So, what notion of nationhood did the archaeologists embrace? Oluf Rygh construed the Viking Age as an era of overseas expansion and conquest, but also of peaceful trade, cultural contacts and progress. Most importantly, he saw it as the period when the land was cultivated, associating the origin of the nation with this agricultural conquest of the land. The birth of the nation was thus not explained in terms of an invasion by a 'Norwegian' people with certain innate mental dispositions, but as an internal process of cultural growth culminating with the Vikings.[32]

These views were also reflected in the campaign to build a new national history museum in the 1880s. The planned museum was intended to display ancient national antiquities, along with the material culture of Norwegian peasants from the sixteenth, seventeenth and eighteenth centuries. According to the young archaeologist Ingvald Undset, this museum display would represent the cultural evolution of the Norwegian people from its primitive stages in the Stone Age up to the rich cultural blossoming of contemporary Norway. In this spirit, the artefacts were to be displayed in a way that would show how 'our' forefathers had migrated to the country and, how, after their arrival, they had cultivated the land and developed those characteristics upon which 'our' Norwegianness and national identity were based. Thus, according to Undset, the nation's forefathers had not been Norwegians when they first entered what later became Norwegian territory. Instead, their Norwegianness emerged as the newcomers adapted themselves to the geographical conditions of the country.[33]

---

31 Jørgen Haavardsholm, *Vikingtiden som 1800-tallskonstruksjon* (Oslo: University of Oslo, 2004), pp. 45-79.

32 Ibid.

33 Ingvald Undseth, *Om et norsk National-Museum* (Kristiania: Cammermeyer, 1885), pp. 5, 10.

Racial nationalism's comeback

The new generation of historians and archaeologists who assumed academic positions in the 1870s rejected the racial theories of the Norwegian School of History. This generation of scholars saw the nation first and foremost as the product of an ongoing historical process, not as a given racial essence. Despite this, however, racial theories of national origins would make a notable comeback in Norwegian academia in the 1890s. This can be explained by a number of factors. One explanation, which will be elaborated upon in chapter 4, is that historians, archaeologists and others who refused to see national history as the unfolding of a set of immutable Germanic virtues still believed in racial differences and thought that these differences could help explain the cultural variations between nations. Another explanation lies in scientific specialisation and the growth of new disciplines. The revival of racial ideas and theories of prehistoric migration was linked to the rise of physical-anthropological research in Norway in the 1880s and 1890s. The practitioners of this new discipline were medical scientists, not humanities scholars, and as such, they underwent different training and worked in their own specific professional and intellectual context. As a consequence, they did not necessarily agree with their colleagues in the historical and philological disciplines on issues involving nation and race.

3. The Germanic Race and Norwegian Anthropology, 1880-1910

The Parisian Society of Anthropology was founded in 1859, which was also the year that Darwin published *On the Origin of Species*. Soon after, similar institutions were established all over Europe. These institutions became important arenas for research and debate on the origin and evolution of the human species and gave rise to the new discipline of anthropology, which replaced 'ethnology' as the most important academic discipline for research on race and human variation.

The main founding father of anthropology was the French anatomist Paul Broca, who initiated the establishment of a number of anthropological institutions and helped turn Paris into an international centre for anthropological research and education. Anthropology, as promoted by Broca, bore many similarities to the ethnology of the mid-nineteenth century. The anthropologists generally assumed that there was a relationship between intellectual ability and the size and shape of the brain and skull. Craniology was the preferred method for classifying and ranking inferior and superior races, and the cephalic index was retained and elaborated upon as an important criterion for classification. The Germanic race was still blond and long-skulled, and debates on racial types and European prehistory were still interwoven with struggles surrounding national narratives and national identities.[1]

---

1   See, for instance: Elisabeth A. Williams, 'Anthropological Institutions in Nineteenth-Century France', *Isis*, Vol. 76, no. 3 (1985), pp. 331-48; Chris Manias, 'The *Race Prussienne* Controversy: Scientific Internationalism and the Nation', *Isis*, Vol. 100, no. 4 (2009), pp. 733-57; Stephen Jay Gould, *The Mismeasure of*

http://dx.doi.org/10.11647/OBP.0051.03

However, there were also some important differences between the ethnology of the 1840s and the anthropology of the 1860s and later decades. Broca and his French colleagues took the lead in developing craniology and racial typology into a quantitative science. They launched new and more rigorous measuring techniques and instruments, undertook increasingly comprehensive studies of living populations and skeletal remains, and adopted increasingly advanced statistical methods to analyse the ever-expanding volume of data on anatomical variation between human groups. In addition, Retzius' scheme of racial succession, which had held a dominant position since the 1840s, was debunked in the 1860s. Employing a range of quantitative methods, Broca proved that the aboriginal Basque population, which had been assumed to have short skulls, was in fact overwhelmingly long-skulled, whilst the Celts were in fact short-skulled, not long-skulled as had been previously assumed.[2]

With the advent of anthropology, racial science became a better organised, comprehensive and institutionalised activity. Given that anthropology's principal aim was to explore the evolutionary history of humankind and to establish a natural system of classification of human races, it was by its very nature a transnational discipline, aimed at the worldwide mapping and numerical description of human anatomical variation. However, anthropology was also strongly linked to the nation-state: it was usually financed and organised on a national level, with national or colonial populations as its preferred research subjects, and various nations fostered different and often competing schools of research.[3]

Norway was a latecomer. It was only in the 1880s, and particularly in the 1890s, that anthropology became established as a field of research in Norway. From the beginning, Norwegian anthropology was inspired by foreign models, but its rise was also entwined with domestic cultural, social and political processes. Anthropological research was mainly funded by the Norwegian government and organised by national institutions. The primary aim of Norwegian anthropology was to study the racial

Man (London: Penguin, 1996), pp. 105-42; Martin Staum, 'Nature and Nurture in French Ethnography and Anthropology, 1859-1914', *Journal of the History of Ideas*, Vol. 65, no. 3 (2004), pp. 475-95.

2   Richard McMahon, *The Races of Europe: Anthropological Race Classification of Europeans 1839-1939* (Ph.D. thesis, European University Institute, 2007), p. 207.

3   The relationship between internationalism, nationalism and the development of anthropology is discussed in Chris Manias, 'The *Race Prussienne* Controversy: Scientific Internationalism and the Nation', *Isis*, Vol. 100, no. 4 (2009), pp. 733-57.

composition and biological history of the Norwegian people, and the discipline arose within the confines of two national institutions that were particularly well placed to facilitate this task: the Norwegian Army and the University of Kristiania. While military recruits served as research objects for studies of the racial composition of the living Norwegian population, the University's Department of Anatomy took responsibility for anthropological research on the skeletal remains of the national past. This meant that racial theories about the Germanic origin of the nation were once again a topic for discussion among Norwegian academics.

The rise of anthropology at the Department of Anatomy

Since its establishment in 1815, the University of Kristiania's Department of Anatomy had, first and foremost, been an educational institution giving basic preclinical instruction to medical students. But from the 1870s onwards, successive heads of department tried to expand its scope and turn it into a key site for biomedical science. These efforts had limited success, however, and it was only after a major revamping in 1915 that the department really became properly equipped for research. More than 300 square metres of the department's premises were then earmarked for physical anthropology, which became a key field of research during the interwar period. Thus, decades of efforts aimed at turning the Department of Anatomy into a leading biomedical research institution ended in a major investment in racial anthropology.[4]

This turn towards anthropology was the culmination of a development that had been ongoing for a couple of decades and must be understood partly against the background of the notions of 'anatomy', 'biology' and 'science' that underpinned the institutional strategy of the department in the late nineteenth century. Jacob Heiberg, head of the department from 1877 to 1887, and Gustav Adolph Guldberg, his successor from 1888 to 1908, advocated a modern 'biological' approach to anatomy at the expense of

---

4   Jacob Heiberg, 'Om et biologisk laboratorium', *Norsk Magazin for lægevidenskaben*, no. 1 (1883-1884), pp. 65-70; Jon Røyne Kyllingstad and Thor Inge Rørvik, *1870-1911: Vitenskapenes universitet*, Universitetet i Oslo 1811-2011, Vol. 2 (Oslo: Unipub, 2011), pp. 195-99, 438; H. Hopstock, *Det anatomiske institutt 23. Januar 1815 -23. Januar 1915* (Kristiania: I kommission hos Aschehoug, 1915), pp. 155-85; Per Holck, *Den fysiske antropologi i Norge. Fra anatomisk institutts historie 1815-1990* (Oslo: Anatomisk institutt, University of Oslo, 1990).

what they both saw as outdated descriptive anatomy. In his programmatic inaugural lecture, Guldberg claimed that biology consisted of two main branches: physiology, which was an autonomous discipline, and morphology, which belonged within the confines of anatomy. Morphology aimed at detecting the natural laws that govern the life-cycles of individual organisms and the overall evolution of life-forms, and it was only by engaging in such research that an anatomy department could earn the right to be regarded as a truly scientific institution.[5]

Guldberg was the first Norwegian professor of anatomy with an extensive scientific education, and he was well versed in morphology. Before assuming the professorship, he had studied with anatomists and zoologists who were at the forefront of morphological research, such as Eduard Van Beneden, Oscar Hertwig, Albert von Koellicker and Ernst Haeckel.[6] In his inaugural lecture, Guldberg divided morphology into two main fields: ontogeny and phylogeny. These fields were interconnected owing to the law of recapitulation, which declared that ontogeny (an organism's life-cycle from the fertilised egg to the fully-developed individual) recapitulates phylogeny (the evolutionary history of the species to which the organism belongs). Morphological research into the life-cycles of individual organisms, as well as comparative studies of anatomical likeness and difference between animal species, could therefore give insight into the evolutionary history and basic causes of the formation of the human body. Furthermore, according to Guldberg, anthropology was, in fact, a branch of morphology as it dealt with the comparative study of 'man's relationship to the anthropoid apes', 'man under diverse conditions of life' and mankind's division into 'human races'.[7] This meant that anthropology naturally belonged within the working field of a modern, research-oriented anatomy department.

Morphology had become a highly important research field following the breakthrough of evolutionary biology, and, like many of his German

---

5   Gustav Guldberg, *Om det anatomiske studium: Tale tale ved tiltrædelsen af professoratet i anatomi ved Christiania universitet d. 7de septbr. 1888* (Kristiania: I kommision hos Dybwad, 1888).

6   Justus Barth, 'In Memoriam! Professor Dr. Med. G.A. Guldberg', *Internationale Monatsschrift für Anatomie und Physiologie* (1908), pp. 101-04; idem, 'Gustav A. Guldberg', *Forhandlinger i Videnskabs-selskabet i Christiania aar 1908.* (Kristiania: I kommission hos Jacob Dybwad, 1909), pp. 11-24; Carl M. Fürst, 'Gustav Adolph Guldberg', *Anatomischer Anzeiger*, Vol. 32, nos. 19/20 (1908), pp. 506-12.

7   Guldberg, *Om det anatomiske studium*.

colleagues,[8] Guldberg's predecessor Jacob Heiberg campaigned intensely to turn the University of Kristiania's Department of Anatomy into a leading institution for morphological research. He tried to obtain public funding for the construction of a new anatomy building that could house laboratories for experimental embryology and microscopy studies of tissues and cells, and which would allow for the expansion and modernisation of the Museum of Comparative Anatomy, and its systematic collection of embryos and organs from various animal species.[9] Such collections were important tools for morphological research, and it was at this museum that Gustav Guldberg began his career in the late 1870s. During his time there, Guldberg managed the collection, undertook embryological and comparative anatomical research on whales, and established a huge collection of whale skeletons.[10]

By the time Heiberg died in 1887, it was becoming increasingly clear that neither the Norwegian political authorities nor the national medical profession favoured the idea of a research-oriented anatomy department. Instead, they wanted the Department of Anatomy to leave morphology and comparative anatomy to the zoologists and to concentrate on practical anatomical training for medical students.[11] Thus, when Guldberg took over as head of the department, it was apparent that Heiberg's grand plan would have to be abandoned. It is probably no coincidence that the Department of Anatomy then began to pursue anthropological research systematically. This was a part of morphology that did not naturally belong within zoology, and at the same time, there was a growing demand for research on the biological history of the nation which the university's Department of Anatomy was able to meet.

---

8   On morphology and anatomy in Germany, see Lynn K. Nyhart, *Biology Takes Form: Animal Morphology and the German Universities, 1800-1900* (Chicago, IL: University of Chicago Press, 1995).

9   Jacob Heiberg, 'Om et biologisk laboratorium', *Norsk Magazin for lægevidenskaben*, no. 1 (1884), pp. 65-70. The comparative anatomical collection (*Det zootomiske museum*) had existed in the Department of Anatomy since the 1840s, but in the 1870s it was transferred to the Zoological Museum. This was against Heiberg's will, as he wanted to keep the collection at the Department of Anatomy and further expand it. See RA: S-2536 UiO Medfak Aa, L0002 Forhandlingsprotokoll 1870-1885: Faculty board meeting, 23 October, 13 November and 11 December 1877.

10 Kyllingstad and Rørvik, *1870-1911: Vitenskapenes universitet*, pp. 295-300.

11 Ibid., pp. 195-99, 212-19, 295-300.

Following Heiberg's death, Guldberg went abroad to study anthropology. Although most of the contacts in his network were part of the German-speaking world, as was the case for Norwegian medical practitioners in general, he went to Paris, where he studied anthropology under Léonce Manouvrier and Paul Topinard, the leading figures in French anthropology after the death of their tutor Paul Broca in 1880. Among the first tasks Guldberg undertook after he returned to Kristiania to resume his professorship in anatomy was to improve the department's facilities for physical anthropological research.[12] According to Guldberg, a comprehensive collection of ancient crania was a basic prerequisite for the study of a nation's 'anthropological physiognomy'.[13]

The anatomical collection and the rise of anthropology

The Department of Anatomy had maintained an anatomical collection since its establishment in 1815. This was basically meant for medical instruction, but by the 1880s it also contained objects considered to be of anthropological interest, such as Sami skulls, skulls from non-European peoples (which Guldberg referred to as *racekranier*) and plaster casts of *racekranier* that the department had received from Anders Retzius in the 1850s. However, the most important items were a growing collection of ancient skulls from southern Norway that derived from archaeological excavations.[14] Thus, the growth of anthropology at the university was to some extent a side effect of the growth of archaeology from the 1860s onwards. The archaeologists were more or less exclusively interested in the history of the Norwegians, and this also became the favourite research topic of physical anthropology.

When Guldberg assumed the professorial chair, he sorted out the anthropologically interesting objects and created a separate anthropological collection. He also purchased a number of anthropological measuring

---

12 Before returning to Kristiania, Guldberg also occupied for some months the chair vacated by anatomist and anthropologist Gustaf von Düben, the successor to Anders Retzius in Stockholm, where it is likely that Guldberg familiarised himself with the Swedish tradition of racial anthropology. See Barth, 'In Memoriam!' and Fürst, 'Gustav Adolph Guldberg'.

13 G. A. Guldberg, 'Udsigt over en del fund af gammelnorske kranier', *Nordisk medicinsk arkiv*, Vol. 30, no. 13 (1897), pp. 1-6.

14 Ibid.

instruments and began to systematically supplement the collection with anthropological specimens that he had acquired from collectors, scholars and missionaries.[15] In the mid-1890s, the department even began to carry out excavations on its own in order to fill in geographical gaps in the Norwegian material that had been obtained from the archaeologists.[16] Guldberg evidently saw it as his task both to build up a collection of *racekranier* from all over the world and, more importantly, to establish a representative collection of ancient Norwegian skulls in order to facilitate research on the racial history of the Norwegian people.

The first major anthropological work undertaken at the university was the doctoral thesis *Norønnaskaller* (1896), written by Justus Barth, a member of staff in the Department of Anatomy. The research for Barth's thesis involved extensive measurements and comparisons of the ancient Norwegian skulls in the collection at that time, most of which came from medieval sites in Kristiania and its vicinity (see Fig. 3). Barth claimed to have identified three racial types among the skulls: two short-skulled types and one long-skulled type. He proposed that the latter was typical for the medieval population of southeast Norway and named it the Viking type (*Vikingtypen*), arguing that it resembled skulls from Viking burial mounds. He also argued that the Viking type coincided with the long-skulled race that Anders Retzius had identified in Sweden in the 1840s, as well as with the so-called *Reihengräbertypus* that German anthropologist Alexander Ecker had detected in South German Iron Age graves in the 1860s.[17]

---

15 See 'Det anatomiske institut', in *Det kongelige norske Frederiks Universitets Aarsberetning for 1889-1890, 1890, 1890-1891, 1891-1892* and *1892-1893* (Kristiania: Universitetet, 1889-1894).

16 Gustav A. Guldberg, 'Skeletfundet paa Rør i Ringsaker og Rør kirke', *Christiania videnskabs-selskabs forhandlinger*, no. 9 (1895), pp. 3-14; G. A. Guldberg, 'Fra det anatomiske institut ved det kgl. Fredriks universitet', in *Foreningen til norske fortidsmindesmærkers bevaring, Aarsberetning for 1900* (Kristiania: [n. pub.], 1901), pp. 1-3.

17 Justus Barth, *Norrønaskaller: crania antiqua in parte orientali Norvegiæ meridionalis inventa: En studie fra Universitetets Anatomiske Institut* (Kristiania: Aschehoug, 1896), pp. 1-3, 57ff. In 1868 the Department of Anatomy received 53 skulls from archaeological excavations in a medieval churchyard and a nearby site in Kristiania (Mariakirken and Sørenga). In 1879, fifty skulls came in from the cemetery of a medieval monastery in Kristiania. In 1890, the collection was further supplemented by 56 skulls assumed to be from a Franciscan monastery in Tønsberg, located on the Kristiania fjord (Oslofjorden) and one of Norway's oldest towns.

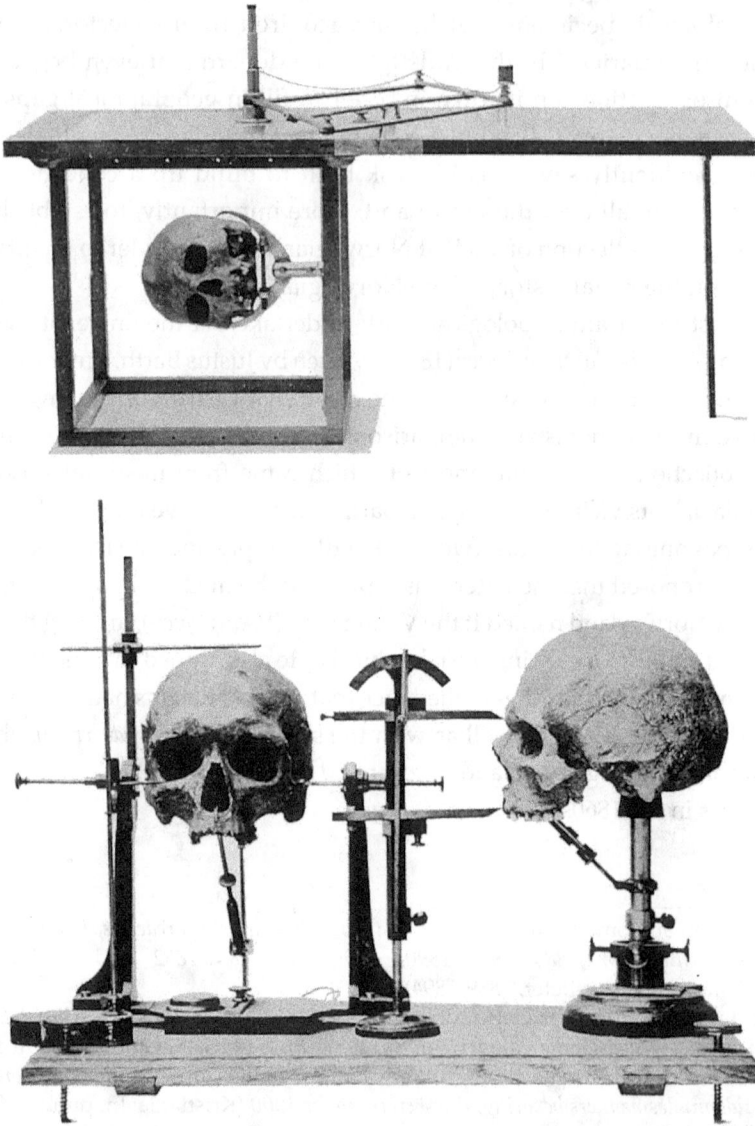

Fig. 3 Craniometrics: a 'diptograph' (top) and a 'craniophor' (bottom) used by Justus
Barth for his drawings of skulls. The diptograph is covered by a glass plate on which a
diopter sight is placed and then connected in turn to a pencil.

During the years that followed, the collection at the University of Kristiania
was further supplemented with a number of skulls from other parts of
southern Norway, and in 1901 the army doctor Carl F. Larsen published
a new study based on this expanded collection entitled *Norwegian Cranial*

Types. In contrast to Barth, Larsen argued in favour of no fewer than seven different skull types. However, he did agree with Barth on the existence of a blond, long-skulled type that he labelled the 'Norse-Germanic dolichocephalic type', identical to Barth's Viking type.[18]

Army anthropology

In parallel with the growth of skeletal anthropology at the Department of Anatomy, army doctors began to study the racial composition of contemporary Norwegians. As a result of the military conscription system, they had easy access to a presumably representative sample of the population and could draw inspiration from countries like France, Germany and Italy, where large-scale racial surveys of conscripts had been undertaken since the 1860s.[19] Racial anthropology was even considered relevant to the medical assessment of conscripts. In the *Norwegian Journal of Military Medicine*, army doctors discussed whether geographical variations in the supply of serviceable recruits were caused by differences in racial quality or by the impact of varying local environments.[20]

In a thesis published in 1875, the army doctor Carl Oscar Eugen Arbo proposed that the scope of the routine medical examinations of new conscripts should be expanded so that they might not only fulfil narrow military aims but also serve broader state interests by functioning as instruments for the collection of medical, statistical, ethnological and anthropological research data. The aim was to assess and explain variations in bodily quality within the national population and between nations, and thus to measure the physical well-being of the people and the strength of the nation.[21] Arbo's enterprise was partly inspired by the work of the leading German medical professor and anthropologist Rudolf Virchow, who, in 1863, had argued in favour of turning the assessments of conscripts

---

18 C. F. Larsen, *Norske kranietyper: efter Studier i Universitetets anatomiske Instituts Kraniesamling*. Skr. Vidensk. Selsk. Christiania MN kl., 1901, no. 5 (Kristiania: Videnskabsselskabet, 1901).

19 Otto Ammon, *Anthropologische Untersuchungen der Wehrpflichtigen in Baden*. (Hamburg: Verlagsanstalt und Druckerei Actien-Gesellschaft, 1890); Ridolfo Livi, *Antropometria Militare* (Roma: Presso il Giornale medico del Regio Esercito, 1896-1905). Manias, 'The *Race Prussienne* Controversy', p. 739.

20 *Norsk tidsskrift for militærmedicin. Kristiania.* First issue, 1897.

21 C. O. E. Arbo, *Om Sessions-Undersøgelsernes og Recruterings-Statistikens Betydning for Videnskaben og Staten med et Udkast til en derpå grundet Statistik for de tre nordiske Riger* (Kristiania: Steenske bogtrykkeri, 1878), pp. 1-8.

into an internationally coordinated system for medical surveys of national populations. Arbo was also influenced by the French state and French military doctors, who since the end of the Napoleonic Wars had been producing national health statistics based on conscript examinations. And last but not least, he took inspiration from French anthropologists, who, under the leadership of Paul Broca, tried to explain regional variations in health and physical strength with the help of anthropological theories. Arbo analysed data from Sweden, Denmark and Norway and found that they concurred with Broca's findings in France: inborn racial differences were more important explanatory factors for regional variations in physical health and bodily strength than differences in natural environment, climate, economic prosperity or livelihood.[22]

Four years after the publication of his thesis, Arbo received an overseas scholarship from the Norwegian government and went to Berlin and Paris to study anthropology. He visited, among others, Broca at the *Ecole d'Anthropologie*,[23] where it is likely that he was confirmed in his deterministic notions of race. Broca was a neo-Lamarckian who believed that the evolution of species was driven by the inheritance of acquired characteristics. He claimed, for instance, to have proved that the average brain size of Parisians (and thus their average mental capacity) had increased since the Middle Ages because of cultural and social improvement. However, the improvement of the human brain was a slow process that spanned many generations, and Broca held that the mental abilities of individual human beings were strongly determined by their class, gender and race. All these differences could be assessed with the help of anthropometrical investigations.[24]

During the two decades that followed his visits to Berlin and Paris, Arbo travelled to various military camps in southern Norway, gathering data on the distribution of bodily traits such as facial length, jaw angle, body height, eye colour, hair colour and, most importantly, the breadth and length of the head. His results were published in a series of *Contributions to the Physical Anthropology of the Norwegians* in the 1880s and 1890s, earning him membership of the Norwegian Academy of Science and Letters, winning him international acclaim and turning him into the foremost Norwegian pioneer of anthropological research.[25]

22 Arbo, *Om Sessions-Undersøgelsernes*, pp. 1-8, 17-18, 154.
23 Axel Johannessen, 'Carl Oscar Eugen Arbo', *Tidsskrift for den norske lægeforening*, Vol. 26 (1906), pp. 516-19.
24 Stephen Jay Gould, *The Mismeasure of Man*, pp. 105-42.
25 Lars Walløe, 'Carl Arbo', in *Norsk biografisk leksikon*, https://nbl.snl.no/Carl_

According to Arbo, the geographical distribution of short skulls and long skulls coincided with variations in dialects and with the ancient political division of Norway into counties (see Fig. 4). Arbo's main explanation for the uneven distribution of skull shapes was that the counties had originally been settled by different peoples with diverse racial origins. A predominantly dark-haired and brown-eyed short-skulled type had a radiation centre in southwest Norway and was strongly represented in the western coastal regions. Blond and blue-eyed long skulls had their radiation centre in eastern Norway, out of which they had pushed westward to settle the inner fjord and mountain areas.[26]

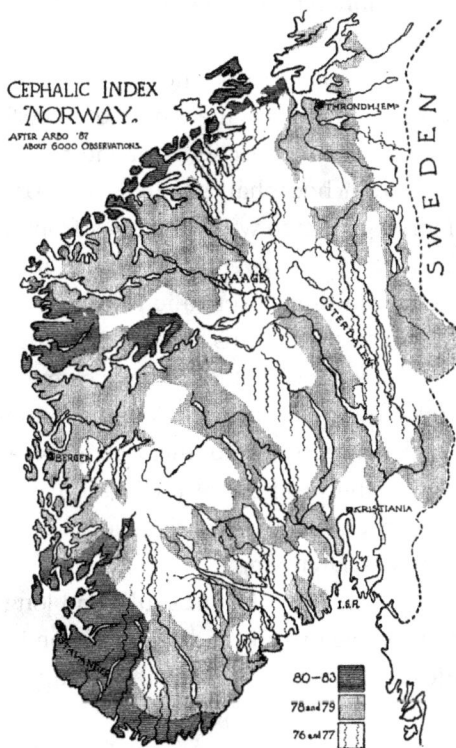

Fig. 4 Map showing the distribution of skull types in Norway based on Arbo's research, as presented in Ripley's *The Races of Europe* (1899).

Arbo. Arbo was cited in detail in William Z. Ripley, *The Races of Europe. A Sociological Study* (London: Kegan Paul, Trench, Trübner & Co., 1899), pp. 205-11. Joseph Deniker also used data from Arbo's works in his 1899 book *Les races de l'Europe* (see Hans Daae, *Militærlægers bidrag til norsk anthropologi* (Kristiania: Gøndahl, 1907), p. 16).

26 Retzius used Broca's system of three categories based on the cephalic index (dolicho-, meso- and brachycephalic), but in his final analysis he merged the dolicho- and mesocephalics into one dolicho-mesocephalic category.

Arbo supplemented this claim with references to mechanisms of natural and social selection that had taken place after the original settlement of the territory. In a monograph from 1897, he argued that the predominantly dark, short-skulled population along the southern coast of Norway was 'psychologically crippled' and weak. However, the short-skulled majority was intermixed with some long-skulled individuals distinguished by their courage. Arbo suggested that the population of the coastal districts had originally included a larger proportion of long-skulled inhabitants, but that most of them had left or died since the area's harsh living conditions did not suit their restless, adventurous and warrior-like nature. Only the calmer, more peaceful and rooted inhabitants—the short skulls—had remained.[27]

Arbo's psychological assessment of local populations was based on other authors' descriptions, on hearsay and commonly-held views, and on his own observations. Referring to the works of historians like Munch and Sars, he put forward detailed accounts of the historical events that had led the adventurous dolichocephalics to leave the coastal districts. He also compared the Norwegian case with examples from abroad. German anthropologists agreed that the average cephalic index of southern Germany had changed from dolichocephalic to brachycephalic since the Iron Age. Some anthropologists saw this as a result of superior Germanics being increasingly intermixed with inferior Slavic elements, whilst others proposed that cultural growth had produced larger brains and that over the centuries this had led to the development of a more spherical skull. Thus, what some saw as the progress of civilisation was considered by others to be a troubling example of racial degeneration. Arbo sided with the theory of detrimental racial mixing.[28]

Arbo compared the distribution of short skulls and long skulls with the relative number of serviceable recruits and with assumed local differences in behaviour and lifestyle. On the basis of this comparison, he argued

27 C. O. E. Arbo, *Fortsatte Bidrag til Nordmændenes Anthropologi IV Lister og Mandals Amt*, Skr. Vidensk. Selsk. Christiania MN kl. 1897 (Kristiania: I Kommission hos Dybwad, 1897), p. 43.

28 C. O. E. Arbo, *Fortsatte Bidrag til Nordmændenes Anthropologi V. Nedenes amt*. Skr. Vidensk. Selsk. Christiania MN kl. 1898 (Kristiania: I Kommission hos Dybwad, 1898), p. 53; Gustaf Retzius, 'Blick på den fysiska antropologiens historia', *Ymer*, Vol. 16, no. 4 (1896), pp. 221-45 (pp. 240-41); Gaston Backman, 'Den Europeiska rasfrågan ur antropologisk och sociala synspunkter', 'Den Europeiska rasfrågen ur antropologisk och sociala synspunkter', *Ymer*, Vol. 35, no. 4 (1915), pp. 330-50 (p. 345).

that racial difference in the Norwegian population could explain regional variations in health, military capability, personality/character, intelligence and behaviour. Whereas people from the typically brachycephalic populations along the coast stood out as weak, nervous, worried, petty and narrow-minded, he argued the overwhelmingly dolichocephalic rural inhabitants of the inland were brave, handsome, resilient, bold and open-minded.[29]

Arbo obviously saw the blond long-skulled race as constituting the core of the Norwegian nation. These people were the present-day equivalent of Barth's Viking type and embodied the nation's most superior mental and physical abilities. Thus, Arbo's work can be seen as a revival of the basic ideas of Munch and Keyser's national narrative, but with one crucial difference: according to Arbo, the Norwegian people were not exclusively drawn from the Germanic race, since the superior long-skulled type was intermixed with an inferior, short-skulled kind. This idea would become a major topic in Norwegian debates on race and nationhood around the turn of the century.

The rise of anthroposociology

Arbo's portrayal of the Norwegian population as made up of a mix of dark short skulls and blond long skulls echoed ideas that had been commonly held by European anthropologists since the heyday of Anders Retzius. Broca, for instance, believed that the French population was a racial mixture dominated by tall, fair and long-headed Kymrics and short, dark and broad-headed Gauls (the true Celtic race), and he claimed that this could explain French regional variations in military ability. Since the Gauls were smaller and weaker, they were more frequently rejected from military service than were the Kymrics. When Arbo discussed the usefulness of military medicine in his 1875 thesis, he referred extensively to this theory, and it is most likely that it was an important source of inspiration for his approach to the study of Norwegian recruits.[30]

---

29 See, for instance: C. O. E. Arbo, 'Udsigt over der sydvestlige Norges anthropologiske forhold', *Ymer*, Vol. 14 (1894), pp. 165-86, (p. 173ff.); *Fortsatte Bidrag til Nordmændenes Anthropologi V. Nedenes amt*, p. 62; idem, *Fortsatte Bidrag til Nordmændenes Anthropologi IV Lister og Mandals Amt*.

30 Arbo, *Om Sessions-Undersøgelsernes*, pp. 17-18, 154.

There was another author, however, to whom Arbo referred more frequently in his anthropological works in the 1890s, namely Otto Ammon.[31] Ammon was a leading figure in anthroposociology, a school of research within which the dichotomy between inferior short skulls and superior long skulls was a key element. Ammon seems to have been an important source of inspiration for Arbo. In order to understand the societal context and ideological implications of Arbo's research, therefore, we need to know more about anthroposociology, its relationship to mainstream anthropology and its impact on Norwegian debates concerning racial identity and origin.

The anthroposociologists were strongly inspired by the French writer Joseph Arthur de Gobineau and his infamous *Essay on the Inequality of the Human Races* (1853-1855). Gobineau was a conservative who lamented the French Revolution and the fall of the *ancien régime*. He saw the aristocracy as the descendants of a warrior caste that had once been the bearers of European high culture, and held that the Revolution had ushered in an epoch of social and geographic mobility that led to racial mixing, threatened the racial purity of the upper class and would ultimately lead to the downfall of Europe.

Gobineau's ideas did not win much acclaim initially, but towards the end of the century, his *Essay* became a rallying point for racial ideologues, and anthroposociology arose as an attempt to establish a quantitative science based on his ideas. The anthroposociologists held that the blond, blue-eyed and long-skulled northern Europeans were descendants of a warrior race that had founded European civilisation and had been the aristocratic rulers over the inferior short-skulled races. They studied the geographical and social distribution of bodily traits such as skull shape and hair colour, and claimed to have quantitative evidence that proved that the stratification of European society mirrored the distribution of racial qualities (see Fig. 5). The anthroposociologists believed that industrialisation and urbanisation stimulated geographical and social mobility, which were over time erasing the natural distinction between classes, leading to racial mixing and biological degeneration. This was a threat to the future of Western civilisation, they argued, and should be counteracted by state intervention in the biological reproduction of citizens.[32]

---

31 The most cited foreign book in Arbo's works in the 1890s was Otto Ammon, *Die natürliche Auslese beim Menschen* (Jena: G. Fischer, 1893).

32 Jennifer Michael Hecht, 'The Solvency of Metaphysics: The Debate over Racial

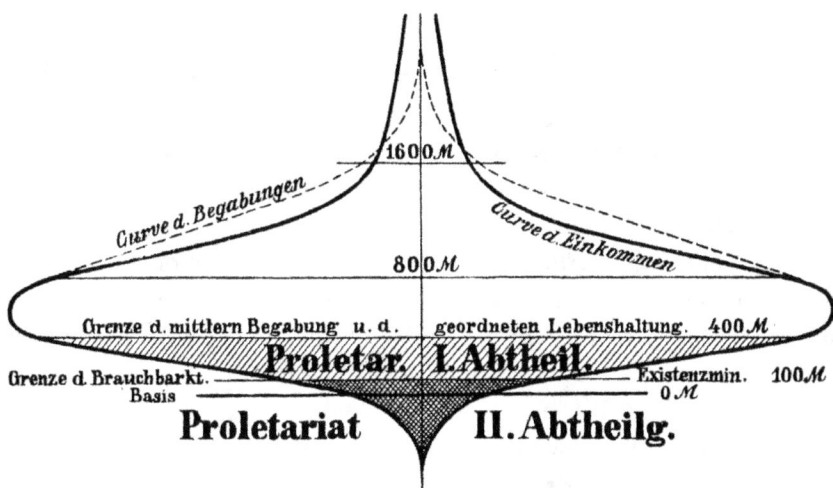

Fig. 5 Ammon's outlook on society: the curve on the right shows the population distributed by income; the curve on the left shows the population distributed according to intellectual endowment. The lower horizontal line indicates the threshold for 'useable' endowment, and this coincides with the line showing the minimum income needed for subsistence.

Anthroposociology represented an attempt to establish a new scientific discipline on the boundary between physical anthropology and the social sciences. This enterprise won different degrees of academic acclaim in France and Germany. In France, Georges Vacher de Lapouge, the chief figure of French anthroposociology, led a comprehensive research programme in the 1890s, gaining sympathisers all over the Western world and some degree of academic legitimacy in his home country.[33] His German colleague Otto Ammon, in contrast, met with strong opposition from the German anthropological establishment when he began putting forward his ideas in the late 1880s and 1890s. After the turn of the century, however, the roles were reversed, with Ammon winning increasing

---

Science and Moral Philosophy in France, 1890-1919', *Isis*, Vol. 90, no. 1 (1999), pp. 1-24 (pp. 3ff.); Benoit Massin, 'From Virchow to Fischer: Physical Anthropology and "Modern Race Theories" in Wilhelmine Germany', in George W. Stocking, Jr., ed., *Volksgeist as Method and Ethic* (Madison, WI: University of Wisconsin, 1996), pp. 106-14.

33 Jennifer Michael Hecht, 'A Vigilant Anthropology: Léonce Manouvrier and the Disappearing Numbers', *Journal for the History of the Behavioral Sciences*, Vol. 33, no. 3 (1997), pp. 221-40.

scientific acclaim in Germany and Lapouge being ostracised from the French scientific community.

The different destinies of anthroposociology in France and Germany were symptomatic of the general development of anthropology and racial science in the two countries. Even though Paul Broca had been strongly opposed to Gobineau's theories, anthroposociology had some important characteristics in common with Broca's school of anthropology: a strong belief in biological determinism and in the use of anthropometry to order human beings into a hierarchy of inferior and superior biological groups. After Broca's death, French anthropology split into competing schools, some of which began to distance themselves from Broca's approach. This is particularly true in the case of Léonce Manouvrier, Lapouge's most outspoken and powerful enemy within the French anthropological community. Manouvrier's attack on Lapouge was coupled with a general criticism of racial determinism and hierarchical thinking. This criticism had a significant impact and helped to marginalise French physical anthropology around the turn of the century.[34]

German anthropology, in contrast, had from the beginning been characterised by a much more liberal attitude to race. The principal figure was the famous anatomist Rudolf Virchow, who, besides having a key position within German science, was a leading liberal-democratic politician. Virchow opposed militaristic nationalism, imperialism and anti-semitism, and he used his scientific knowledge and prestige to criticise the idea of pure, static and ancient races, to argue against racial superiority and to counteract the adulation of the Germanic race.[35]

From the 1890s, however, racial thought gained an increasingly strong foothold in German culture and public discourse, and, among radical nationalists, the nation became increasingly associated with the idea of a Germanic master race. The national-conservative *völkisch* movement, which advocated a romantic and racialised style of nationalism, achieved increasing popular support. While Virchow and other leading anthropologists tried to counter this wave of racial romanticism by the use of arguments from their strongly quantitative and positivist science, Otto Ammon and the anthroposociologists tried to bridge the gap between *völkisch* racial philosophy and scientific anthropology.[36]

---

34 Hecht, 'A Vigilant Anthropology', pp. 221-40.
35 Massin, 'From Virchow to Fischer', pp. 79-153 (pp. 86ff.).
36 Ibid., pp. 100ff., 132.

In the 1880s, Ammon was funded by the German Anthropological Society to carry out a conscript survey in Baden. He found a high frequency of dolichocephalics in the cities, which he explained as the product of social selection: the dynamic and adventurous dolichocephalics were drawn to the city, while the more down-to-earth brachycephalics stayed in rural areas. This theory, which was later termed 'Ammon's Law', met with strong opposition in the German Anthropological Society. In 1889, Ammon was refused additional funding for his project, and during the 1890s his work was rejected by the leading anthropological journals. After the turn of the century, however, his ideas began to win growing support, reflecting a more general shift in German anthropology from 'racial liberalism' in the nineteenth century to racial determinism after the turn of the century.[37]

Anthroposociology and Scandinavia

A key building block in the theoretical edifice constructed by the anthroposociologists was the notion of a convergence between the Aryan and the Germanic races. In contrast to Anders Retzius and his generation, the anthroposociologists did not believe that the original speakers of the Aryan or Indo-European language had wandered into Europe from somewhere in Central Asia. Instead, they held that the original Indo-Europeans were an indigenous European race that had arisen in northern Germany and southern Scandinavia during the Stone Age, and that the Germanic peoples were their true descendants. Thus, the Aryans were identical to the Germanics, and it was this Aryan-Germanic race that was responsible for European civilisation.

This theory was launched in the 1880s by freelance writers who stood outside or on the margins of the academic world, but who based their views upon selective reading of mainstream archaeological, linguistic and anthropological research. Since this group of writers saw Scandinavia as the cradle of the master race and the home of a particularly pure Aryan-Germanic population, they were greatly interested in research on the prehistory and racial composition of the Scandinavian populations. An important prerequisite for the rise of the Aryan-Germanic theory was the rejection of Retzius and Nilsson's racial succession scheme in the 1860s,

---

37 Massin, 'From Virchow to Fischer', pp. 126-43.

and the establishment of scientific consensus regarding Germanic presence in Scandinavia during the Stone Age.[38]

Although the Aryan-Germanic theory was at odds with Retzius and Nilsson's account of European prehistory, these theories had some important ideological implications in common: southern Scandinavia was designated as a centre of gravity for the Germanic race, which stood at the peak of the racial hierarchy and whose members were the true bearers of European civilisation. Thus, anthroposociology seems to have provided a good starting point for the revival of glorified and racialised national narratives in Scandinavia. How, then, did Scandinavian scholars respond to these ideas? Let us take a brief look at Swedish anthropology before returning to Norway.

The leading figure in Swedish anthropology around the turn of the century was Gustav Retzius, the son of Anders Retzius. His most influential anthropological works were 'Crania Suecica Antigua' (1900),[39] which was based on practically all existing prehistoric skulls from Sweden, and *Anthropologia suecica* (1902),[40] which was based on a major survey of Swedish conscripts and co-written with his younger colleague Carl Magnus Fürst.

In parallel to Arbo's findings in Norway, Retzius and Fürst found a slightly higher frequency of short skulls along the coasts and in northern Sweden. They explained this as being the result of an 'attack' on the pure Swedish type from alien racial elements. However, the main conclusion of Gustav Retzius' studies was that Sweden, from the Stone Age until the present time, had been inhabited by a relatively racially-pure Germanic population.

These conclusions seemed to fit well with the Aryan-Germanic theory and attracted considerable interest among German nationalists and anthroposociologists. Gustav Retzius himself, however, was initially opposed to such an interpretation of his findings. Indeed, in concurrence with the views of leading Swedish archaeologist Oscar Montelius, he considered Scandinavia and northern Germany to be the ancestral home of the Germanics, but denied that the Germanics were identical to an ancient

---

38 Olof Ljungström, *Oscariansk antropologi. Etnografi, förhistoria och rasforskning under sent 1800-tal.* (Hedemora: Gidlund, 2004), pp. 262ff.

39 Gustav Retzius, 'Crania Suecica Antigua', *Ymer*, Vol. 20, no. 76 (1900), pp. 76-87.

40 Gustav Retzius and Carl M. Fürst, *Anthropologia suecica: beiträge zur Anthropologie der Schweden nach den auf Veranstaltung der schwedischen Gesellschaft für Anthropologie und Geographie in den Jahren 1897 und 1898 ausgeführten Erhebungen* (Stockholm: [n. pub.], 1902).

Aryan or Indo-European race. Retzius held that the Germanics were only one of a number of Indo-European peoples, and he was sceptical about the anthroposociologists' dogmas.[41]

However, less than seven years after the publication of *Anthropologia suecica*, Retzius changed his mind and lent his strong, public support to the anthroposociological research programme. In a so-called Huxley Lecture in London in 1909, he hailed Lapouge and Ammon as pioneers of a 'modern' race typology according to which there were three European races: the Mediterraneans, the Alpines and the Nordics. Retzius even went so far as to portray the conflict between the dark, short-skulled Alpines and the blond long-skulled Nordics as a main driving force in North European prehistory. After the lecture, Retzius received a letter from Ammon, welcoming him into the 'circle'.[42]

Historian Olof Ljungström has explained the shift in Retzius' opinion by pointing to his close ties with German science and by arguing that he was a typically mainstream scientist who became strongly influenced by the rise of anthroposociology within German anthropology. Retzius was a close friend of the famous German paleoanthropologist Gustav Schwalbe, who advocated similar ideas to Otto Ammon, but who possessed far greater scientific credibility and was instrumental in winning academic acceptance for anthroposociology in Germany. In 1903, the year after Rudolf Virchow's death, Schwalbe was the first influential anthropologist to speak in favour of Ammon and Lapouge's theories at a meeting of the German Anthropological Society. At a national anthropology conference four years later, he even embraced Gobineau's writings, and, according to Ljungström, it was Schwalbe who finally managed to convince Retzius that Ammon and Lapouge's ideas were sound.[43]

The Aryan roots of the Norwegian nation

In contrast to Gustav Retzius' initial dismissal of anthroposociology, we have seen that Arbo, his foremost Norwegian colleague, was already referring extensively to Ammon's work in the 1890s. However, the most ardent, outspoken and well-known Norwegian spokesman of anthroposociology

41 Ljungström, *Oscariansk antropologi*, pp. 301, 303-06, 322.
42 Ibid., p. 341.
43 Ibid., p. 333ff.

was not Arbo but rather the scientific freelancer Andreas M. Hansen, a scientific freelancer who, in the latter half of the 1890s, developed a grandiose national narrative based on the Aryan-Germanic theory. If we wish to assess the degree of academic success enjoyed by these ideas in Norway, as well as the impact they had on dominant national narratives, we need to consider the reception of Hansen's ideas.

Hansen held a teacher's degree in science from the University, which at the time was the highest level of natural-scientific education that could be achieved in Norway. For most of his life, he worked as a freelance researcher and author in disciplines such as geography, geology, anthropology and archaeology. He was the first person in Norway to demonstrate the existence of inland shorelines—traces of the post-glacial land rise—and developed a method for using these shorelines to date Stone Age settlements. This aspect of his work was pioneering, won academic acclaim and is still recognised as scientifically valid. However, these studies also provided a starting point for Hansen's racial account of the history of the Norwegians, which he launched in the latter half of the 1890s and which became both widely known and hotly disputed.[44]

Hansen's account was underpinned by an impressive array of arguments from plant geography, geology, archaeology and linguistics, as well as racial anthropology. The core idea was that the regional boundaries discovered by Arbo between short-skulled and long-skulled populations coincided with the boundaries of the glaciers during the last Ice Age. This, according to Hansen, proved that a short-skulled aboriginal population had survived along the ice-free Norwegian coast during the Ice Age. Long-skulled people had later wandered in and established themselves north and east of the glacier, and then followed the frontier of the melting ice south and westward.

Hansen proposed that the ancient Aryans had their roots in Europe. They had been the first speakers of the original Aryan/Indo-European language and were the forefathers of the long-skulled Germanic peoples. After the Ice Age, they had established themselves as a ruling caste in Europe and had imposed their Aryan language and superior culture upon the inferior and short-skulled Anaryan peoples. In line with this, the short skulls along the west coast of Norway were descendants of an Anaryan race of slaves,

---

44 Werner Werenskiold, 'Andreas M. Hansen', in *Norsk biografisk leksikon*, Vol. 5 (Oslo: Aschehoug, 1931) pp. 358-63.

while the long-skulled population in eastern Norway and in the interior valleys and mountains belonged to the Aryan master race; they were the ones who had created the Old Norse culture.[45]

Hansen believed his theory could shed light on a number of cultural, social and political features of contemporary Norway. In his 1899 book *Norwegian National Psychology*, he demonstrated that the geographical distribution of short and long skulls coincided with the distribution of votes in the parliamentary elections, and claimed that this could be explained by the double racial origin of the nation (see. Fig. 6). Individuals from the predominantly Anaryan rural population on the west coast were distrustful, bigoted, backward-looking and politically conservative, and were therefore inclined to vote for the *Høyre* Party, while the predominantly Aryan population in the south eastern inland were more open-minded, courageous and intelligent, and thus they represented the progressive forces of society and would most likely vote for the *Venstre* Party.[46]

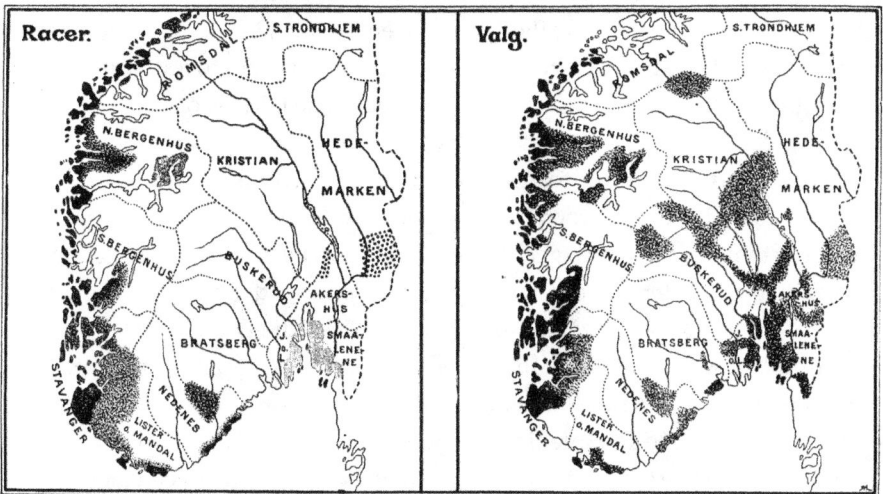

Fig. 6 The map to the right shows the distribution of conservative votes in the Parliamentary election of 1897. The map to the left highlights the areas with a majority short-skulled population.

45 Andreas M. Hansen, *Menneskeslektens ælde* (Kristiania: Jacob Dybwad, 1899), pp. 46, 69-75. Hansen refers to Karl Penka's *Die Herkunft der Arier. Neue Beiträge zur historischen Anthropologie der europäischen Völker* (Vienna: K. Prochaska, 1886).

46 Andreas M. Hansen, *Norsk folkepsykologi: med politisk kart over Skandinavien* (Kristiania: Jakob Dybwad, 1899).

Hansen's account of the origin of the Aryans and Anaryans was partly based on theories developed by German philologist Karl Penka in the 1880s. Penka was a pioneer of the Aryan-Germanic hypothesis and an important source of inspiration for Otto Ammon.[47] In his work Hansen also referred frequently to Otto Ammon and Vacher de Lapouge, and his racial analysis of the political and social landscape in Norway was typical of the anthroposociological school of research. According to Carlos Closson, an American advocate of anthroposociology, the findings presented in *Norwegian National Psychology* confirmed the basic anthroposociological idea of a correlation between bodily and psychological racial traits.[48]

Otto Ammon himself acknowledged Hansen's book and discussed it in the German journal *Centralblatt für Anthrophologie*. Ammon was well informed about Scandinavian anthropological research, but argued that it was Hansen who had come up with the true explanation for the geographical distribution of long skulls and short skulls, and that this explanation was also relevant for attempts to understand the racial composition of Germany. Ammon was particularly thrilled by Hansen's analysis of the psychological differences between the two races, contrasting the aristocratic, freedom-loving attitude of the long skulls with the excessive ideas of equality held by the short skulls, who lacked any sense of freedom. Hansen's work demonstrated, according to Ammon, that the slave-like mentality of the short skulls and the aristocratic mentality of the long skulls were not the result of the centuries in which the Anaryans had been slaves to the Aryans; instead, the master/slave relationship had emerged naturally from the ancient inborn psychological differences between the two races.[49]

Ammon even discussed the objections that had been raised against Hansen's theories, such as the claim that there was no proof of any relationship between skull shape and intelligence. According to Ammon and Hansen, this critique was beside the point, and neither man believed in a direct relationship between skull shape and mental faculties. They rejected, implicitly, the theories on brain anatomy that had been the rationale behind Anders Retzius'

---

47 In *Menneskeslektens ælde*, pp. 46, 69-75. Hansen refers to K. Penka's *Origines Ariacæ* (1883) and *Die Herkunft der Arier* (1886).

48 Carlos C. Closson, 'A Critic of Anthropo-Sociology', *Journal of Political Economy*, Vol. 8, no. 3 (1900), pp. 397-410 (p. 403); Josep R. Llobera, 'The Fate of Anthroposociology in L'année Sociologique', *Jaso*, Vol. 27, no. 3 (1996), pp. 235-51 (p. 242).

49 Otto Ammon, 'Zur Anthropologie Norwegens', *Zentralblatt für Anthropologie, Ethnologie und Uhrgeschichte*, Vol. 5, no. 3 (1900), pp. 129-37.

invention of the cephalic index sixty years earlier, though this index was still a key concept in their research. They declared that the cephalic index was nothing more than a method for identifying racial difference; however, since the races were equipped with different mental abilities, there was an indirect relationship between the geographical distribution of short skulls and long skulls and psychological characteristics.[50]

This idea of an indirect relationship between skull shape and mental faculties meant that Ammon and Hansen were able to dismiss critics who took the existence of brave and highly intelligent short-skulled individuals as evidence against the anthroposociological dogmas. They claimed that even if the races were mentally different on average, there could still be great variation within each race. Thus, the existence of some superior non-Aryan individuals did not disprove claims that the non-Aryans were, on average, inferior to the Aryans.

The controversy over the blond short skull

A linchpin of Hansen's account was the notion of the two races within the Norwegian people.[51] However, Hansen did not base this view upon his own empirical research; instead, he leaned strongly on the work of Arbo and others. This meant that Hansen ran into trouble when Arbo discovered that blondness tended to coincide with brachycephaly in southeast Norway and began arguing for the existence of a third race, one that was blond and short-skulled. Arbo termed this the 'North Sea race' (Nordsjørasen) on account of its similarity to racial elements found on the European North Sea coast.[52]

In his book *Norrønnaskaller*, Justus Barth also proposed the existence of two different short-skulled types, and in 1901 Carl F. Larsen claimed to have identified no fewer than seven different racial types in the University's skull collection.[53] Over the following years, Larsen undertook a series of

---

50 Ibid.

51 Barth, Justus, *Norrønaskaller: crania antiqua in parte orientali Norvegiæ meridionalis inventa: En studie fra Universitetets Anatomiske Institut* (Kristiania: Aschehoug 1896).

52 C. O. E. Arbo, *Den blonde Brachycephal og dens sandsynlige udbredningsfelt* (Kristiania: Kristiania Videnskabs-Selskab, 1906).

53 C. F. Larsen, *Norske kranietyper*, pp. 1-20. Larsen used a system invented by the Italian anthropologist Guiseppe Sergi and classified the skulls according to geometrical types: ellipsoid, rhomboid, etc.

surveys of conscripts from the central Norwegian counties of Trøndelag and Nordland, and claimed to have identified a certain long-skulled *Trønder* type that differed from the eastern Norwegian long skulls. He even suggested that the existing Norwegian population contained a number of different short-skulled types, arguing that the most common of these were not the dark, Alpine race, but rather a blond type.[54]

These views, and in particular the idea of a blond short-skulled race, ran counter to the simple racial dichotomy upon which Hansen's grand theory was based. Hansen therefore set out to prove that the blond brachycephal was not a true race but the product of racial mixing between a dark bracycephalic and a blond dolichocephalic race. He tried to prove his point with the help of arguments drawn from a number of disciplines, such as philology, archaeology and history, as well as anthropology. Larsen responded by accusing Hansen of interpreting any empirical evidence in ways that would fit his overarching theory, and he countered Hansen's grandiose theorising with quantified data on anatomical variations within past and present Norwegian populations.[55] Hansen, in turn, claimed that Larsen's empiricist, inductive and descriptive approach would only lead to the splitting up of any population into an increasingly fine-graded, descriptive and meaningless typology of races.[56]

The strong disagreement over the number of Norwegian races and the controversy between Hansen and Larsen must be understood against the background of ongoing international debates over the meaning of the anthropological concept of race. Around the turn of the century, American sociologist William Z. Ripley published *The Races of Europe*,[57] while the French anthropologist Joseph Deniker issued *The Races and the Peoples of the Earth*.[58] Both men studied the geographical distribution of traits such

---

54 C. F. Larsen: *Trønderkranier og trøndertyper*, Skr. Viden. selsk. Christiania MN kl. 1903 (Kristiania: I kommission hos Dybwad, 1903); idem, *Nordlandsbefolkningen: antropologiske Undersøgelser 1904*, Skr. Viden. selsk. Christiania MN kl. 1905 (Kristiania: I kommission hos Dybwad,1905).

55 Ibid., pp. 23-26.

56 Andreas M. Hansen, *Landnåm i Norge. En udsigt over bosætningens historie* (Kristiania: Fabritius, 1904), pp. 219ff.

57 William Z. Ripley, *The Races of Europe. A Sociological Study* (London: Kegan Paul, Trench, Trübner & Co., 1899).

58 Joseph Deniker, *Les races et les peuples de la terre: elements d'anthropologie et d'ethnographie* (Paris: Schleicher, 1900). I refer to the English version of this work: *The Races of Man* (London: Walter Scott, 1900).

as skull shape, body length, hair and eye colour, but while Deniker split the Europeans into six main races and four secondary races, Ripley, in line with the anthroposociologists, argued for three: the dark, long-skulled Mediterranean race in the south, the blond, long-skulled Nordic race in the north, and the dark, short-skulled Alpine race in the middle.[59] According to Ripley, their conflicting results were caused by different understandings of the concept of race: Deniker's typology was purely descriptive and did not identify the underlying original races. When Deniker detected a frequently-appearing combination of traits, he characterised them as a race and gave them a name, and this meant that Deniker did not address what Ripley considered the real task of anthropology—that of identifying the inheritable, ideal 'types' within the population.[60]

The controversies between Deniker and Ripley and between Larsen and Hansen had to do with a built-in ambiguity in the anthropological idea of racial types. When anthropologists talked about 'types', this could mean an average bodily type that was assumed to be typical of a certain race. However, it could also mean an anatomical 'building plan' inherited by members of a race. This double meaning led to problems for the anthropologists. The theories of Anders Retzius, Sven Nilsson and Rudolf Keyser had been based on the assumption of a concurrence between skull shape, ethnic identity and racial type. Since their time, however, it had become increasingly clear that there was a complicated relationship between 'people' and 'race': it was commonly accepted that all observed populations were racially mixed. There was no easy way to detect the basic racial types within racially-mixed populations.[61]

Perhaps the turn-of-the-century debates over racial types can be best understood against the background of the approach to heritability put forward by the anthropologist, statistician, biologist and eugenicist Francis Galton in the 1880s. Galton studied the frequency of various quantifiable traits in a population and showed that they tended to vary around an average value. He also showed that deviations from the average were distributed according to a normal distribution curve, meaning that when biological traits were inherited over generations, it was this tendency to vary around a norm that was passed down. Singular individuals who

---

59 Ripley, *The Races of Europe*.
60 Ibid., pp. 597-608.
61 See, for instance: Massin, 'From Virchow to Fischer', pp. 106-14.

deviated from the average norm would therefore produce offspring who, on average, were closer to the norm than their parents. Accordingly, a reversion to the average type took place.[62]

For racial anthropology, this meant that any human race had a series of racially-specific features that could be described with the help of figures, such as body length, facial length, arm span and cephalic index. If one examined these figures in a purebred population, one would find that the values that deviated from the race-specific figure occurred with a frequency that was normally distributed around this average figure. The question was how to detect the true racial types within a racially-mixed population.[63] Hansen believed that he had found an answer to this question. With the help of his own statistical invention—the so-called *affinitetstallet* (affinity figure)—he claimed that he could demonstrate that blondness was statistically correlated with dolichocephaly, and darkness with brachycephaly. This would indicate that the 'blond brachycephal' represented a mixture of blond dolichocephalics and dark brachycephalics. Hansen also produced graphs showing the frequency of various cephalic indices in the population. These graphs proved to have three peaks, and the highest peak was located between the two others, indicating that the most frequent cephalic index was neither the assumed typical index of the short-skulled Alpine race, nor the assumed typical index of the Nordic race, but something in between. Somewhat counter-intuitively, Hansen took this as evidence of racial mixing. He explained the curve as the sum of two overlapping standard distribution curves, which peaked around the average cephalic index of the Alpine (non-Aryan) and the Nordic (Aryan) race (see Fig. 7). The highest peak occurred in the middle because negative deviation in one racial group and positive deviation in the other overlapped, so that individuals could have the same cephalic index and still belong to different races.[64]

---

62 Daniel J. Kevles, *In the Name of Eugenics: Genetics and the Uses of Human Heredity* (Berkeley, CA: University of California Press, 1985), pp. 13-19.

63 See, for instance, Andreas M. Hansen, 'To grundraser i det danske folk', *Nyt magasin for naturvidenskaberne*, Vol. 53, no. 3 (1915), pp. 203-67; Søren Hansen, 'Om Grundracer i Norden'. *Forhandlinger ved De skandinaviske naturforskeres 16. møte i Kristiania den 10.-15. juli 1916* (Kristiania: A.W. Brøggers boktrykkeri 1918), pp. 822-38; C. O. E. Arbo, 'Er der foregået nye invandringer i Norden? Foredrag på det skandinaviske naturforskermöde i Stockholm 1897', *Ymer*, Vol. 20, no. 1 (1900), pp. 25-49.

64 Hansen, *Landnåm i Norge*, pp. 230-51.

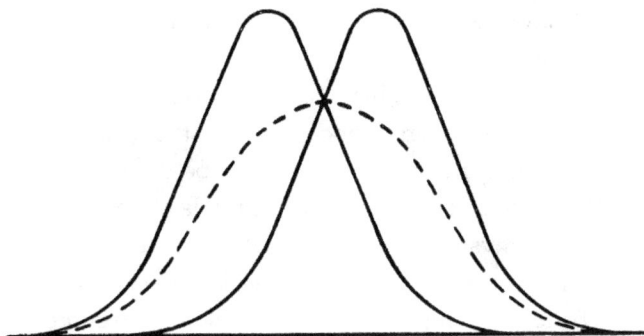

Fig. 7 Illustration of the issue of racially-mixed populations from Rudolf Martin's *Lehrbuch der Anthropologie*. The dotted line shows the relative distribution of cephalic indices in the overall population. The two overlapping curves show the relative distribution of cephalic indices among the two races assumed to comprise the whole population.

In order to prove that brachycephaly and dolicocephaly were deeply-rooted, inheritable racial traits, Hansen also referred to research that indicated that individuals could be identified as dolichocephalics or brachycephalics at an early stage of embryological development, and that these traits were not blurred in mixed offspring. Children with a brachycephalic father and a dolichocephalic mother would either be dolichocephalic or brachycephalic, not something in between. He claimed that the task of anthropology was to identify such inborn racial traits in the population, and that Larsen's purely descriptive typology was irrelevant to this task.[65]

Hansen's racial theories turned him into a well-known public figure in Norway, and his theories were taken seriously both by the academic community and by the general public. Hansen never held a regular academic position, but in 1908, at the age of 51, he was awarded a lifelong state scholarship by the Norwegian Parliament to enable him to continue his studies of the history and anthropology of Norwegians.[66] Such state scholarships were usually given to individual scholars whose work did not fit within the scope of established institutions, particularly scholars doing research in the humanities that was considered to be of national importance. In 1910, Hansen even attained membership of the Norwegian Academy

---

65   Hansen, *Landnåm i Norge*, pp. 230-51.
66   *Statsstipendium* from 1908, cited in Per Holck, *Den fysiske antropologi i Norge*, p. 38.

of Science and Letters, meaning that in spite of his fanciful racial theories, he was clearly acknowledged as a legitimate member of the Norwegian academic community.

However, while he may not have been regarded as a pseudo-scientist, Hansen was clearly a controversial one. He was a stubborn and opinionated man who moved freely and without humility between disciplines, often quarreling with respected experts in various fields of knowledge. We have already seen that his physical anthropological views were strongly disputed by Larsen, and in the next chapter we will see that experts were also critical of many of his historical, linguistic and archaeological arguments.

Professor Guldberg and anthroposociology

If Hansen was an *enfant terrible* who thrived on the outskirts of the academic establishment, Gustav Adolf Guldberg was his antithesis. As head of the Department of Anatomy, Professor Guldberg held one of the most influential and prestigious positions within the national system of medical research and education. In 1903, he was even elected president of the Norwegian Academy of Science and Letters, consolidating his position as a key figure in the Norwegian academic world. At the same time, he was also a driving force behind the anthropological research at the Department of Anatomy. How, then, did Guldberg respond to anthroposociology?[67]

Despite taking the lead in establishing anthropological research at the university, Guldberg produced relatively few anthropological works himself. The most important of these were an investigation of two female skeletons from the Oseberg Viking ship and a study of Norwegian medieval and prehistoric bones that sought to determine body length through a comparison of shin bones.[68] These studies reveal little about his attitude towards race, but they do show that Guldberg was an empirically

---

67 Barth, 'In Memoriam!', pp. 101-04.
68 Gustav Guldberg, *Die Menschenknochen des Osebergschiffs aus dem jüngeren Eisenalter: eine anatomisch-anthropologische Untersuchung*, Skr. Vidensk. Selsk. Christiania MN kl. 1907 (Kristiania: I komission hos Dybwad, 1907); idem, *Anatomisk-anthropologiske Undersøgelser af de lange Extremitetknokler fra Norges Befolkning i Oldtid og Middelalder, 1, Undersøgelsesmethoderne, Laarbenene og Legemshøiden*, Skr. Vidensk. Selsk. Christiania MN kl. 1901 (Kristiania: Brøggers bogtrykkeri, 1901).

accurate and thorough scientist who—in contrast to Hansen, Lapouge and Ammon—was reluctant to draw bold conclusions.

Guldberg's attitude can also be discerned in a popular-science book from 1890 in which he argued that Darwinism should be confined to natural science and not turned into a social philosophy. Guldberg strongly opposed the idea of an evolution driven solely by random variation and natural selection, and he characterised Ernst Haeckel, the famous zoologist who is often referred to as the main German advocate of Social Darwinism,[69] as 'a literary gifted fanatic' surrounded by 'blind', arrogant and narrow-minded supporters.[70] In sum, Guldberg's book espoused a type of evolutionism and a view on the social (ir)relevance of evolutionary theory that were strongly at odds with the anthroposociological research programme. Fourteen years later, however, Guldberg appears to have changed his thinking. In 1904, he launched a plan for a racial survey of Norway that was explicitly inspired by Ammon and Lapouge. In a speech to the Norwegian Academy of Science and Letters, he proposed a nationwide investigation of regional variations in bodily characteristics such as head shape, body length and eye colour, and even suggested gathering data on regional variations in mentality and behaviour. He argued that the national population was composed of different races that were not only physically but also psychologically unique, and that this, *more than anything else,* could explain certain social phenomena and shed light on historical and political issues.[71]

Guldberg seems to have moved a long way from his dismissal of the Social Darwinian faith a decade earlier. This may in part have been due to the fact that, like his Swedish colleague Gustav Retzius, most of Guldberg's international professional network was located in Germany. He was thus influenced by the growing acceptance of anthroposociology within German anthropology after the turn of the century. Guldberg's proposal for a national survey was put forward at the request of Gustav Schwalbe, who headed an initiative by the German Anthropological Society for a 'Statistical-Anthropological' survey of Germany. Schwalbe suggested similar surveys

---

69 Richard Weikart, 'The Origins of Social Darwinism in Germany, 1859-1895', *Journal of the History of Ideas*, Vol. 54, no. 3 (1993), pp. 469-88.

70 Gustav A. Guldberg, *Om Darwinismen og dens rækkevidde* (Kristiania: Dybwad, 1895), p. 85.

71 Gustav A. Guldberg, *Om en samlet anthropologisk undersøgelse af Norges befolkning*, Christiania videnskabs-selskabs forhandlinger for 1904, no. 11 (Kristiania: I commission hos Dybwad, 1904), p. 6.

in Scandinavia, and Guldberg's speech to the Academy of Science was in part a word-for-word translation of Schwalbe's original proposal, which was strongly inspired by the anthroposociological research programme.[72] Given that the request came from a respected scientist like Schwalbe, acting on behalf of the German Anthropological Society, the project may have appeared to Guldberg to be an uncontroversial, mainstream scientific undertaking. In addition, it can be argued that anthroposociology offered a convenient set of arguments for the social utility of anthropological research. But the important fact is that these arguments actually won support from the scientists assembled at the Academy meeting. Guldberg's speech led to the establishment of an 'Anthropological Central Committee' consisting of Guldberg, Arbo, Larsen and the army doctor A. L. Faye.[73] The initiative, however, proved unsuccessful; no national survey was ever undertaken by the committee, and over the next four years Guldberg, Arbo and Larsen passed away. It was not until the interwar years that the vision of a national survey would finally be realised by a new generation of anthropologists.

---

72 Ibid., p. 339.
73 Ibid., p. 5.

4. Norwegian Nationhood and the Germanic Race, 1890-1910

While the Norwegian historians, philologists and archaeologists who attained academic positions in the 1870s and 1880s were generally opposed to the racial ideas of 'the Norwegian School of History', Arbo's anthropological research and Andreas Hansen's grand theory can be seen as revivals of these ideas. So how did Norwegian humanities scholars respond to the rise of racial science, and what impact did the notion of Germanic racial supremacy have upon the scholarly debate over Norwegian history and national identity? These questions can be elucidated by studying Andreas Hansen's relationship to Ernst Sars, the most influential public intellectual among Norwegian historians around the turn of the century.

The evolution of morality

We have seen that in the 1870s and 1880s Darwinism and positivism were introduced into Norwegian public debates and turned into watchwords for the *Venstre* movement. Hansen and Sars belonged to the same urban *Venstre* intelligentsia, and they both hailed the *Venstre* movement as the vanguard of 'evolution', each man producing national narratives that were based on 'scientific', 'positivist' and 'evolutionary' ideals.[1] A basic prerequisite

---

1   Narve Fulsås, *Historie og nasjon. Ernst Sars og striden om norsk kultur* (Oslo: Universitetsforlaget, 1999), p. 159; Knut Kjeldstadli, 'Andreas M. Hansen', in *Norsk biografisk leksikon*, Jon Gunnar et al. (ed.) (Oslo: Kunnskapsforlaget, 1999-2005), http://nbl.snl.no/Andreas_Hansen.

http://dx.doi.org/10.11647/OBP.0051.04

of these national narratives was the use of 'evolution' as a yardstick for normative evaluations: everything that was in line with evolution was good, but everything that was out of step with evolution was bad. This was not only an implicit notion underpinning Sars and Hansen's social views; they explicitly put forward this viewpoint in public, notably when they participated in the moral debates of the 1880s which were closely followed by the Norwegian public.

The controversy arose when a group of cultural radicals began criticising what they regarded as a blatant example of social hypocrisy: extramarital sex was considered acceptable for men, but unacceptable for women, and prostitution was common. The so-called bohemians wanted to replace this moral double standard with sexual liberation for both sexes, but they were opposed by a group of 'neo-moralists' who held that both men and women should abstain from extramarital sex. While the established morality was often defended with religious arguments, both bohemians and neo-moralists were inclined to use evolutionary arguments to advance their views.[2] Ernst Sars and Andreas Hansen belonged to the neo-moralist camp, and their main adversary was the leading figure of the bohemian circle, the author Hans Jæger. Both Sars and Hansen agreed with Jæger that morality should no longer be based on religion and that the idea of free will had to be abandoned, because all human acts, including moral choices, were determined by biology. However, they disagreed on the role of morality within this evolutionary-determinist worldview. Jæger claimed that the very idea of guilt should be abandoned: since human actions are determined by biological dispositions, individuals cannot be held responsible for their actions.[3] Hansen, on the contrary, claimed that the feeling of guilt was a natural phenomenon, and that morality was a physiological function embedded in the central nervous system of human beings. According to Hansen, we only imagine that we make free moral choices, while in reality our 'choices' are determined by nature: it is our 'moral organisation' that reacts, partly without involving our consciousness.[4]

---

2   Gro Hagemann, 'Det moderne gjennombrudd 1870-1905', in *Aschehougs Norgeshistorie. Vol. 9* (Oslo: Aschehoug, 1997), pp. 119-21.

3   Andreas M. Hansen, *Om determinisme og moral. Foredrag den 27. januar 1886. Den frisinnede studenterforenings foredrag og diskussioner I* (Kristiania: [n. pub.], 1886); idem, *Om pressefrihedens grænser i tilknytning til diskussionen om justitsforfølgningen mod Hans Jæger. Den frisinnede studenterforenings foredrag og diskussioner II* (Kristiania: [n. pub.], 1886).

4   Hansen, *Om determinisme og moral*, p. 11.

Thus the moral feelings of the bourgeoisie were just as natural as Jæger's sexual drives, and the bohemian revolt against morality was in fact a revolt against nature. Moral instincts were products of evolution, according to Hansen, and their evolution was driven by the evolution of society—'the social organism'—towards ever-greater complexity. Increasing division of labour led to the development of improved social abilities among members of society, resulting in inheritable biological changes in their brains. In line with this conception, Hansen claimed that Jæger's promiscuous lifestyle was an 'atavism', a step backwards in the evolution of social instincts that put him on the level of 'a wretched polar Indian'.[5]

Sars embraced Hansen's arguments, and his way of reasoning implies that he, like Hansen, ranked individuals and social groups in a moral hierarchy according to their level of evolutionary development. He placed himself and his peers at the top of this hierarchy.[6] According to his biographer Narve Fulsås, Sars saw himself as a member of an intellectual elite whose progressive ideas were often out of tune with the general public but who still had a greater right than others to make decisions about the future of society, since the elite represented the evolutionary avant-garde.[7]

Hansen and Sars' arguments may have been indirectly or directly inspired by the ideas of Auguste Comte and Herbert Spencer. Both Comte and Spencer believed that the rise of civilisation was intertwined with growth in intelligence and progress in morality, and that these developments led to inheritable changes in the anatomy of the brain. Spencer held that increasing division of labour and an increasingly complex society led to the formation of progressively more advanced human brains, enhanced social abilities and strengthened faculties for rational, abstract reasoning. This meant that there were average inherited differences in intellectual abilities between both social groups and nations. Thus, like Paul Broca, Herbert Spencer believed that the social hierarchy and the hierarchy between civilised and less civilised nations to some extent mirrored a hierarchy of intellectual and cerebral evolution.[8]

---

5   Hansen. *Om determinisme og moral*. pp. 15-20.
6   *Om pressefrihedens grænser*, p. 19.
7   Fulsås, *Historie og nasjon*, p. 225.
8   J. D. Y. Peel, *Herbert Spencer: The Evolution of a Sociologist* (Aldershot: Gregg Revivals, 1992), pp. 108-09, 124, 150; Mary Pickering, *Auguste Comte: An Intellectual Biography* (Cambridge: Cambridge University Press, 1993), pp. 353, 563ff., 600 ff., 617-20, 626, 631.

Narve Fulsås has characterised Sars as an idealist evolutionist. Sars believed that the nation was organised around certain core ideas that underwent a historical process of growth and were more strongly embodied by some social groups than others. In accordance with this belief, Sars saw cultural evolution and the hierarchy of nations and of social groups as purely cultural phenomena, not as biological ones.[9] However, given the neo-Lamarckian idea that cultural growth can lead to the biological transformation of the human brain, it is difficult to distinguish this kind of socio-cultural evolutionism from a biological theory of evolution.

Norwegian Folk Psychology and the struggles over national identity

Hansen's book *Norwegian Folk Psychology* (1899) was founded on the same basic assumptions as his arguments a decade earlier in the debate over sexual morals. These assumptions were that mankind is undergoing a psychological and moral evolution, that nations and groups of people within nations are ranked in a hierarchy of evolutionary stages which also indicates their moral worth, and that a national elite exists with higher intelligence and greater moral worth entitling them to a leading role in society and culture. However, there was one crucial change in Hansen's point of view: he no longer believed that moral progress was driven by a mutual interplay between nature and nurture, and regarded their association instead as a one-way causal relationship. Culture was reduced to race: moral superiority and national virtues were embedded in the central nervous system of the Aryan-Germanic race, and social progress required the dominance of this race over others. This idea was incompatible with Sars' school of evolutionary nationalism, on which Sars, in contrast to Hansen, never changed his opinion.

In 1900, the year after the launch of *Norwegian Folk Psychology*, Sars, along with the folklorist Moltke Moe, published an article in which they discussed the psychological characteristics of the Norwegian people. They cited as a generally known scientific fact that Norwegians were a mixture of two or more races, but they rejected the notion that psychological characteristics had anything to do with skull shape. By doing so, Moe

---

9　Fulsås, *Historie og nasjon*, p. 225.

and Sars were implicitly dismissing the basic theoretical assumptions of anthroposociology. They rejected the idea that racial anthropology was relevant to the study of political, cultural and social questions, and they disregarded Hansen's theories on Norwegian national psychology. According to Sars and Moe, the Norwegian national character sprang from a common Germanic *Nationalkarakter* or race, which had given birth to the different 'racial' characters of a number of nations. But they argued that both the Germanic and the Norwegian race or *Nationalkarakter* had arisen through gradual socio-historical evolution, not through the struggle for survival between anthropological races with set intellectual abilities.[10] There are two probable reasons behind Moe and Sars' dismissal of racial explanations. Racial determinism conflicted with the idea of socio-cultural evolutionary growth, which was at the core of Sars' national narrative. At the same time, Hansen's idea of a racially divided nation was at odds with a national ideology of cultural unity, another linchpin of both Sars' and Moe's cultural, political and academic activities.

Hansen developed his theory of national psychology in response to an ongoing cultural and political conflict that divided the *Venstre* movement. *Venstre* was an alliance between progressive urban elites and rural national-democratic, anti-establishment elements. The latter had their stronghold in rural communities in southwestern Norway and advocated low taxes, resistance to growth in state bureaucracy and a cultural policy aimed at building a national culture founded on the cultural heritage of agrarian society. Hansen argued that political tensions coincided with racial differences. As we have already discussed, the dark, short-skulled Anaryans from western Norway represented cultural conservatism, irrationality, backwardness, detrimental populism, greed, envy and pettiness, and were thought more likely to vote for *Høyre*, the conservative party. However, those Anaryans who did not champion the conservative party tended instead to support the 'mainly anti-bureaucratic rural fraction' in the *Venstre* movement.[11] This was in contrast to the blond, long-skulled Aryan-Germanics in eastern Norway, who represented the racial backbone, the Viking heritage of the nation, and were the pinnacle of progress and scientific rationality. The Aryan-Germanics were most likely to support

10 Nordahl Rolfsen et al., *Norge i det nittende aarhundrede*, Vol. 1 (Kristiania: Cammermeyer, 1900), pp. 431-32.

11 Andreas M. Hansen, *Norsk folkepsykologi: med politisk kart over Skandinavien* (Kristiania: Jakob Dybwad, 1899), p. 49.

the 'liberal' ideas—in a European sense—that were the true essence of the *Venstre* movement. It is unsurprising, then, that due to 'Ammon's Law' the long skulls were most prevalent among the urban elite of the capital.[12]

Among the rural, democratic nationalists, it was common to argue that Norway consisted of two nations. One of these nations was made up of the urban elite with foreign roots who had established themselves during the years of Danish rule and who were the bearers of a foreign, academic, urban culture. The other was the true Norwegian nation grounded in a traditional rural culture with historical roots in the golden age of the Norwegian medieval state. Hansen's theory was an uncompromisingly urban, elitist negation of this ideology, while Moe and Sars were leading figures in a group of intellectuals who tried to mitigate the conflict and maintain that Norwegian nationality was a product of historical interaction between the peasantry and the educated elite.[13]

It seems clear that professors Sars and Moe had both professional and ideological reasons for dismissing Hansen's racial notion of nationhood, and it is likely that their views had greater academic, public and political impact than Hansen's. Sars was the leading historian of his generation and an influential ideologue of the *Venstre* movement. Moltke Moe was also a well-known and influential figure in the Norwegian cultural sphere. His father, Jørgen Moe, was famous for his key role in collecting and publishing Norwegian folktales. These had an impact on Norwegian national identity comparable with that of the Brothers Grimm in Germany. Moltke Moe had followed in his father's footsteps, becoming the first Norwegian professor of folkloristics and the founding father of Norwegian folklore studies. He was also well-known and respected for his role as a mediator in the political struggles over language and national identity.[14]

Moreover, the book in which Sars and Moe's article on Norwegian national psychology appeared was highly prestigious. The grandiose, richly-illustrated two-volume work, *Norway in the 19th Century*, was initiated by university professors, funded by the government and published on the centennial. Written and illustrated by the country's foremost artists, scientists and authors, the book described Norway's natural environment,

---

12 Hansen, *Norsk folkepsykologi*, pp. 50-51, 57.
13 Ole Dalhaug, *Mål og meninger. Målreisning og nasjonaldannelse 1877-1887* (Oslo: Norges forskningsråd, 1995), p. 54; Bodil Stenseth, *En norsk elite: nasjonsbyggerne på Lysaker 1890-1940* (Oslo: Aschehoug, 1983), pp. 56-58.
14 Knut Liestøl, *Moltke Moe* (Oslo: Aschehoug, 1949).

society, science, literature and art, and aimed at promoting national pride among Norwegians and at demonstrating a distinct Norwegian nationality to the Swedes and the outside world.[15] *Norway in the 19th Century* was backed by leading members of the academic and cultural establishment and can be described as a state-led attempt at nation-building. Moe and Sars' article concluded Volume One and served as an introduction to the first part of Volume Two, which featured a series of articles describing people's temperament, culture and way of life in different parts of Norway. The articles suggest that racial interpretations of local mindsets and national psychology were commonly shared by leading Norwegian scholars and intellectuals. Nevertheless, most of the articles did not have racial determinism and the idea of a Germanic master race as principal features.

Many of the contributors to the book used words like 'race' or 'type' when characterising local populations, with some even referring directly to an anthropological concept of race and to anthropological theories. However, most writers used the word 'race' in a vague Lamarckian sense, often combining it with loose comments on pigmentation, skull shape or other anatomical traits. Local differences in psychological dispositions were mainly explained by social factors and variations in natural environment. The description of the population in the Gudbrandsdalen valley by Hans Aanrud, one of the authors, is typical. The people in Gudbrandsdalen are self-conscious, strong, honest and mindful, but never talkative, adventurous or dangerous.[16] Aanrud claimed that the people living in the valley had been moulded by their natural environment, and this in turn had resulted in a 'harmonic configuration of humans and society', with people living in concord with one another and their environment.

The articles in *Norway in the 19th Century* seem to indicate that Hansen's style of racial thought had some support among the Norwegian intellectuals who engaged in cultural nation-building at the turn of the twentieth century, but that Ernst Sars and Moltke Moe's reasoning was more commonly accepted. According to Sars and Moe's narrative, Norwegian nationhood

15 Rolfsen et al, *Norge i det nittende aarhundrede*; Geir Hestmark, 'En nasjonal-evolusjonær katekisme', in *Norsk litteraturhistorie, sakprosa fra 1750 til 1995, Vol. 1, 1750-1920* (Oslo: Universitetsforlaget, 1998), pp. 708-17; Torben Hviid Nielsen, Arve Monsen, Tore Tennøe, *Livets tre og kodenes kode Fra genetikk til bioteknologi Norge 1900-2000* (Oslo: Gyldendal akademisk, 2000), p. 34.

16 Rolfsen et al., *Norge i det nittende aarhundrede*, Vol. 2, citation at pp. 63-65.

was not a biological entity inherited from the ancient Germanics, but first and foremost a social and cultural entity that had arisen as the result of a slowly evolving historical process.

It is important to note, however, that although Ernst Sars rejected the supremacy of the Germanic race, he did not reject white supremacy. In 1903 he gave a lecture in which he dismissed the historical relevance of any psychological differences between European races, while simultaneously arguing for a deep and significant racial divide between 'the Indo-European race, the Negro race, the Malay race and the Mongolian race'.[17] Sars claimed these major races of humankind were so different that intermixture would lead to racial deterioration, and this belief affected his views on Norwegian nationhood. It implied that the Sami (who supposedly belonged to the 'Mongolian' race) were so racially different that Norwegians did not see them as fellow countrymen, even though they were citizens of the same nation. How, then, could Sars still believe in the unity of the Norwegian nation? According to Narve Fulsås, Sars solved this problem by ignoring the Sami, claiming that they were so few in numbers that it was not necessary to take them into account.[18] Thus, although Sars saw Norwegian nationhood as a socio-cultural entity, it was also in part a racially-delineated entity: there was a biological limit to the racial variation that could be assimilated into the Norwegian 'social organism'.

Was the Norwegian nation a racial entity?

We have so far discussed what impact the idea of Germanic superiority had on notions of nationhood among Norwegian scholars. It is now time to ask what influence the idea of European racial supremacy had upon Norwegian nationalism. And since the Sami were generally seen as a non-European people, the best way to shed light on this question is to study Norwegian scholars' attitudes towards the Sami. Despite the fact that the Sami were Norwegian citizens, they were not generally regarded as members of the Norwegian *people*. The question is whether they were considered to be outside the nation because of their cultural and linguistic distinctiveness, or because of their perceived racial inferiority. Norwegian scholars who

---

17 Fulsås, *Historie og nasjon*, p. 240.
18 Ibid.

studied Sami language, culture, history and race in the nineteenth and early twentieth centuries had differing attitudes on this issue.

In the 1830s and 1840s, the Norwegian state and the Church of Norway implemented a paternalist and pluralist minority policy. The Sami and the Kvens were encouraged to preserve their language, and the university gave language training to pastors destined for service in Sami and Kven communities. This laid the foundation for the discipline of 'lappology' — the philological and historical study of Sami language and culture. One of the principal goals of the discipline was to develop the written language and create a Sami literature that could give its readers access to enlightenment and the Christian gospel.[19] The great pioneer of lappology was Jens Friis, who was a lecturer in the Sami language from 1851 and in 1874 became the first Norwegian professor of Sami and Finnish languages. He undertook comprehensive studies of the Sami language, religion and culture, wrote fiction and travel literature about the Sami and advocated a liberal minority policy.[20]

The debate on minority policy shifted during Friis' years at the university. The last decades of the nineteenth century saw rising threats towards Sami culture. Agricultural and industrial expansion into Sami districts coincided with the emergence of evolutionary ideas in public debates, and it became common to argue that Sami culture was a relic of the past, destined for extinction. An increasingly harsh policy of cultural and linguistic assimilation, directed at both the Sami and the Kvens, was implemented in the schools. At the end of the century, the political debate was not about whether the minorities should be 'Norwegianised', but about the methods by which the process could be accelerated. An important motivation for this assimilationist policy lay in national security concerns and fears of Russian expansionism. The Norwegian state wanted to secure its territorial control through linguistic and cultural assimilation of the territories bordering the Russian empire.[21]

---

19 Helge Dahl, *Språkpolitikk og skolestell i Finnmark 1814-1905* (Oslo: Universitetsforlaget, 1957), pp. 1-13, 36.

20 Lars Ivar Hansen and Einar Niemi, 'Samisk forskning ved et tidsskifte: Jens Andreas Friis og lappologien—vitenskap og politikk?', in Eli Seglen (ed.), *Vitenskap, teknologi og samfunn* (Oslo: Cappelen akademisk forlag, 2001), pp. 372f, 358f.

21 Knut Einar Eriksen and Einar Niemi, *Den finske fare. Sikkerhetsproblemer og minoritetspolitikk i nord 1860-1940* (Oslo: Universitetsforlaget, 1981).

The scholarly study of the Sami was affected by this change in the political climate. When Friis died in 1896, Parliament decided not to renew the chair in Sami and Finnish. They determined that the sole obligation of the Norwegian state towards the Sami and the Kvens was to educate pastors who could speak their language: there was no need to conduct scientific research on their language and culture. In 1911 the professorship was re-established, but by now its justification was purely scientific. Lappology and Finno-Ugrian linguistics were prestigious research fields in which Norway could achieve international acclaim, and it would be embarrassing to leave this research to neighbouring countries. Thus, from the mid-nineteenth century, the social legitimacy of lappology had changed. It was no longer part of a paternalist and pluralist policy aimed at developing the Sami language and culture into tools for cultural progress. Instead, it was legitimised as a purely academic study of a language and a culture that the state, ironically, wanted to eradicate.[22]

The Sami as an object of ethnographic interest

Apart from the professorship in lappology, a main institutional impetus for the study of Sami culture was the Ethnographic Museum in Kristiania. This museum was established following the first World's Fair in London in 1851. Among the enterprises that moved into the spectacular Crystal Palace exhibition hall at the end of this great event was an ethnographic museum directed by Robert Latham. In order to obtain Sami objects to exhibit, he relied on the assistance of his friend, Ludvig Kristensen Daa, to arrange a trade with the University of Kristiania. A number of Sami artifacts were shipped to London, along with plaster casts of the heads of three Sami men. In return, the university received cultural objects from Sumatra, Borneo, Australia and British Guinea.[23] This prompted the establishment of a Norwegian Ethnographic Museum in 1853.

The Ethnographic Museum was initially a rather modest institution. Its first director was the history professor Peter Andreas Munch, who put little effort into this aspect of his professorial duties. But when Daa took

---

22 Harald Dag Jølle, 'Nordpolens naboer', in Einar-Arne Drivenes and Harald Dag Jølle (eds.), *Norsk polarhistorie 2* (Oslo: Gyldendal, 2004), pp. 259-326 (p. 302).

23 Yngvar Nielsen, *Universitetets ethnografiske samlinger 1857-1907* (Kristiania: W. C. Fabritius og sønner, 1907), pp. 3-7.

over the professorship ten years later, he began expanding and renewing the museum. Daa believed that the museum had a special obligation to maintain a representative collection of Sami artefacts and to display Sami culture. He established an open-air exhibition featuring a replica Sea Sami farm in the garden of the university building, and in 1867 he undertook an ethnographic field trip to the Finnish-Norwegian-Russian border region along with his friend, the lappologist Jens Friis.[24] As we saw in chapter 2, Daa had a paternalistic and philanthropic attitude towards the Sami. He thought they had an inferior culture, but in line with his monogenist views, he did not consider this inferiority to be racially determined or immutable. Daa believed that the Norwegians should help the Sami become civilised.

According to Daa, the museum ought to provide a coherent picture of all the cultures in the world, as illustrated by their 'industrial products'. Thus he split the museum's exhibits into thirteen cultural-historically, climatically, 'ethnologically' and religiously defined groups. Four of these were European and included both the Norwegian and the Sami cultures. In Daa's vision, both Sami and Norwegian cultural artefacts were to be exhibited along with objects from distant, 'primitive' tribes as examples of the cultural variety of humankind.[25] After Daa's death in 1877, however, the museum changed its character: from being a museum of human cultures, it became a museum of non-Western cultures. During this transformation, the Norwegian and Sami collections assumed new meanings. While the Sami artefacts were kept at the Ethnographic Museum as objects of great interest, the Norwegian items were removed and transferred to a national museum of culture and history.

In the 1860s, Daa had initiated a campaign for collecting artefacts typical of early-modern Norwegian rural culture. The enterprise was continued by his successor at the museum, Yngvar Nielsen, but Nielsen abandoned the plan of displaying the Norwegian artefacts at the Ethnographic Museum, since he held that such museums should only 'represent the primitive peoples and those peoples, whose civilisation is based on a foundation totally different from Europe'.[26] From the 1880s onwards, the rural culture campaign received funding from the government, but even among the politicians the idea of putting 'the Norwegian farmer' on display

---

24 Ibid., p. 46.
25 Ibid., pp. 31, 76.
26 Ibid., p. 77; Stortingsforhandlinger, 1880, p. 241.

side by side with 'half-wild peoples from the South Sea Islands' was highly controversial.[27]

The debates over Norwegian rural culture and the Ethnographic Museum were entwined with the proposal to build a new national history museum, which was to house both the Ethnographic Museum and the National Antiquities Collection. The planned museum was meant to include the Norwegian rural artefacts, not as part of the ethnographic department, but as a separate exhibition connected to the National Antiquities Collection. The aim of this arrangement, as previously mentioned, was to offer the visitor a journey through national history from the Stone Age to the present day, thus illustrating the cultural development of 'our' nation.[28] There were mainly pragmatic reasons for locating the Ethnographic Museum in the same building as the national-historical collections, but this was also justified pedagogically: visitors would get a better understanding of past stages in the cultural evolution of Norway if they could compare it to the culture of contemporary primitive peoples, including the Sami.

By the time the new historical museum was finally opened in 1904, after decades of debates, quarrels and setbacks, the Norwegian rural artefacts had already been transferred to another institution, the *Norsk Folkemuseum* (Norwegian Museum of Cultural History), a new type of museum focusing on the daily life of pre-industrial Norway. Cultural objects were displayed in an open-air museum, its old buildings located in a scenic landscape on the outskirts of the capital. The *Norsk Folkemuseum* was the first of a number of similar establishments established in Norway over the following decades. These museums have had a significant impact on Norwegian notions of cultural roots, and they became a key site for research into the material culture of pre-industrial society.[29]

However, the Sami collection was not transferred to the *Norsk Folkemuseum*, most likely because it was not regarded as part of the nation's cultural heritage. Instead it was retained with the non-European cultures at the Ethnographic Museum, where it fed the more general ethnographic interest in 'Arctic cultures' represented at the museum. With the Arctic expeditions of Fridtjof Nansen and Roald Amundsen around the turn of the

---

27 Stortingsforhandlinger, 1880, p. 251.

28 Ingvald Undseth, *Om et norsk National-Museum* (Kristiania: Cammermeyer, 1885), pp. 5, 10.

29 Haakon Shetelig, *Norske museers historie* (Oslo: J. W. Cappelens, 1944), pp. 214-31.

century, Norway became renowned as a 'polar nation', and Arctic research became highly prestigious.[30] The Arctic explorers were mainly interested in natural science, but they also undertook studies and collected artefacts from the people they encountered, some of which ended up at the Ethnographic Museum. When, after the turn of the century, the museum became a site for professional ethnographic research for the first time, interest focused on 'Arctic cultures' and special attention was paid to the Sami.[31]

A primitive people or a primitive race?

We have seen that minority policy was influenced by the notion of the Sami as a relic of the evolutionary past. We have also examined how the study of Sami culture was separated from that of the national heritage and was institutionally categorised as a subject for ethnographic study—defined as a non-European, 'primitive' and Arctic culture. This raises the question of whether this categorisation of Sami culture was based on notions of race. Were the Sami considered an object of ethnographic research and a vanishing people because they were assumed to be culturally primitive, or because they were considered to be racially inferior? Yngvar Nielsen, the head of the Ethnographic Museum, gave a straightforward answer to this question. In an article in *Norway in the 19th Century*, he claimed that the Sami belonged to an 'inferior race', one that stood outside 'the European civilisation' and that was going to go extinct in their encounter with the superior Norwegian people. It was both natural and legitimate that Norwegians should take over the traditional lands of the Sami, he argued, claiming that 'our' civilised 'concepts of law' should triumph over outdated Sami notions of 'divine right' to the land. The Sami people were doomed, and the only thing 'we, the superior, the stronger people' could do about this was 'to show gentleness and kindness' in the times to come.[32] Yngvar Nielsen's line of reasoning suggests that he used the word 'folk' in a biological sense and that he saw the Sami as racially inferior.

The difference in attitude between Nielsen and his predecessor Daa bears witness to the emergence of Social Darwinism and racial determinism

---

30 Jølle, 'Nordpolens naboer', p. 299.
31 Gutorm Gjessing and Marie Krekling Johannessen, *De hundre år: Universitetets etnografiske museums historie 1857-1957* (Oslo: Universitetets etnografiske museum, 1957).
32 Rolfsen, *Norge i det nittende aarhundrede*, Vol. 2, p. 120f.

in Norwegian attitudes towards the Sami. It is important to note, however, that the ideas Nielsen advocated were not universally accepted. Ole Solberg, who became assistant professor at the museum in 1906 and succeeded Nielsen as head of the museum in 1916, was most likely opposed to Nielsen's style of racial thinking. Around the turn of the century, Solberg had studied anatomy and physical anthropology under Gustav Guldberg in Kristiania and the Professors Wilhelm von Waldeyer-Hartz and Rudolph Virchow in Germany. It is likely that he was familiar with Virchow's liberal attitude to race when he decided to switch to ethnography in 1901. Over the next decade he spent a total of six years at German ethnographic museums, and he also visited the U.S., where he did field work among the Hopis in Arizona and studied the ethnographic collections in New York, Washington and Chicago. According to his successor, Gutorm Gjessing, Solberg did not adhere to any particular school of research.[33] However, he seems to have been particularly influenced by Adolf Bastian, head of the Berlin *Museum für Völkerkunde* (1873-1905), and by the leading figure of German ethnography during the last decades of the nineteenth century, Friedrich Ratzel, who was famous for his studies of the interaction between human populations and their environments. Solberg's ideas also appear to have been shaped by Franz Boas, the founding father of American cultural anthropology.[34] The research of all three men was based on the idea of the psychic unity of mankind; they dismissed racial differences as an appropriate explanation for cultural differences. This attitude was especially typical of Franz Boas who, in the early decades of the century, engaged in a long-running campaign against scientific racism.

Solberg was personally acquainted with Boas, who visited Norway in 1924 in connection with the launching of a cross-disciplinary programme for the study of 'Arctic' cultures. The programme, which Solberg had designed, was based on the assumption that all the Arctic peoples, regardless of their racial roots, shared a common Arctic way of life. As they were all forced to adapt to the harsh Arctic environment, there were basic similarities between their cultures across Norway, Russia, Siberia, Alaska, Canada and Greenland. According to this line of reasoning, though the Sami stood

33 Gjessing and Johannessen, *De hundre år.*

34 Jon Røyne Kyllingstad, '*Menneskeåndens universalitet*' *Instituttet for sammenlignende kulturforskning 1917-1940. Ideene, institusjonen og forskningen* (Ph.d. thesis, University of Oslo, 2008), pp. 334-41.

outside European civilisation, the essential dividing line was not racial, but rather the fact that the Sami belonged to an Arctic cultural region.[35]

The Sami: indigenous people or newcomers?

As we saw in chapter 2, the racial succession scheme advocated by Retzius, Nilson, Keyser and Munch was rejected in the 1860s. This implied that the Sami had lost their status as the descendants of the original inhabitants of the Scandinavian Peninsula. In 1866 and 1867, the Swedish archaeologist Karl Hildebrand and his Norwegian colleague Oluf Rygh put forward a hypothesis of two Scandinavian Stone Age cultures. The Sami were descended from 'Arctic' hunters who used slate tools and were culturally connected with peoples further east, whereas the Norwegians were descended from a Germanic, long-skulled, agricultural people, who used flint tools and were connected to cultural areas further south.[36] As the archaeologist Ole Furset has demonstrated, this theory was characterised by ethnic stereotypes. While a steady line of progress led from the dynamic southern Scandinavian Stone Age to contemporary Norwegian society, the 'Arctic' Stone Age was seen as a stagnant culture, fitting well with the past of the supposed primitive Sami people.[37] This theory went unquestioned for forty years and implied that even if the Sami had never inhabited all of Scandinavia, they were still the indigenous people of the north. But at the turn of the century, even this assumption was contested. Over the years, an increasing number of slate tools and other artefacts associated with the 'Arctic' Stone Age had been found in south Scandinavia, demonstrating that geographic distribution of the assumed 'Arctic' Stone Age culture did not match the distribution of the present-day Sami population.

Andreas Hansen was one of the first to raise questions regarding the two Stone Age cultures. He argued that the distribution of typical 'Arctic' Stone Age findings coincided with the present-day geographical distribution of dark, short-skulled individuals, and he claimed that the short-skulled

---

35 ISKF-archive: Arktisk utvalg, ring binder 'Arktisk utvalg', 21.10.23, Memorandum from Solberg to Institutt for sammenlignende kulturforskning/ Institute for Comparative Research in Human Culture.

36 Inger Storli, 'Fra "kultur" til "natur". Om konstitueringa av den "arktiske" steinalderen', *Viking*, Vol. 56 (1993), pp. 7-22.

37 Ole Jacob Furset, *Arktisk steinalder og etnisitet. En forskningshistorisk analyse* (Master's thesis, University of Tromsø, 1994).

Anaryan race had been the representative of both the southern Scandinavian (flint-using) Stone Age and the northern Scandinavian (slate-using) Stone Age. These were the forefathers of the dark, short-skulled Norwegian coastal dwellers in the south as well as the dark, short-skulled Sea Sami in the north. But while the Anaryans along the south Norwegian coast had adopted the Aryan-Germanic language of 'our' forefathers, the Anaryans along the northern coast had taken up the Sami language of the reindeer-herding nomads of the inland. These nomads, the original Sami people, had not settled in Norway before the tenth century.[38]

Hansen even claimed that the Anaryan, non-Sami ancestors of the Sea Sami had continued to exist as a distinct people into historical times. One of his arguments was the existence of respectful descriptions of the Sea Sami written by Norwegians in the seventeenth and eighteenth centuries. These descriptions may have matched the Anaryans, he argued, but they did not match the Sami, since the Norwegians had always scorned the Sami for their 'dwarf-like stature', their 'thin limbs' and their 'characteristic inferiority'. In spite of Hansen's generally negative assessment of the short-skulled Anaryans, when he compared them to the 'true' Sami, they appeared brave, strong and clever. His reasoning was based on a racial hierarchy with the long-skulled Aryans at the top, the Anaryans at a lower level, and the Sami at the bottom.[39]

One of Hansen's key arguments was the discovery of what he saw as Anaryan skulls in a number of ancient graves in Eastern Finnmark, excavated by the merchant and 'gentleman-archaeologist' Andreas Nordvi in the mid-nineteenth century. Before Christianisation in the seventeenth and eighteenth centuries, the Sami had a tradition of building burial sites in screes, where stone slabs were erected as roof and walls around the deceased. In the 1840s, Andreas Nordvi, who ran a trading company in Eastern Finnmark, began excavating these 'stone-coffins'. Nordvi had studied archaeology in Copenhagen and wanted to understand the pre-Christian burial customs of the Sami; he was not primarily interested in the skulls. But in the 1870s and 1880s, he faced financial problems and began selling Sami skulls to scientific institutions. Some of these skulls found

---

38 Andreas M. Hansen, *Landnåm i Norge. En udsigt over bosettingens historie* (Kristiania: Fabritius, 1904).

39 Hansen, *Landnåm i Norge*, cited after Audhild Schanche, *Graver i ur og berg. Samisk gravskikk og religion 1000 f.kr. til 1700 e. Kr.* (Ph.D. thesis, University of Tromsø, 1997), p. 40.

their way into the anatomy department at the University of Kristiania, and became the object of Hansen's interest.[40] He claimed to have found marked anatomical differences between the typical Sami skull and the typical Anaryan skull, and argued that the 'stone coffin graves' of Eastern Finnmark were Anaryan, not Sami.[41]

The Arctic-Baltic Stone Age

Hansen's theory was at odds with a number of established historical, linguistic, anthropological and folkloristic views of Sami and Norwegian prehistory. He dismissed established interpretations of ancient and medieval sources that were taken as evidence of ancient Sami presence, and he rejected established folkloristic theories about remnants of Norse mythology in Sami folk traditions, as well as linguistic theories about Norse or proto-Scandinavian loanwords in the Sami language which implied ancient Sami settlement in Scandinavia. However, as Hansen himself had to admit in 1901, the leading Norwegian lappologists—Professor Konrad Nielsen and the rector Just Qvigstad—were not willing to accept Hansen's views and abandon their theory of ancient Sami presence in Scandinavia.[42]

Even if Hansen's theory did not win general scientific acclaim, it led to a public debate, shaking established views and causing doubt about the Sami's status as first-comers in northern Scandinavia. This uncertainty became even stronger when the young, aspiring archaeologist Anton Wilhelm Brøgger published *Studies of Norwegian Stone Age* (1906) and *Arctic Stone Age* (1909).[43] Brøgger dismissed Hansen's theory and upheld the hypothesis of a separate Arctic Stone Age, but in the latter work he agreed that the Sami did not descend from the Arctic Stone Age people. When he published these studies,[44] Brøgger was still in his early twenties and untrained as an archaeologist, but his work was instrumental in establishing

---

40 Schanche, *Graver i ur og berg*, pp. 23-28.
41 Hansen, *Landnåm*, pp. 259-68.
42 Andreas M. Hansen: articles appearing in the newspaper *Verdens Gang* on 16, 18, 19 March 1910.
43 Anton W. Brøgger, *Den arktiske stenalder i Norg*, Skrifter, Videnskabselskapet i Kristiania, HF-kl. (Kristiania: I kommisjon hos Dybwad, 1909); idem, *Norges Studier over Norges steinalder* (Kristiania: I kommission hos Jacob Dybwad, 1906).
44 Waldemar C. Brøgger, *Strandliniens beliggenhed under stenalderen i det sydøstlige Norg* (Kristiania: Aschehoug, 1905), pp. v-vi.

Stone Age archaeology as an academic field of research in Norway. These publications helped launch a career that would culminate in Brøgger's appointment as head of the University's Antiquities Collection in 1915.

As with Hansen, the young Brøgger based his arguments in part on notions of racial superiority and inferiority. According to the archaeologist Wenche Helliksen, Brøgger's Stone Age studies were partly inspired by Gustav Kossinna,[45] the Berlin archaeology professor who championed the Aryan-Germanic theory and developed the influential school of 'settlement-archaeology'. Kossinna linked cultural superiority to biologically superior races and assumed that cultures spread through human migration (in particular through the spread of the Aryan-Germanic race). By studying the geographical distribution of different types of archaeological finds, Kossinna established a mosaic of distinct cultural regions, and by presupposing that each region's culture was tied to a certain ethnic group, he thought this method enabled him to reveal the prehistoric distribution and movement of peoples.

Brøgger's Stone Age studies were based on similar ideas. By analysing the spatial distribution of certain types of artefacts, in particular slate tools and a certain type of ceramics, he drew a boundary between two cultural areas: a dynamic southern Scandinavia connected southwards to the continent, and a more backward Arctic-Baltic area, later swallowed by the southern Scandinavian culture. Brøgger claimed that it was likely that the Arctic Stone Age had been dominated by a clearly-defined race, and by matching historical, archaeological, linguistic and physical anthropological evidence, he thought he could show that it was not 'lappish'. The Arctic-Baltic Stone Age sites had been inhabited instead by a dolichocephalic people, who resembled the contemporary population in the assumed Scandinavian distribution area of the Arctic Stone Age.[46]

Brøgger explicitly claimed that there was no necessary overlap between physical-anthropologically defined races, linguistically-defined 'peoples', and archaeologically-defined cultural regions. Still, his reasoning was based on the assumed existence of such a correlation, and he also presupposed a racial hierarchy with the Sami at the bottom. Brøgger assumed the Sami had lived in a Stone Age society until historical times,

45 Wenche Helliksen, *Evolusjonisme i norsk arkeologi: Diskutert med utgangspunkt i A.W. Brøggers hovedverk 1909-25* (Oslo: Universitetets oldsaksamling, 1996).
46 Anton W. Brøgger, *Den arktiske stenalder i Norge*. Skrifter, Videnskabselskapet i Kristiania, HF-kl. (Kristiania: I kommisjon hos Dybwad, 1909), pp. 174, 182.

but claimed there was no historical evidence to indicate that they had ever had the advanced ceramics or stone tool production found in the Arctic-Baltic Stone Age. He also noted that such an industry would have been difficult to combine with the life of nomadic reindeer herders. This implies that he believed that Sami culture, static and unchanged, had been defined by reindeer husbandry since the Stone Age, and that such a culture was inferior to that of the Arctic Stone Age.[47]

The Sami Iron Age

The same year that Brøgger wrote his work on the Arctic Stone Age, Ole Solberg published his first and most important study of the Sami, demonstrating the existence of a Sami Iron Age and refuting the commonly-held view that, until historical times, the Sami had lived in a Stone Age society. Simultaneously, Solberg established beyond any reasonable doubt that there had been Sami settlements in Finnmark since the early eighth century at least. Solberg's work was based on the excavations of two ancient settlements at Kjelmøya, an island near the Norwegian-Russian border. The settlements had already been excavated in the mid-nineteenth century by Andreas Nordvi, who had assigned them to a Sami Stone Age. Solberg's new investigations showed that the Kjelmøya settlers had used iron tools, and this convinced him that the previously-mentioned 'stone coffin graves' in the same area also belonged to a Sami Iron Age. He did not, however, offer any racial, anthropological proof for the Sami identity of the Iron Age inhabitants of Kjelmøya. His key evidence was a written source from the Viking age—a travelogue recorded by the English King Alfred in the ninth century. In this text, the Viking chief Othere describes a trip along the coast of Finnmark and the Kola Peninsula and his encounters there with a people called 'Finns', the traditional Norwegian name for the Sami.[48]

Solberg's conclusion was severely criticised by Andreas Hansen, who argued that Othere's 'Finns' were identical to the Anaryans, and that it was the Anaryans, not the Sami, who had populated the Kjelmøya dwellings.[49]

---

47 Ibid., p. 165.
48 Ole M. Solberg, *Eisenzeitfunde aus Ostfinmarken* (Kristiania: I Kommission bei Dybwad, 1909), 125ff.
49 Ibid., p. 127. Hansen: articles in *Verdens Gang*, 16, 18, 19 March 1910.

Hansen was not able to prevent Solberg's conclusions from winning general scientific acceptance, however. For many decades, the Kjelmøya settlement was recognised as the oldest Sami finding in Scandinavia, and it became an uncontested starting point for explorations of the prehistory of the Sami.[50]

The political implications of Sami prehistory

The public controversy between Hansen and Solberg must be understood against the background of the political implications of Sami prehistory. The indigenousness or foreignness of the Sami were opposing arguments in the debate over the policy of cultural assimilation. This debate flourished after the turn of the century when additional pressure in favour of Norwegianisation provoked the rise of an ethno-political Sami movement.[51] The dissolution of the Norwegian-Swedish union in 1905 also helped to place these issues on the public agenda. One of the disputes that the Norwegian and Swedish negotiators were unable to resolve in 1905 was that of the Sami nomads' right to move their reindeer herds across the Norwegian-Swedish border. The negotiations, which continued until 1919, were primarily over the traditional rights of the Swedish Sami to summer pastures in Norway; the Swedish government wanted to retain them, and the Norwegian government wanted them abolished. The Swedish argument centred on the idea that the 'Lapps' were an aboriginal people, perfectly adapted to their nomadic way of life, who should be allowed to continue their ancient customs. The Norwegian government, in contrast, denied the indigenousness of the Sami and argued that their backward nomadic culture had to give way to a 'higher social goal'—the expansion of Norwegian agriculture.[52]

The negotiations over reindeer pastures created a demand for research on Sami culture and history, and particularly on the question of Sami prehistoric presence in Scandinavia. Andreas Hansen's theories about the Sami as latecomers to Scandinavia were well-adapted to the position of the Norwegian government. In public debates he accused his academic opponents of lacking not only scientific rigour, but also patriotism;

---

50 Bjørnar Olsen, 'Kjelmøyfunnenes (virknings) historie og arkeologi', *Viking*, Vol. 54 (1991), pp. 65-88.

51 Regnor Jernsletten, *Samebevegelsen i Norge* (Tromsø: Senter for samiske studier, University of Tromsø, 1998).

52 Eriksen and Niemi, *Den finske fare*, pp. 93, 118-19.

by assigning the Sami a more ancient presence in Norway than they themselves could rightly claim, his opponents weakened the bargaining power of the Norwegian government. Solberg countered this critique by mocking Hansen for attempting to serve up 'scientific' arguments to the Norwegian government. If Norwegian negotiators based their argumentation on Hansen's fanciful and dubious theories, he claimed, they were bound to fail.[53]

There is much to suggest that the Norwegian government agreed with Solberg. The fact is that the government commissioned not Hansen, but his academic adversaries — Ole Solberg and the lappologists Konrad Nilsen and Just Qvigstad — as expert advisors in the negotiations with Sweden. This indicates that despite the potential political usefulness of Hansen's theories, they lacked the scientific credibility necessary to be politically effective. But though the government did not engage Hansen as a scientific expert in the reindeer-pasture negotiations, his research was still financed by the state, and even if his theories of Sami prehistory met with strong criticism from leading experts, they did not disappear into oblivion. Instead, in the interwar years, Hansen's theories became an important starting point for anthropological research into the racial history of the Sami when the Department of Anatomy launched a huge project of excavating and investigating Sami skulls.

Race and nationhood

At the turn of the century, a number of Norwegian academics believed in the superiority of the Germanic race and held that the struggle between races was a main driving force of human history. These ideas were accepted as scientifically valid and were discussed within academic institutions, but this does not mean that they were scientifically uncontroversial, nor does it mean that Norwegian scholars in general championed a national ideology centred on the idea of a Germanic master race. The notion that Europeans could be split into a hierarchy of races was controversial, as was the idea of Norwegians as members of a Germanic elite among the European races.

In fact, it is arguable that Norwegian academia was dominated by the concept of the nation as a social organism shaped by certain historical preconditions and by adaptation to a particular geographical environment.

---

53 Kyllingstad, *'Menneskeåndens universalitet'*, p. 331.

The Norwegians were commonly thought to have originated with groups of Germanic-speaking peoples who had settled in Norwegian territory during a long prehistoric period. These peoples did not, however, become Norwegians until they had cultivated the land and undergone a slow evolutionary process of adaptation to the Norwegian landscape. This process was construed as the establishment of a hierarchy of cultural-evolutionary levels, as the growth of a characteristic Norwegian national character and as an increasing and still ongoing social integration to certain national values.

But even if 'race' was not the core feature of this prevailing notion of Norwegian nationhood, it was still an important element in the national identity. It was common to assume that peoples could be ranked in a hierarchy from primitive to civilised, and even if there were differing views about the extent to which these distinctions were racially determined or culturally malleable, there were few who would totally rule out the significance of inherited racial characteristics. In addition, although not everyone supported the idea of a Germanic master race, few questioned the notion of white supremacy. It was common to consider Norwegians racially superior to non-Europeans. The scholarly works we have discussed were all formulated within a frame of reference whereby peoples could be ranked in a hierarchy of evolutionary levels, but there were huge differences in the extent to which this hierarchy was considered racially-determined or not. While race was irrelevant to Solberg when construing the boundary between the Sami and the Norwegians, it was the decisive criterion for Yngvar Nielsen and Andreas Hansen. The majority of other works were situated somewhere between these extremes, though in most cases race was given some significance in the delineation of the national community.

It is important to note, however, that if we leave the academic debates for a moment and instead look at the minority policy that was actually implemented in Norway, we find that 'race' was of little relevance. Not only the Sami, but also other minorities, notably the Kvens and the Roma, were subjected to a harsh policy of assimilation from the late nineteenth century until the middle of the twentieth century. This policy rested on the assumption that these peoples could, and should, be transformed into Norwegians, even though they were assumed to be racially different and even inferior. Thus, notions of huge racial difference were no impediment to the implementation of a hardline policy aimed at melting together different ethnic groups into an ethnically homogeneous Norwegian nation.

5. Racial Hygiene and the Nordic Race, 1900-1933

The nineteenth century saw the rise of a scientific worldview whereby humans were ranked in a hierarchy according to their degree of biological, cultural and moral advancement. This evolutionary worldview was marked by profound faith in human progress, but also by dread of degeneration. Around the turn of the century, members of the educated Western elite began to fear that the evolution of the human species was coming to a halt because modern society was out of step with nature. This anxiety fuelled the growth of the racial hygiene movement to counteract the biological degeneration of humankind. After the turn of the twentieth century Mendelian genetics arose as a new and prestigious field of research. This helped strengthen the notion of human nature as something innate, unchangeable and calculable. In such a setting, anthropological racial science acquired new social relevance by being linked to racial hygiene and new meaning in light of the Mendelian approach to biological heredity.

The rise of Mendelian genetics

It was in the 1860s that the Austrian monk Gregor Mendel conducted his famous hybrid experiments. When he crossed white- and purple-flower pea plants, the result was not a blend: in fact, all the offspring had purple flowers. However, when he allowed the bean plants to self-fertilise, he obtained a second generation of pea flowers that were purple and white at a ratio of 3 to 1. Based on this discovery, he conceived the idea of heredity units, which he called 'factors' and which determined the inheritance of biological traits. For each singular trait, the organism inherits one factor from each parent. These may be similar or different. If they are different, only one of them, the dominant factor, will determine the organism's appearance. The other factor,

http://dx.doi.org/10.11647/OBP.0051.05

the recessive factor, will only be expressed if the individual inherits a double dosage of it.

Initially Mendel's work did not attract much attention. He had a peripheral status in the world of science, and contemporary biological research was mainly oriented towards other issues. In 1900, however, his work was rediscovered and in the following years genetics emerged as a new discipline that explored the field of biological inheritance using controlled crossing experiments and a new conceptual and theoretical framework. Mendel's hereditary units were given the name 'genes'. The concept of genes became linked to chromosomes and identified as a materially existing phenomenon located in the nucleus of all living organisms—the terms 'phenotype' and 'genotype' were coined to distinguish between an organism's observable characteristics and its underlying genetic makeup.

Mendelian genetics did not, however, provide clear answers to all issues related to biological heritability, and both Lamarckism and the orthogenetic theory of directional evolution continued to exist alongside the new genetics. Biology was marked by an incoherent and disputed theoretical foundation into the interwar years, and it was unclear what implications the new insights of genetics would have for evolutionary theory. This situation started to change in the 1930s, with the advent of the neo-Darwinian synthesis of genetics and selection theory, which turned genes and populations into key variables in the explanation of biological evolution. A 'population' was construed to be a group of organisms that share a set of genes. Reproduction and the exchange of genes occur mainly within and not between populations, and evolution occurs when the composition of a population's gene pool is changed.

It may seem logical to assume that scientists who rejected the old theories of heritability and began to apply Mendelian genetics to anthropological issues would soon lose interest in the old morphological concept of race and instead turn their attention towards the flow of genes within and between populations. One might expect that the concept of race would be replaced by those of 'population' and 'genes'. Something along these lines did happen, but not until the 1940s and 1950s, when a number of influential geneticists began criticising traditional physical anthropological race research for being based on outdated nineteenth-century ideas. However, in the early decades of the twentieth century, many maintained that Mendelian genetics was a good argument for revitalising the anthropological concept of race.[1]

_____

1   For an account of the relation between genetics and anthropological racial science in Germany in the early twentieth century, see Veronika Lipphardt,

Race and Mendelism

Around the turn of the century, German anthropologists went through what the historian Benoit Massin has described as a conceptual, theoretical and methodological crisis. Decades of extensive anthropometric measuring had led to the accumulation of huge amounts of data on morphological variations within humankind, but there was increasing frustration over the meaning of the concept of race and its usefulness in making sense of these data.[2] In 1901, the Hungarian anthropologist Aurel von Török claimed that anthropology had reached a dead end because it was based on a faulty premise—the notion that the arithmetic mean of a population coincided with the inheritable 'type' of the race. Török argued that the anthropological enterprise rested on a circular argument: it took for granted what it was designed to demonstrate—the existence of pure races.[3]

Török traced the origin of this fatal flaw back to Anders Retzius and his belief in a number of original, pure races, each of which was characterised by a certain skull shape. Since it was assumed that modern populations were racially mixed, Retzius' theory implied that the further back in time you searched, the more racial purity you would find. According to Török, however, decades of research on ancient skulls had not confirmed this notion of primordial pure races.[4] Török's criticism was directed towards the basic conceptual and theoretical underpinnings of the anthropological study of race, and he was not alone in voicing this reservation. A number of anthropologists argued that racial traits were distributed between and within populations in a gradual and irregular manner that made it impossible to delineate distinct racial types. Adding to this, many even maintained that some of the most measured racial characteristics, like the cephalic index, were determined by environmental impact as well as by inheritance and were therefore unreliable as racial markers. Taken seriously, this criticism would mean that racial anthropology was a largely unfounded science.

'Isolates and Crosses in Human Population Genetics, or: A Contextualization of German Race Science', *Current Anthropology*, Vol. 53, no. S5 (2012), pp. 69-82.

2   Benoit Massin, 'From Virchow to Fischer: Physical Anthropology and "Modern Race Theories" in Wilhelmine Germany', in George W. Stocking, Jr. (ed.), *Volksgeist as Method and Ethic* (Madison, WI: University of Wisconsin, 1996), pp. 106-14.

3   Massin, 'From Virchow to Fischer', p. 109.

4   Ibid., pp. 109-10.

It was in this context that Mendelism made its breakthrough in the anthropological study of race. Eugen Fischer's study of the so-called 'Rehoboth bastards' in 1908-1913 was often referred to by interwar anthropologists as a trailblazing work bringing together Mendelism and anthropology.[5] The population of the Rehoboth village in southwest Africa comprised descendants of European settlers and local Khoikhoi people. Fischer undertook genealogical studies of the inheritance of traits presumed to be race-specific—like eye colour, skin colour and the cephalic index—in racially-mixed families, and he analysed the occurrence and distribution of such traits in the mixed population. The goal was to determine whether these traits were inherited in a Mendelian fashion. The work elaborated upon similar studies that had recently been made by the American eugenicist and geneticist Charles Davenport.

Fisher's main conclusions were that racial traits are not inherited as a coherent type and that racial mixing does not lead to intermediate types. Instead, the crossing of races leads to the dissolution of race-specific combinations of physical traits. The traits themselves do not disappear, but are sustained as singular traits that are combined in new ways among the 'bastards' and inherited in a Mendelian fashion. Fischer claimed, for example, to have detected a 3-to-1 ratio between the occurrence of curly versus straight hair in the second generation after the mixing of the parental races, and argued that this matched a predicted pattern of dominant and recessive inheritance of hair types. He also claimed to have demonstrated genealogically that skull shape, as described by the cephalic index, is inherited in accordance with Mendel's rules.[6] Thus, racial traits that had been 'discovered' in the nineteenth century, and mapped using classification criteria based on pre-Mendelian theories of hereditary types, were now reinterpreted and redefined as Mendelian traits.

Physical anthropology as a descriptive science

In 1914 Rudolf Martin, an anthropologist at the University of Zurich, published the extensive textbook *Lehrbuch der Anthropologie*,[7] which became a

---

5   Lipphardt, *Isolates and Crosses*, p. 71.
6   Eugen Fischer, *Die Rehobother Bastards und das Bastardierungsproblem beim Menschen* (Jena: G. Fischer, 1913), pp. 142-43, 156.
7   Rudolf Martin, *Lehrbuch der Anthropologie in systematischer Darstellung mit besonderer Berücksichtigung der anthropologischen Methoden* (Jena: Gustav Fischer, 1914).

standard reference work in the German-speaking academic world, including Sweden and Norway.[8] The textbook was written in the aftermath of 'the conceptual crisis' of the discipline at the turn of the century, when leading anthropologists had questioned the basic theoretical and methodological foundations of racial typology. According to Martin's preface, the textbook was meant to represent the 'young' discipline as it stood in 1914, without taking into account its internal debates. *Lehrbuch der Anthropologie* was first and foremost a catalogue of methods for measuring the human body, and as such it strongly advocated a descriptive style of research.[9] Martin claimed that the goal of anthropology was to investigate the bodily variations within humankind, and he thought that the study of psychological differences lay outside its domain. He argued that anthropologists should stick to the purely physical concept of 'race' and entrust to ethnologists the task of studying the culturally-defined 'people' (*Völker*) and its expressions of individual psychology (*die Völkerseele*, or national soul).[10]

In a systematic presentation of the discipline, Martin defined 'psychology' as an anthropological topic. *Lehrbuch der Anthropologie* touched upon the question of interrelations between psychology, craniometry and brain anatomy, and gave a thorough presentation of the theories concerning the relationship between 'cultural level' and skull shape. However, there was no mention of psychological differences between races. The textbook referred to Eugen Fischer's studies and advocated a Mendelian understanding of heritability and race. 'Race' was defined as a group of humans sharing a *merkmalkomplex*, a complex of bodily traits which were inherited independently of each other according to Mendelian rules. Even though Martin held that these variations were mainly caused by genetics, he allowed

---

8   Robert Proctor, 'From *Anthropologie* to *Rassenkunde* in the German Anthropological Tradition', in George W. Stocking, Jr. (ed.), *Bones, Bodies, Behavior* (Madison, WI: University of Wisconsin Press, 1988); Benoit Massin, 'From Virchow to Fischer: Physical Anthropology and "Modern Race Theories" in Wilhelmine Germany', in George W. Stocking, Jr. (ed.), *Volksgeist as Method and Ethic* (Madison, WI: University of Wisconsin, 1996), pp. 79-154 (pp. 140-42); Andrew D. Evans, 'Race Made Visible: The Transformation of Museum Exhibits in Early-Twentieth-Century German Anthropology', *German Studies Review*, Vol. 31, no. 1 (February 2008), p. 91. Matin's textbook was published in several editions starting from 1914. The fourth version was rewritten by Rainer Knussman and published in 1988. Swedish and Norwegian researchers used Martin's textbook as their main frame of reference when they undertook racial studies in the 1920s. (See chapter 8).
9   Rudolf Martin, *Lehrbuch der Anthropologie*, pp. v-vii.
10 Ibid., pp. 1-2.

for environmental influence and its interactions with the physiological mechanisms of bodily growth.

However, as Martin saw it, these questions were not central to anthropology; the discipline's main task was to measure and describe the phenotypic variations within mankind. The study of the causes behind these variations was very much a secondary priority. Martin claimed there was too little knowledge about these issues and that bold theorising would be counterproductive: anthropology should not concentrate on theories about cause and effect, but on the gathering of empirical facts (see Figs. 8 and 9).[11]

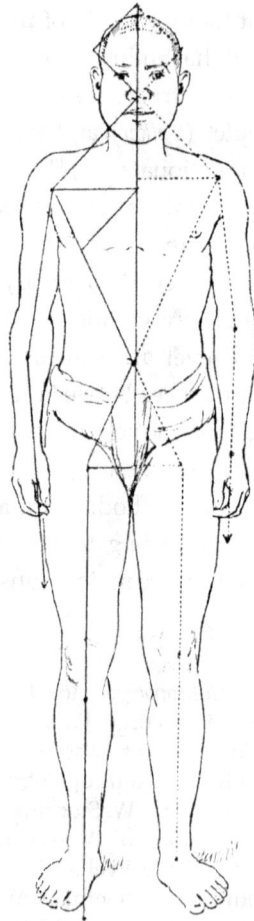

Fig. 8 Chart of human body proportions from Martin's *Lehrbuch der Anthropologie*.
Different races were thought to have different proportions.

11 Ibid., Preface and chapter 1.1.

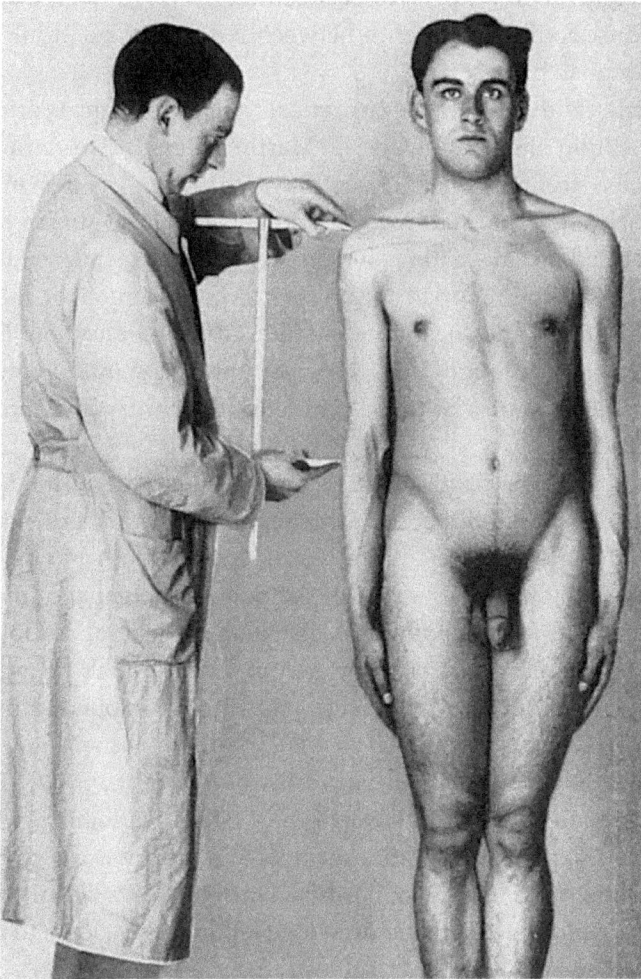

Fig. 9 Measurement of upper arm length as demonstrated in
Martin's *Lehrbuch der Anthropologie*.

There was no place for the inheritance of acquired properties in Martin's
textbook. Nevertheless, he maintained an interest in studies of the
relationships between social environment and bodily growth, which
resembled the Lamarckian standpoint within nineteenth-century
anthropology. A group of individuals sharing a *merkmalkomplex* did not
necessarily share racial origin. An alternative explanation for their likeness
could be that all the individuals in the group had been affected by the
same type of environmental influences and had therefore developed the
same bodily characteristics. Systematic differences in living habits, living

conditions and environmental impact could therefore result in systematic differences in bodily appearance between socially or politically defined groups of human beings.[12]

Scientists with different theoretical and ideological orientations operated within the framework of Martin's descriptive anthropology. Many of the techniques used by the anthropologists for measuring, observing and quantifying the anatomical shape of the human body had also been used by the anthropologists of the nineteenth century. The extent to which the mapped 'properties' were products of inheritance or of environment and lifestyle was still a disputed question. Despite a changed theoretical foundation, there was much continuity between the anthropological debates of the late nineteenth century and those of the early twentieth century.

Among the German anthropologists of the later days of the *Kaiserreich* and the early days of the Weimar Republic, there were many who championed the supremacy of the Nordic race and others who strongly opposed it, with both sides aware of the political potential of these ideas. Karl Saller, a respected anthropologist and student of Rudolf Martin, was opposed to *völkish* nationalism, and in the late 1920s he argued that the concept of a Nordic race was an empirically unfounded theoretical construction. Other anthropologists were members of the *Nordischer Ring* which aimed to promote a 'Nordic worldview' (*nordische Weltanschauung*). The combination of racial philosophy and Social Darwinism which had entered the discipline in the first decade of the century was a scientifically-accepted, though still disputed, position. During the 1920s, however, these ideas spread and the discipline drew correspondingly closer to the racial hygiene movement.

The idea of racial hygiene

The idea of racial hygiene, or eugenics, was developed in the 1880s and 1890s; two of its leading advocates were the Englishman Francis Galton and the German Alfred Ploetz. In 1905, the world's first organisation for racial hygiene was established in Germany on the initiative of Ploetz. During the first two or three decades of the twentieth century, the idea of racial hygiene became increasingly popular, and eugenics organisations

---

12 Ibid., p. 10.

were established all over the world. In the period from World War I until the late 1920s, much of the international scientific research and debate on human genetics and race was strongly related to the eugenics debate.[13]

The eugenics movement was nourished by a general worry about the biological degeneration of the populations of the Western world. There was a widespread belief that the mechanisms of natural evolution had been corrupted by modern, industrialised society, and that 'inferior' individuals were therefore reproducing faster than the 'superior'. The task of racial hygiene was to make sure that valuable genetic material was passed on at the expense of the less valuable. Advocates of racial hygiene usually assumed that the lower social strata, and in particular the 'asocial' groups at the bottom of society, were of generally lesser biological quality than the middle class and the elites.

Racial hygiene, however, was not a scientifically or politically homogeneous movement. Ploetz and Galton, who developed their ideas independently of each other, represented two different strands of eugenic thought. Ploetz was a *völkish* nationalist, and the idea of the Nordic race played a crucial role in the type of racial hygiene that he advocated. But Galton's style of eugenics was closely connected to the British movement for social reform and social hygiene. Adherents of this version of eugenics were less concerned with 'race' in the physical-anthropological sense of the word and were more interested in questions about the inheritance of positive and negative individual traits. There was no clear and unambiguous boundary between these two strains of eugenic thought, and they should not be confused with the terminological distinction between 'racial hygiene' and 'eugenics'. Racial hygiene was the common term in Germany and Scandinavia, while eugenics was used in the Anglophone world. However, both the explicitly racist and the more social-reformist types of racial hygiene/eugenics were current in all these countries and partially overlapped.

---

13   The following analysis draws on Daniel J. Kevles, *In the Name of Eugenics: Genetics and the Uses of Human Heredity* (Berkeley, CA: University of California Press, 1986); Stefan Kühl, *Die Internationale der Rassisten* (Frankfurt am Main: Campus, 1997); Sheila Faith Weiss, 'The Race Hygiene Movement in Germany', *Osiris*, 2nd series, Vol. 3 (1987), pp. 193-236; Paul Weindling, 'Weimar Eugenics: The Kaiser Wilhelm Institute for Anthropology, Human Heredity and Eugenics in Social Context', *Annals of Science*, Vol. 42, no. 3 (1985), pp. 303-18.

Eugenic ideas were advocated by a wide variety of organisations and movements, often as part of broader programmes of social reform. Feminist organisations were interested in eugenics. When promoting rational family planning, they were able to make use of arguments about positive and negative genetic properties and claim that contraception and sexual education should be made publicly available so that the lower classes, as well as the upper, could reduce their number of offspring. Many socialists were also committed to eugenics, believing that the scientific management of the biological quality of the population was a necessary element in a rationally-ordered socialist economy.

According to the historian Stefan Kühl, there was a general difference in the political strategies of the race-oriented and more social-hygienically oriented eugenicists. The latter were inclined to operate in a national arena and work for a more rational national population policy, often arguing that this would make the country more fit for the competition between nations. Eugenicists who were more concerned with the 'blond race' and its struggle to survive in competition with supposedly inferior races often had a more international strategy: they advocated cooperation between eugenicists in nations where the Nordic race was assumed to be in the majority.[14]

The first initiatives for organised international cooperation came from a *völkish*-oriented group of racial hygienists in Munich, and by 1907 they had established an International Society for Racial Hygiene, the objective of which was to promote cooperation between nations with predominantly 'Nordic' populations. Attracting members from Scandinavia—the presumed heartland of the Nordic race—was high on the agenda, and the first foreign members included the Norwegian chemist Jon Alfred Mjøen and the famous Danish geneticist Wilhelm Johannsen. In 1909, a recruitment campaign in Sweden led to the enrolment of twenty new members and the establishment of the Swedish Racial Hygienic Society (*Svenskt sällskapet för rashygien*). Ten years later, when Sweden founded a State Institute for Racial Biology (*Statens institut för asbiologi*) in the university town of Uppsala, it became an important centre for a strand of racial hygiene that was strongly committed to preserving the Nordic race.

The race-oriented style of eugenics was strong in the U.S. as well. The anthropological concept of a 'Nordic race' coincided to a great degree with the politically, socially and economically dominant ethnic

---

14   Kühl, *Die Internationale der Rassisten*, pp. 11-17, 19-20.

group in American society—white Anglo-Saxon Protestants. Increasing immigration from southern and eastern Europe, a growing number of African-Americans and their own declining fertility rates, led to WASP fear of being outnumbered by 'non-Nordic' racial elements. The geneticist Charles Davenport attained a leading position in American eugenics and managed to raise money for a comprehensive research programme. By gathering extensive genealogical and medical data, Davenport's research project aimed to uncover the genetic causes behind psychological disorders and other supposedly heritable pathologies. He also led research on the effect of racial mixing and differences on intelligence.

In 1912 there was a huge eugenics conference in London, assembling people from all over the Western world and representing a broad range of political and scientific views. It was a mixed group of feminists, industrial capitalists, religious leaders, statisticians, sociologists, anthropologists, politicians, military officers, biologists, medical doctors and others. The heterogeneity of the participants is exemplified by the two Norwegian attendees, Katti Anker Møller and Jon Alfred Mjøen. Møller was a feminist who advocated sexual education and legalising the marketing of contraceptives. Mjøen was primarily worried about what he saw as the dangers fall in the fertility of the blond, fair-skinned population of northwestern Europe, and he was opposed not only to contraception but also to sexual education and feminism.[15]

Support for eugenics grew after the conference. A committee was entrusted with the task of writing a joint policy statement and establishing an international organisation. In the following years, international cooperation between eugenicists would come to be dominated by this organisation, which from 1925 was called the International Federation of Eugenics Organizations (IFEO). The conferences arranged by the IFEO were, until the late 1920s, the most important international meeting-place for scientists doing human genetic research. Public interest in racial hygiene was fuelled by World War I. The physically fittest young men were sent to the front where they were systematically killed in the worst bloodshed the world had ever witnessed. The first 'industrialised' war was seen as an extreme example of the counter-evolutionary forces that threatened modern society and caused many influential people to worry about the biological quality of European populations.

---

15 Torben Hviid Nielsen et al., *Livets tre og kodenes kode. Fra genetikk til bioteknologi i Norge 1900-2000* (Oslo: Gyldendal akademisk, 2000), p. 66.

Scandinavian champions of racial hygiene

It was during the years around World War I that Herman Lundborg established himself as the leading figure in the Swedish racial hygiene movement. Lundborg was a noted scientist both in Sweden and internationally. His academic prestige was mainly based on his mammoth work *Medical-biological family studies within a 2232-person strong peasant family in Sweden*.[16] In this work, which mirrored studies undertaken by Davenport in the U.S., Lundborg argued that a series of apparently different diseases occurring within this big family were, in reality, various manifestations of an inherited type of epilepsy.[17]

Like Davenport and Ploetz, Lundborg was worried about the future of the Nordic race, and he did not limit himself to the scientific study of the question. Along with a network of likeminded adherents of eugenics, he worked hard to preach the gospel of the Nordic race. In 1918 he set up an exhibition of 'folk types' (*folktypsutställning*) that toured Sweden with models of 'Swedish racial types', and he also helped organise a beauty contest to find the ideal 'Swedish-Germanic racial type'. After its establishment in 1922, the State Institute for Racial Biology became, under Lundborg's leadership, a key institution for physical anthropology and human genetics in Sweden.[18]

Jon Alfred Mjøen was the foremost spokesman for racial hygiene in Norway. He considered himself a member of the 'first small circle of believers' and had been a personal friend of Alfred Ploetz since the late 1880s. Like Lundborg, Mjøen had an influential network of contacts within the eugenics movement and became internationally renowned as one of the movement's pioneers. At a meeting in 1908 of the Association of Norwegian Medical Students (*Medicinerforeningen*) he put forward the first

---

16 Herman Lundborg, *Medizinisch-biologische Familienforschungen innerhalb eines 2232köpfigen Bauerngeschlechtes in Schweden (Provinz Blekinge)* (Jena: G. Fischer 1913).

17 Gunnar Broberg, 'Eugenics in Sweden: Efficient Care', in his and Nils Roll-Hansen (eds.), *Eugenics and the Welfare State, Sterilisation Policy in Denmark, Sweden, Norway, and Finland* (East Lansing, MI: Michigan State University Press, 1996), pp. 84f.

18 Gunnar Broberg, 'Statens institut för rasbiologi–tilkomståren', in Gunnar Broberg, Gunnar Eriksson and Karin Johannisson (eds.), *Kunskapens trädgårdar: om institutioner och institutionaliseringar i vetenskapen och livet* (Stockholm: Atlantis, 1988); idem, 'Eugenics in Sweden', pp. 85-91.

version of what was later to be known as the Norwegian Programme of Racial Hygiene (*Det norske program for rasehygiene*). This was the model for the international statement on eugenics written after the First International Eugenics Congress in 1912.[19]

Mjøen held that the goal of racial hygiene was to fight for the survival of 'our own race' — the Germanics.[20] In his view, the future of the Norwegian nation and indeed of Western civilisation was at stake. The Norwegians had a responsibility towards their own nation and the world to protect their racial purity and quality, a national resource comparable to 'our waterfalls, our woods and our wonderful nature'.[21] According to Mjøen, modern civilisation had disrupted the natural struggle for existence among human beings. New medical therapies, bacteriology and better individual hygiene had ruined the quality of the race by helping weak individuals to survive. The same was true of social insurance and the establishment of institutions to take care of mentally retarded, insane, deaf or epileptic children. Even modern warfare counteracted natural selection, with the strongest men killed at the front while the weak were allowed to stay at home and procreate. Mjøen, who had a German doctoral degree in organic chemistry, also held that various chemical substances, like alcohol and industrial emissions, were leading to genetic deterioration. Moreover, he feared that the ongoing mass migration from Norway to America was draining the country of its most superior racial elements, while immigration to Norway from countries to the south and east was allowing inferior elements into the country.[22]

To combat these evils, Mjøen prescribed positive racial hygienic measures that could promote the reproduction of superior individuals: eugenic education, decentralisation of the population in order to avoid the degenerating effects of city life and the reorganisation of taxation and social insurance schemes. He prescribed 'prophylactic' measures like health declarations before marriage, the combating of chemical poisons and the establishment of a progressive system for taxing alcoholic drinks. Finally,

---

19   On Mjøen and the First International Eugenics Congress, see also Kühl, *Die Internationale der Rassisten*, p. 35. On the historiography of Norwegian eugenics, see Introduction.

20   Alfred Mjøen, *Racehygiene* (Oslo: Dybwad, 1914), p. 238: '[...] en kamp for vor egen races — germanernes — bestaaen'.

21   Mjøen cited in Monsen, *Politisk biologi*, pp. 46-47.

22   Mjøen, *Racehygiene* (1914).

he outlined 'negative' eugenic measures to counteract the procreation of inferior individuals. Declaring that 'we must learn to distinguish between the right to live and the right to give life', he advocated forced segregation and in some cases even sterilisation of the mentally retarded, of epileptics and of individuals he believed to have inborn criminal tendencies.[23]

In 1906, Mjøen established the private Vinderen Biological Laboratory, which became the institutional base for eugenic propaganda and research. The Laboratory did not receive any public funding, and it provided Mjøen with no substantial revenue. However, in 1907 Mjøen became government inspector of the production of liquor and beer in the Kristiania region, and by 1916 he owned a pharmacy that provided him with the financial freedom to pursue his main interest.[24] Mjøen belonged to the cultural and political elite, and his ideas garnered support from politicians in different political camps. Mjøen himself was politically active in the *Venstre* Party, and several times he gave talks at the national party congress. In 1914 he spoke about 'turning the treatment of racial and national diseases into a public task'. The speech was well received, and the Minister of Justice Lars Abrahamsen declared his support for Mjøen's ideas.[25]

The attack on Mjøen and the rise of genetics in Norway

It is clear that Mjøen had an impact on the social-political debate in Norway, and he may have had good reason to believe, in the years before World War I, that a Norwegian eugenics movement under his leadership was about to become an influential force in the Norwegian political and academic landscape. In 1914, however, his campaign suffered a severe setback. Mjøen published the book *Racial Hygiene*, in which he substantiated his racial hygienic programme, and was met with devastating criticism from a group of university-based scientists. This led to a lasting conflict that thwarted the establishment of a unified eugenics movement in Norway and hindered the International Federation of

---

23 Mjøen, *Racehygiene* (1914), pp. 140, 190f.

24 Christopher Hals Gylseth, 'Jon Alfred Mjøen', in *Norsk biografisk leksikon*, http://nbl.snl.no/Jon_Alfred_Mjøen

25 Helge Pedersen, *'Gud har skapat svarta och vita människor, jäfvulen derimot halfnegeren'. En komparativ analyse av Jon Alfred Mjøen og Herman Lundborgs rasehygieniske ideer i Norge og Sverige. Ca. 1900-1935* (Master thesis, University of Oslo, 2003), pp. 121f.

Eugenics Organizations from establishing a proper foothold in the Norwegian scientific community.[26]

Mjøen's opponents claimed that his extensive proposals for political action were based on weak scientific foundations. His main critics were Ole Malm, Kristine Bonnevie, Otto Lous Mohr and Kristian Emil Schreiner. They strongly questioned his competence in biology and tried to brand him as a pseudo-scientific dilettante. Ole Malm was the national director and main architect of the Norwegian Veterinary Administration. He was a well-known social conservative who vigorously opposed feminism, abortion, sterilisation, contraception and everything else that could threaten traditional family values and lead to declining birth rates. He not only dismissed Mjøen's scientific credibility, he dismissed the very idea of eugenics, which he saw as an example of dangerous social radicalism.[27]

Malm had academic degrees in both medicine and veterinary science. In his younger years, he had worked at the Louis Pasteur Institute in Paris and had published scientific works on bacteriology, hygiene and vaccination; but he was no expert in genetics or racial anthropology. The other three critics, however, constituted the foremost experts on chromosomes, genetics and race at the University of Kristiania, and as such they were in an excellent position to delegitimise Mjøen. Kristine Bonnevie was a professor of zoology and head of the zoological laboratory, and Kristian Emil Schreiner was Guldberg's successor as head of the anatomy department. Both Schreiner and Bonnevie had worked with internationally-leading cytologists, embryologists and geneticists like Arnold Lang in Zürich, Theodor Boveri in Würzburg and Edmund B. Wilson at Columbia University in New York. Both had won international repute for their cytological research, which was directly relevant to the breakthrough of modern genetics and to the understanding of the relationship between genes and chromosomes (see chapter 7). Even the young medical researcher Otto Louis Mohr had international experience in laboratory research on cells and chromosomes, and was, in 1914, at the beginning of a successful career as a geneticist.[28]

---

26 Nils Roll-Hansen, 'Norwegian Eugenics: Sterilization as Social Reform', in Gunnar Broberg and Nils Roll Hansen (eds.), *Eugenics and the Welfare State: Sterilization Policy in Denmark, Sweden, Norway, and Finland* (East Lansing: Michigan State University Press, 1995), pp. 151-94 (pp. 158-61); Monsen, *Politisk biologi*, pp. 40, 45.

27 Monsen, *Politisk biologi*, pp. 42-43.

28 Inger Nordal, Dag O. Hessen and Thore Lie, *Kristine Bonnevie: Et forskerliv* (Oslo: Cappelen Damm, 2012), pp. 97-222.

In contrast to Ole Malm, Bonnevie, Schreiner and Mohr were not opposed to the general idea of racial hygiene. Instead, they criticised the scientific quality of Mjøen's book, and their attack on his scientific credibility was intertwined with struggles concerning research funding and professional legitimacy. Racial hygiene was on the public agenda and served as an argument for raising funds for genetic research. Mjøen's success in establishing himself as a leading proponent of racial hygiene in Norway and abroad made him a rival to the biological and medical scientists at the University in their pursuit of public funding and professional prestige.[29]

When Mjøen published his book, genetics was not yet established as an institutionalised discipline at the Norwegian university. As a direct result of the debate, however, a new Institute of Genetics was established in 1916, on the initiative of Kristine Bonnevie and a group of medical professors. The new institute was to study human genetics, and the academic initiators, government bureaucrats and parliamentary politicians involved in its establishment all argued that it was urgent to undertake this type of human genetic research because of its social implications. New scientific insight into human genetics was seen as having great potential implications for future social policy and legislation related to 'antisocial elements in the population' and 'psychic abnormities'. Advocates of the new institute also claimed, implicitly alluding to Mjøen, that one of the main tasks of the new institution would be to serve as a guarantee against dilettantism in the fields of eugenics and genetics.[30]

Compared to Lundborg's State Institute for Racial Biology in Sweden, the Norwegian Institute of Genetics was a very modest institution. It was housed on the premises of the University's Department of Zoology and had a minimal annual budget, but it allowed Kristine Bonnevie to move from cytology into genetics. She argued that Norway, with its isolated, inbreeding rural populations, was a good place for compiling genealogical pedigrees and for studying the prevalence and inheritance of genetic traits. Her research aimed at solving basic scientific issues, but at the same time it had relevance for eugenics. She studied the inheritance of abnormal traits like mental disabilities, the tendency towards twin births and polydactylism (in which a person is born with extra fingers or toes). In the 1920s Bonnevie also began to study the genetics and ontogenesis of

---

29 Roll-Hansen, 'Norwegian Eugenics', pp. 158-167; Monsen, *Politisk biologi*, p. 59.
30 Monsen, *Politisk biologi*, p. 61.

the papillary patterns on the fingertips—a research field closely related to racial science.[31]

Research on the inheritance of fingerprints was first initiated by Francis Galton—the British founder of eugenics—in the 1890s, and was based on the assumption that fingerprint patterns were genetically determined and could correlate with race, ethnicity, disease propensity, mental abilities and behavioural characteristics. In a series of studies published around the turn of the century, it was argued that fingerprint patterns varied between different races and could be used as a criterion for ranking races on a scale of proximity to our anthropoid ancestors. This kind of research continued into the 1920s and was the starting point for Bonnevie's investigations.[32]

In 1924 Bonnevie published a study of the different frequencies of papillary patterns in various ethnic groups and races. Using a scheme invented by Galton, she divided fingerprints into three types—whorls, loops and arches—and demonstrated that Asians had a higher proportion of whorls, and fewer arches, than Europeans. In the late 1920s Bonnevie published three studies in which she attempted to clarify the relation between genetic and environmental causes in the embryological development of papillary patterns,[33] followed in 1927 by a study of Norwegian schoolchildren in which a correlation between fingerprint patterns and intelligence was made. Furthermore, Bonnevie suggested that this was due to a causal relationship between the embryonic development of the papillary pattern and the nervous system. Finally, she argued for the social value of this type of research by claiming that papillary patterns might be developed into a criterion for identifying mentally weak individuals.[34]

It is reasonable to assume that anatomy professor Kristian Emil Schreiner, like Bonnevie, regarded Mjøen as a competitor for funding, since anthropological concepts of race played a role in Mjøen's brand of

31 Nordahl, Hessen, Lie, *Kristine Bonnevie*, pp. 205-18.

32 Simon A. Cole, 'Twins, Twain, Galton and Gilman: Fingerprinting, Individualization, Brotherhood, and Race in Pudd'nhead Wilson', *Configurations*, Vol. 15, no. 3 (2007), pp. 227-65.

33 Kristine Bonnevie, 'Studies on Papillary Patterns of Human Fingers, *Journal of Genetics*, Vol. 15, no. 1 (1924), pp. 1-111; idem, 'Was lehrt die Embryologie der Papillarmuster über ihre Bedeutung als Rassen- und Familiencharakter?', *Molecular and General Genetics*, Vol. 50, no. 1 (1929), pp. 219-48; idem, 'Zur Mechanik der Papillarmusterbildung 1 & 2', *Development, Genes and Evolution*, Vol. 117, no. 1 (1929), pp. 384-420 and Vol. 126, no. 2 (1932), pp. 348-72.

34 Kristine Bonnevie, 'Papillarmuster und Psychische Eigenschaften', *Hereditas*, Vol. 9, nos. 1-3 (1927).

eugenics. The fact is that anthropological research at the Department of Anatomy, which had been dormant since Guldberg's death in 1908, was given a boost in the aftermath of the controversy over Mjøen's book; it is likely that this was partly stimulated by the debate over racial hygiene (see chapter 7). It was also in the aftermath of the Mjøen controversy that the anatomy department turned to genetics. In 1917, Otto Lous Mohr went to New York to work at Professor Thomas Hunt Morgan's famous laboratory of experimental genetics at Columbia University. He came home with a colony of fruit flies — Morgan's preferred research object — and established a small laboratory for fruit fly experiments in the anatomy department. During the next decade he became internationally recognised for his genetic research and, like Bonnevie, supervised a number of colleagues and students, helping to establish a Norwegian tradition of genetics research.[35]

Even if Mohr's fruit fly research was of little direct relevance to eugenics, he became an important contributor to the debate on eugenics in Norway. By the late 1920s he had become a key member of the Norwegian scientific community and took a leading role in public debates on family planning and population policy. Mohr was married to the daughter of Katti Anker Møller, the aforementioned participant at the First International Eugenics Congress. Like his wife and his mother-in-law, both feminists, he championed birth control, sexual education and other socially radical and socialist ideas, and he was strongly opposed to Mjøen's brand of racial hygiene. Mohr became one of Mjøen's most outspoken critics.[36]

The scientific opposition against Mjøen was highlighted in 1919 when the new Norwegian Association of Genetics (*Norsk forening for arvelighetsforskning*) was established. Mjøen did not obtain membership, and the association was dominated by Otto Lous Mohr and Kristine Bonnevie, as well as by psychiatry professor Ragnar Vogt. Mjøen continued to maintain the private Vindern Biological Laboratory, which became his main institutional bridgehead for racial hygiene research and activism. He also initiated and managed the Norwegian Consultative Committee for Racial Hygiene (*Den norske konsultative komiteen for rasehygiene*), a national committee connected to the IFEO, and edited the journal *The Nordic Race* (*Den nordiske rase*) along with an international board of directors consisting

---

35   Lars Walløe, 'Otto Lous Mohr', in *Norsk biografisk leksikon*, http://nbl.snl.no/ Otto_Lous_Mohr

36   Walløe, 'Otto Lous Mohr'.

of likeminded eugenicists from Sweden, Great Britain, Germany and the U.S. Mjøen's leading position in the IFEO made it difficult for the organisation to establish itself in the Norwegian scientific community. During the 1920s, Kristine Bonnevie, Ragnar Vogt and the Norwegian Association of Genetics turned down a number of offers to join the federation.[37]

Although it seems clear that the Norwegian controversy over racial hygiene was intertwined with struggles over economic and institutional resources, this does not necessarily imply that the criticism put forward by Mjøen's opponents consisted purely of vicarious arguments aimed at blackening a rival's reputation. On the contrary, it is likely that Bonnevie, Schreiner and Mohr were seriously concerned about what they considered to be Mjøen's misuse of scientific arguments, and that their attack on him was motivated by a sense of duty to educate the public and contribute to an informed debate on eugenics. It is important to note, however, that it was neither his racism—his ranking of superior and inferior races—nor his worship of the Nordic race that made them brand him a pseudo-scientist. The book that Mjøen launched in 1914, *Race Hygiene*, was not primarily about the supremacy of the Nordic race; in fact, it was mainly about how to protect the biological quality of the national population. This included measures to prevent racial mixing with foreign and inferior races, but this topic was treated at little length compared to public health issues, temperance policy and questions about the inheritance of singular pathological traits within the national population. It was only in a later edition of the book that racial purity and the propagation of the Nordic race became the key issues.[38]

Furthermore, while attacking Mjøen's book, Bonnevie, Schreiner and Mohr referred in positive terms to another book on eugenics published in the same year, namely *Heredity and Racial Hygiene* (*Arvelighetslære og racehygiene*) by Ragnar Vogt, who agreed with Mjøen in placing the long-skulled and blond northern European race at the top of a racial hierarchy and in affirming that a main goal of racial hygiene was to strengthen this race. Vogt believed that the progress of human civilisation went hand in hand with the worldwide expansion of the Germanic peoples. Like Mjøen, he upheld racial purity as an ideal, believed miscegenation to be detrimental and welcomed the dying-out of inferior races. He claimed that

---

37 Monsen, *Politisk biologi*, pp. 59-74; Nordahl, Hessen Lie, *Kristine Bonnevie*, p. 196.
38 Jon Alfred Mjøen, *Racehygiene* (Oslo: Dybwad, 1914).

a racially-pure nation would share common ideals and mentalities and have a strong sense of community and loyalty. These views were inspired by, among others, the German writer Ludwig Wilser, the author of *The Origin of the Germanic* (*Die herkunft der Germanen*). He was also a key ideologue in the *völkisch* movement, a main architect behind the Aryan-Germanic theory and a friend of Otto Ammon.[39]

With respect to their view on the Nordic race, there was no deep, principled difference between Vogt and Mjøen. Yet Mjøen was branded a pseudo-scientist, while Vogt was considered a respected member of the scientific establishment. This indicates that the attack on Mjøen's scientific credibility in 1914 was a controversy over neither the scientific credibility of the idea of a superior Nordic race, nor the notion of racial superiority and inferiority. This would change during the subsequent years, however. From the late 1920s, the debate on race became progressively polarised, and the notion of a superior Nordic race became increasingly contested both in Norway and within the international eugenics movement.

A polarising debate over racial hygiene

From the late 1920s onwards, the International Federation of Eugenics Organizations (IFEO) was more and more dominated by a distinctly racist brand of eugenics. The federation initiated research on topics like the psychological differences between races and the effects of racial mixing. A clique of dogmatic racists tried to turn the organisation into a 'Blond International' aimed at protecting the Nordic race against 'bastardisation'. They also worked to exclude socialists, feminists, Lamarckians and people of non-European origin from the federation. This group consisted mainly of people from the U.S. and Germany, as well as the Scandinavians Jon Alfred Mjøen and Herman Lundborg.[40]

In contrast to the IFEO's turn towards a racist strand of eugenic thinking, the debates over eugenics that were ongoing at a national level in many countries became increasingly influenced by a more social hygienic style of eugenics in which the idea of a racial hierarchy was fairly irrelevant. In the late 1920s and early 1930s, leading British and

39 Ragnar Vogt, *Arvelighetslære og racehygiene* (Kristiania: Cammermeyer, 1913), pp. 105, 120-23.
40 Kühl, *Die Internationale der Rassisten*, pp. 71-94.

American biologists, anthropologists and psychologists launched an attack on scientifically legitimated racism. Biologists like Julian Huxley and L. C. Dunn claimed that the concept of race had become scientifically irrelevant because of the new insights from population genetics. They did not reject the soundness of the basic idea of eugenics, but advocated a liberal or socialist vision untainted by racial and social prejudice.[41] This type of criticism also had an impact in Scandinavia. The internationally renowned geneticist Gunnar Dahlberg advocated anti-racist ideas and had already begun criticising Lundborg in the early 1930s. In 1936 he succeeded Lundborg as director of the Swedish State Institute for Racial Biology, a contested decision strongly influenced by Dahlberg's political connections within the powerful Social Democratic Party.[42]

In Norway a growing opposition to racist eugenics also began to emerge in the late 1920s, and there much of the impetus came from academics of socialist leaning. In 1934 the Norwegian Parliament passed a law on sterilisation,[43] legalising its use as a contraceptive method for individuals with an 'honourable reason'. The law also authorized and regulated the forced sterilisation of mentally 'retarded' (*åndssvake*) and mentally 'sick' persons (*sinnsyke*) who were assumed to lack a basic understanding of their own situation. A decade-long debate over sterilisation as a racial hygienic measure and over castration as a way to 'treat' sexual offenders had preceded the enactment of the law. In the leading social-democratic newspaper *Arbeiderbladet*, the politically engaged physician and socialist Johan Scharffenberg ran an extensive campaign in favour of the sterilisation act. His arguments for the law were coupled with a rejection of the type of racist racial hygiene that the Nazis embraced. This helped make racial hygiene more acceptable to members of the labour movement, which from the mid-1930s was the dominant political force in Norway.[44]

---

41 Kevles, *In the Name of Eugenics*, pp. 123-27; Elazar Barkan, *The Retreat of Scientific Racism: Changing Concepts of Race in the United States between the World Wars* (Cambridge: Cambridge University Press, 1992).

42 Gunnar Broberg, *Statlig rasforskning: en historik över Rasbiologiska Institutet* (Lund: Avdelningen för Idé och lärdomshistoria vid Lunds Universitet, 1995), pp. 60-87 (p. 70).

43 For a detailed account of the background of the sterilisation act and the sterilisations authorised under the act, see Per Haave, *Sterilisering av tatere 1934-1977. En Historisk undersøkelse av lov og praksis* (Oslo: The Norwegian Research Council, 2000).

44 Nielsen, Monsen and Tennøe, *Livets tre og kodenes kode*, pp. 105f.

Scharffenberg, however, was not a consistent anti-racist, despite his unequivocal stand against the racial ideology of the Nazis. He advocated the use of sterilisation as a racial hygienic measure against the propagation of Roma travellers. This ethnic group, who had travelled the Scandinavian country roads for centuries, were called *tatere* or, more commonly, *omstreifere* (vagrants) by the majority Norwegian population. In public debates in the late nineteenth and early twentieth centuries, their culture and lifestyle was mainly seen as a social problem that should be dealt with by the state. From the late nineteenth century onwards, the Norwegian government pursued a policy aimed at eradicating their traditional way of life and turning them into permanently settled, 'productive' members of an ordered society. Scharffenberg, however, claimed that this policy was doomed to fail because the *Taters* were of partly 'Gypsy' origin: the urge to wander was an inborn, inherited racial trait. Since the *Taters* and the Gypsies were dysfunctional remnants of a nomadic stage in human evolution and all efforts to settle them had failed, sterilisation was the best solution to the 'problem'.[45]

In contrast to Scharffenberg, the radical socialist and eugenicist Karl Evang was consistently anti-racist. Evang was a prolific writer and participant in the debate on social health policy and sexual education who, in 1938, became the Director of the National Health Services. In 1934 Evang wrote an introduction to the proposal for a Norwegian sterilisation law, published by the Association of Socialist Physicians, in which he harshly attacked racial determinism and what he saw as a reactionary strand of eugenics.[46] According to Evang it was uncontroversial that individuals with serious genetic conditions should be prevented from proliferating. However, he deemed racial hygiene to be in conflict with the basic principles of capitalist society and therefore only fully implementable in a rationally ordered socialist society.[47]

---

45 Haave, *Sterilisering av tatere*, pp. 34-37. Between the late 1930s and the late 1940s, Romani were overrepresented among the women who became sterilised under the 1934 Act. According to Haave, the Romani population was not specifically targeted for sterilisation by the national health authorities; rather, the imbalance in the number of sterilisations was due to widespread negative views of Roma lifestyle and culture (Haave, pp. 169, 391).

46 'Det norske forslag til sterilisasjonslov', in Karl Evang, *Rasepolitikk og Reaksjon*, Socialistiske lægers forenings småskrifter no. 2 (Oslo: Fram, 1934).

47 Karl Evang, *Rasepolitikk og reaksjon*, Socialistiske lægers forenings småskrifter no. 2 (Oslo: Fram, 1934), p. 8. For a more detailed account, see Haave, *Sterilisering av tatere*, pp. 41-44.

Evang believed that racial hygiene theory was misused by reactionary political forces, a fact that held true for the most extreme faction within the racial hygiene movement. The notion of human races having different degrees of moral worth had helped to legitimise the colonial suppression of non-European peoples and to depict capitalism and class society as nature-given. Evang portrayed the racist policy of the Nazis as the ultimate consequence of this bourgeois racial ideology, and he dedicated an entire chapter of *Rasepolitikk og reaksjon* to an extensive critique of the Nordic idea (*den nordiske tanke*).

Racial hygiene as applied anthropology

Evang was not alone in putting forward such ideas in the mid-1930s. The Nazi takeover of Germany in 1933 led to an increased polarisation of the international scientific debate on race. The racial ideology of the Nazis provoked anti-racist campaigns among scientists in countries such as France, the U.S. and England. These campaigns were then opposed by a host of German anthropologists, racial hygienists and human geneticists, turning international scientific arenas into battlegrounds over interwoven scientific and political racial issues. While racial determinism and the idea of the Nordic master race were beginning to lose ground in Scandinavia and the English-speaking world, they gained momentum in Germany. Soon after the Nazi takeover, 'anthropology' was redefined as *Rassenkunde* (racial science). *Rassenkunde* became a crucial provider of scientific legitimacy and tools for the implementation of racial policy, and many anthropologists assumed important positions in the new regime's machinery of power.[48]

The shift from anthropology to *Rassenkunde* during the Nazi period, however, was not simply the result of the forced or voluntary adjustment of German scientists to a new political situation. It was also the culmination of a trend in German anthropology whose momentum had steadily increased since World War I. Already in the 1920s, according to Robert Proctor, the discipline was becoming dominated by a 'therapeutic logic' aimed at protecting the Germanic race against internal and external enemies.[49]

---

48 Elazar Barkan, 'Mobilizing Scientists against Nazi Racism 1933-1939' and Proctor, 'From *Anthropologie* to *Rassenkunde*', pp. 180-205 and pp. 138-79.

49 Ibid. A number of historical studies in recent years have charted the trajectory of German anthropology from a discipline dominated by 'racial liberalism' in the nineteenth century to one strongly affected by biological determinism and

As already pointed out, and according to Rudolf Martin's influential *Lehrbuch der Anthropologie*, 'race' was by definition nothing more than a descriptive device aimed at classifying bodily differences; it had no relevance for psychological or cultural properties. During the 1920s, however, Martin's view of anthropology was challenged by a growing number of German anthropologists. One of Martin's foremost opponents was the leading eugenicist Fritz Lenz. In 1921, with Eugen Fischer and Erwin Baur, he published a textbook on *Human Heredity and Eugenics* (*Grundriss der Menschlichen Erblichkeitslehre und Rassenhygiene*) which strongly influenced the German debate on racial hygiene. Fritz Lenz believed in psychological differences between races, and advocated a Nordicist brand of racial hygiene; he wanted to associate anthropology closely with the racial hygiene movement and turn the discipline into the study of human genetic variation.[50]

Lenz's reasoning was at odds with two crucial aspects of Martin's anthropology. It redefined the objective of anthropological research from describing bodily variations within mankind to studying genetic variations. The established division of labour between anthropology and cultural research was consequently challenged, because genetics was increasingly seen as the key to understanding both bodily and cultural variation.[51]

During the 1920s, Fritz Lenz gained growing support for his definition of anthropology. A new generation entered the discipline, bringing in new ideas. Anthropology was drawing closer to racial hygiene, and after the death of Rudolf Martin in 1925, the idea of physical anthropology as a purely descriptive science began to wane. In the late 1920s, a new set of research problems were incorporated into the scope of anthropology: human genetics, constitutional medicine, blood group research, genetic psychology and genetic pathology. Questions about the mental abilities of

---

völkisch racism. Benoit Massin, 'From Virchow to Fischer: Physical Anthropology and "Modern Race Theories" in Wilhelmine Germany', in George W. Stocking, Jr. (ed.), *Volksgeist as Method and Ethic* (Madison, WI: University of Wisconsin, 1996), pp. 106-14; Andrew D. Evans, *Anthropology at War: World War I and the Science of Race in Germany* (Chicago, IL: University of Chicago Press, 2010).

50 Proctor, 'From *Anthropologie* to *Rassenkunde*', p. 139; Sheila Faith Weiss, 'The Race Hygiene Movement in Germany', *Osiris*, 2nd series, Vol. 3 (1987), pp. 214ff.

51 Rudolf Martin, *Lehrbuch der Anthropologie* (Jena: Fischer, 1928), Introduction; Proctor, 'From *Anthropologie* to *Rassenkunde*', pp. 142ff.

races, which in Martin's textbook were an untreated topic, became a core field of inquiry. A new style of anthropology arose, one that combined the established anthropological study of bodily variation with a new interest in the psychological differences between races.[52]

After Martin's death, Eugen Fischer attained a key position in the German anthropological community. He became Professor of Anthropology at Berlin University, as well as director of the Kaiser Wilhelm Institute for Anthropology, Human Genetics and Eugenics (founded in 1927). In a speech in 1928, he claimed that the great progress of genetics during the preceding two decades had led to a major transformation of anthropology. From descriptive mapping the distribution of bodily characteristics, anthropologists were now moving into a new scientific era, one in which they would examine how these bodily characteristics were formed and transformed.[53]

According to Fischer, this genetically-informed anthropology was of great societal value. He saw the deterioration of the population's biological quality as one of the greatest challenges for Western civilisation. Different genetic lineages had differing cultural abilities, he claimed, but the low fertility, disrupted social structures and racial mixing typical of modern industrial societies were helping to destroy the culturally creative biological elements.[54] Fischer hailed eugenics as the cure against this evil. It had the same function in the life of a people as medical expertise had in the life of individual human beings. The task of eugenics was to consider what was good and what was bad for the social organism, and to implement proper treatment. The cure should be based on scientific knowledge of the biological quality of human beings, and it was anthropologists first and foremost who possessed this necessary knowledge. Eugenic assessment should therefore be based on anthropological knowledge. Eugenics was applied anthropology.[55]

Six months after the Nazi takeover, Fischer became rector of Berlin University. In a speech given just before the inauguration, he praised the Nazis for being the first ones to take racial hygiene seriously. Soon after, he published the pro-Nazi essay *Der völkische Staat biologisch gesehen*. In 1934,

52 Ibid.; Evans, *Anthropology at War*, pp. 189-221.
53 Eugen Fischer, 'Der untergang der Kulturvölker im Lichte der Biologie', *Volkausartung, Erbkunde, Eheberatung* (December 1928).
54 Ibid.
55 Ibid.

at a *Festschrift* in honour of his 60th birthday, he was praised by colleagues as the 'Führer' of German anthropology. It was asserted that Hitler's regime was the first in the world to make race, genetics and selection part of practical politics, and that these tools had been put into the hands of the politicians by Fischer.[56]

The Nordic race and anthropology as applied science

To sum up, the 'Nordic race' existed as a relatively unproblematic scientific concept within both racial hygiene and physical anthropology until the mid-1920s. In those nations assumed to have an overwhelmingly 'Nordic' population, there were influential scientists who claimed that the future of Western culture depended on the protection of this race against racial mixing. In the late 1920 and 1930s, however, this type of racial thought was subjected to a growing wave of scientific and ideological criticism, and an increasingly polarised debate on racial issues arose. By the end of the 1920s, the leading international eugenics organisation (the IFEO) was increasingly dominated by proponents of the racist strand of the racial hygiene movement. An influential group of men tried to turn the organisation into a 'Blond International' aimed at the purification and propagation of the Nordic race. Jon Alfred Mjøen and Herman Lundborg were part of this group, but by the early 1930s they were increasingly out of step with the development of debates on racial hygiene in their own countries.

The Nordic idea, and the racist style of eugenics, faced an increasingly united and well-articulated scientific opposition in Scandinavia and the Anglophone world. At the same time, however, these ideas gained support among German anthropologists, who redefined the discipline from being fundamentally descriptive to being closely linked with racial hygiene and the study of the presumed psychological properties of the races. After 1933, this type of anthropology became increasingly hegemonic in Germany.

Norway had three professional physical anthropologists in the interwar years: Kristian Emil Schreiner, his wife Alette Schreiner and the military doctor Halfdan Bryn, who from 1917 onwards continued the research tradition established by Carl Oscar Eugen Arbo. Bryn and the two Scheiners undertook extensive anthropological studies of past and present Norwegian populations. They also participated in debates on eugenics and

---

56 Proctor, 'From *Anthropologie* to *Rassenkunde*', p. 157.

race within the Norwegian scientific community, the Norwegian public arena and among physical anthropologists in Scandinavia, the German-speaking world and beyond

This meant that they had to deal with an academic and political landscape that underwent significant transformations and became increasingly polarised. Racial views that had been uncontroversial in 1914 became extremely controversial in the early 1930s. As we will see in the following chapters, this had a significant impact on the life and work of the Norwegian anthropologists.

Fig. 10 Halfdan Bryn at his desk.

6. Halfdan Bryn and the Nordic Race

Physical anthropology virtually vanished in Norway after the deaths of Arbo, Guldberg and Larsen; when it re-emerged in the interwar years, eugenics had become one of its major social justifications. As noted in the previous chapter, physical anthropology was particularly relevant to the faction of the racial hygiene movement concerned with purifying and propagating the Nordic race. In the years immediately following World War I, the leading physical anthropologist in Norway was Halfdan Bryn, who would become an increasingly ardent proponent of the superiority of the Nordic race. This chapter deals with Bryn's theoretical and methodological approach to the study of race, and how this related to his increasingly racist outlook on society.

Halfdan Bryn's career in anthropology

Halfdan Bryn (1864-1933) was born into the educated elite and the medical profession. His grandfather was an *embetsmann* (a senior official), a politician and a member of the assembly that drafted the Norwegian constitution in 1814. His father was a *stadsfysikus* (a leader of the public health authority) in Trondheim, Norway's third largest town, located in the central Trøndelag counties. His father's job as a *stadsfysikus* was to protect public health and maintain municipal hygiene through the implementation of a variety of measures. Bryn's lifespan coincided with a period in which science made tremendous progress and the medical profession gained a principal position in society. Advances in bacteriology provided an increasingly self-confident medical profession with new tools to fight diseases, while the

http://dx.doi.org/10.11647/OBP.0051.06

government increasingly undertook public health measures resulting, in turn, in larger and more powerful public health bodies.

Halfdan Bryn followed in his father's footsteps and graduated with a medical degree from the University of Kristiania in 1889. After a short interlude in the United States, he settled with his young family in his hometown of Trondheim, where he ran a private practice and worked as an army doctor. Bryn was a respected member of the local elite of this provincial capital. From 1898 to 1914, he was a Liberal Party, or *Venstre*, representative to the Trondheim City Council, and from 1905 to 1910 he was one of its chairmen. In this role Bryn was particularly interested in municipal sanitation and hygiene, urban planning and housing policies. He travelled overseas to study sanitation and housing for workers, and became involved in the international garden city movement.[1] Bryn was also a prominent member of Trondheim's small academic community, contributed to the establishment of a biological research station on the Trondheim fjord in 1899 and was a leading member of the Trondheim-based Royal Norwegian Society of Sciences and Letters, Norway's oldest scientific society and the little brother to the Norwegian Academy of Science and Letters in Oslo. Bryn was also a respected member of the national academic and medical community—his public offices included the presidency of the Norwegian Medical Association (*Den norske lægeforening*, 1921-1922)—and he gained international recognition for his anthropological studies of the racial character of the Norwegian nation in the 1920s.[2]

Like Arbo and Larsen before him, Bryn's anthropological research was rooted in his job as an army doctor. The army medical service was headed by Hans Daae, who was deeply interested in physical anthropology, and in 1915 he relieved Bryn of many of his non-scientific responsibilities to allow him to concentrate on anthropological research. Two years later, at the age of 53, Bryn published his first major anthropological work based on measurements taken during his routine medical examinations of army conscripts from Trøndelag.[3] The work received a prestigious national

---

1   *Studentene fra 1882* (Kristiania: [n. pub.], 1907 and 1932); S. Schmidt-Nielsen, 'Halfdan Bryn: Minnetale i Fellesmøtet 10 de april 1933', *Det kgl. n. Vid. Selsk. Forhandlinger*, Vol. 6, no. 16 (Trondheim: I kommisjon hos F. Bruns bokhandel, 1933); Per Holck, 'Halfdan Bryn', in *Norsk biografisk leksikon*, http://nbl.snl.no/ Halfdan_Bryn

2   Ibid.

3   Halfdan Bryn, *Trøndelagens antropologi. Bidrag til belysning av det norske folks*

award,[4] and Bryn gained access to research funds from the most important funding body in Norway, the Nansen Fund. In 1924, he abandoned private medical practice and the post of army doctor to engage in full-time anthropological research. In the 1920s, Bryn published several scientific articles that attracted significant national and international attention.[5] In 1920, he received a letter from Rudolf Martin which was full of praise for his work and which offered to help him publish in Germany.[6] Over the following few years, Bryn established a large network of colleagues in the German and Scandinavian scientific communities. He was elected to the Norwegian Royal Academy of Science and Letters in Kristiania in 1923, the German Society of Physical Anthropology in 1925, and in 1929 to the Anthropological Society of Vienna and the German Society for Blood Group Research. During the 1920s, he made several study trips to Germany and cooperated with Lundborg at the Institute for Racial Biology in Uppsala.[7]

In the interwar years the other two main professional anthropologists in Norway were Kristian Emil Schreiner at the University's Department of Anatomy and his wife Alette Schreiner. Since the two Schreiners did not begin publishing their findings until the late 1920s, Bryn had a virtual monopoly over anthropological publications in Norway during the first decade after World War I and was described by Kristian Emil as 'our most famous anthropologist'.[8]

---

anthropologi i begyndelsen av det 20de aarhundrede, Det kgl. n. Vid. selsk. Skr. 1917 (Trondheim: Aktietrykkeriet, 1918).

4   *Aftenposten*, 3 September 1917. The *Kongens guldmedalje* (Royal Gold Medal) was awarded by the university. Bryn's work answered the Faculty of Medicine's call for a paper entitled 'A Survey of the Anthropology of a District in Norway' ('En undersøgelse over de antropologiske forhold i et større eller mindre distrikt af vort land'). The evaluation committee (K. E. Schreiner and Justus Barth) praised the great wealth of empirical knowledge put forward in Bryn's work, but was skeptical about the actual scholarly analysis, arguing that Bryn had underestimated the difficulties of his chosen research topic and exaggerated the importance of his findings.

5   From 1917 to 1925 he produced 19 scientific publications. See Per Holck, *Den fysiske antropologi i Norge. Fra anatomisk institutts historie 1815-1990* (Oslo: Anatomisk institutt, University of Oslo, 1990), p. 95ff.: Bibliography of Physical Anthropological Research in Norway.

6   Bryn's archive: R. Martin to Bryn, 20 September 1920.

7   On his cooperation with Lundborg, see Bryn's archive: correspondence between Bryn and Lundborg. Bryn was awarded an honorary doctorate at the University of Uppsala in 1927.

8   Bryn's archive: copy of a letter from K. E. Schreiner to Rector Stang at the

Halfdan Bryn's racial science

In the early years of his anthropological research, Bryn collaborated closely with Andreas Hansen, who was then the only living member of the first generation of Norwegian racial-anthropological authors. Hansen helped Bryn with statistical calculations, they discussed research topics of common interest and Bryn supported Andreas Hansen's pet theories, notably the ideas that the Sea Sami were unrelated to the Sami nomads and that the Norwegians were a mixture of blond dolichocephalics and dark brachycephalics.[9]

As noted in chapter 3, Hansen's simplistic racial dichotomy had come under heavy criticism shortly after the turn of the twentieth century, with Arbo and Larsen arguing for the existence of more than two Norwegian racial types. While Arbo claimed to have identified an additional blond, short-skulled 'North Sea Race' in southwestern Norway, Larsen argued for the existence of a distinct, mesocephalic, local Trøndelag race, which he called the 'Trønder-type'. In his first, award-winning anthropological work, Bryn dismissed the existence of Larsen's 'Trønder-type', arguing that it was not a distinct race but a 'bastard' resulting from the admixture of blond dolichocephalics and dark brachycephalics.[10] This first publication was followed by a series of papers in which Bryn continued to defend the theory that two races gave rise to the Scandinavian peoples.

One year before Bryn's debut as an anthropologist, the Danish anthropologist Søren Hansen had launched a severe critique of this two-race theory. In a speech given at a Scandinavian scientific conference, he claimed that the thesis of short-skulled and long-skulled parental races was scientifically outdated. He argued that the cephalic index was a useless racial marker, since it varied significantly within each race and since the shape of the skull was related, ontogenetically and physiologically, to the size of the head and body. According to Søren Hansen there was only one undivided European race.[11] In a paper of 1920,

University of Kristiania, 31 March 1924.

9   Bryn's archive: a number of letters from A. M. Hansen to H. Bryn in the years 1919-1920 (see, for example, letters dated 30 January and 30 November 1919).

10 Bryn, *Trøndelagens antropologi*, pp. 5ff., 69ff.; idem, *Møre fylkes antropologi.* Skr. D. n. Vidensk. Selsk. MN kl. (Kristiania: I kommission hos J. Dybwad, 1920), pp. 66-67.

11 Søren Hansen, 'Om Grundracer i Norden'. *Forhandlinger ved De skandinaviske naturforskeres 16. møte i Kristiania den 10.-15. juli 1916* (Kristiania: A. W. Brøggers

Bryn presented a number of counterarguments to this critique, accusing Hansen of focusing too narrowly on present-day appearances instead of searching for historical patterns. According to Bryn, Hansen failed to recognise that each race had developed their typical characteristics–such as head shape, skin, eye and hair colour–hundreds of thousands of years ago, during a long prehistoric period of isolation. According to Bryn, the ensuing mixing of different racial groups had diluted these original race-specific combinations of inherited traits, but had not obliterated them. Bryn considered racial traits like blondness and dolichocephalism to be basic attributes inherited according to Mendelian rules, and he believed that the anthropologist's role was to reconstruct the original pure races by mapping the distribution of the various features in racially-mixed modern populations.[12]

Bryn was influenced by Eugen Fischer's famous study of the 'bastards' of Rehoboth,[13] in which Fisher suggested that racial mixing led to the dissolution of the original race-specific combinations of traits and to their random distribution within the population of mixed offspring. Bryn, however, claimed to be able to reconstruct the ancestral races of a bastard population through correlation analysis, using the 'affinity quotient' (*affinitetstall*) invented by Andreas Hansen. Racial mixing was seldom complete, he argued, and so the racial markers would not be completely randomly distributed through the population. It would be possible to detect individuals and regional populations that were carriers of the originally race-specific combinations of markers.[14] The admixture ratio of the original races would vary in different geographic regions, and the original race-specific combinations of traits could therefore be estimated by comparing their relative distribution in different regions. Despite the fact that neither dark short skulls nor blond long skulls were overrepresented in Trøndelag, Bryn thought he could demonstrate that

boktrykkeri, 1918), pp. 822-38.
12 Halfdan Bryn, 'To grundraser i Norge', *Nyt Mag. f. Naturvidensk* (1920), pp. 32-33.
13 Bryn's copy of Fischer's book on Rehoboth (now held at the Gunnerus Library, University of Trondheim (NTNU)) is full of underlining and comments in the margins. Eugen Fischer, *Die Rehobother Bastards und das Bastardierungsproblem beim Menschen: anthropologische und ethnographische Studien am Rehobother Bastardvolk in Deutsch-Südwest-Afrika* (Jena: G. Fischer, 1913).
14 Bryn argues against Fischer in his *Selbu og Tydalen. En antropologisk undersøkelse av mænd, kvinder og barn i to norske indlandsbygder*, Skr. D. n. Vidensk. Selsk. MN kl 1921, no. 5 (Kristiania: I kommisjon hos Jacob Dybwad, 1921), p. 81.

the population consisted of a mix of the two types. Regions with a high frequency of brown-eyed individuals also tended to have many short and brachycephalic individuals, while regions with a high frequency of blue-eyed people had a higher percentage of dolichocephalic, tall people.[15]

The theoretical edifice underpinning Bryn's racial research was based on the assumption that racial traits are inherited independently of each other, and that there is a simple one-to-one relationship between racial traits and Mendelian factors. This basic assumption was challenged by Hansen's insistence on the variability of skull shapes and on the physiological and ontogenetic relationship between skull shape and other presumed racial traits, like body length and head size. It was therefore urgent for Bryn to show that traits like the cephalic index and eye colour were inherited according to simple Mendelian rules. In his reply to the challenge from Søren Hansen, he drew upon arguments taken from his own genetic studies which supposedly demonstrated the Mendelian inheritance of the cephalic index and eye colour.[16] We will return to these arguments in chapter 8. For now, Bryn's research strategy can be summed up as follows: he studied the inheritance of assumed race-specific traits in order to establish that they were in fact inherited in accordance with Mendelian rules and could be regarded as true, inherent racial markers. He performed correlation analyses to ascertain the extent to which certain sets of racial markers were present in the population of a certain area. If he found a correlation, he concluded that particular combinations of traits derived from the original, ancient races. By studying the occurrence of racial traits in different geographic areas, Bryn could then ascertain the relative distribution of various racial elements in the Norwegian population (see Fig. 11).[17]

---

15 Bryn, *Trøndelagens antropologi*.

16 Halfdan Bryn, 'Researches into Anthropological Heredity. On the Inheritance of Eye Colour in Man. II. The Genetic of Index Cephalicus', *Hereditas*, Vol. 1, no. 2 (1920), pp. 186-212; Arvelighetsundersøkelser. Om arv av øienfarven hos mennesker', *Tidsskrift for den Norske Lægeforening*, Vol. 40, no. 10 (1920), pp. 329-42; idem, 'Arvelighetsundersøkelser vedrørende index cephalicus', *Tidsskrift for den Norske Lægeforening*, Vol. 41, no. 10 (1921), pp. 431-52.

17 See for example the following works by Bryn: *Trøndelagens antropologi*, *Selbu og Tydalen*, *Anthropologia Nidarosiensis*, 'Anthropologia Nidarosiensis' and *Møre fylkes antropologi*.

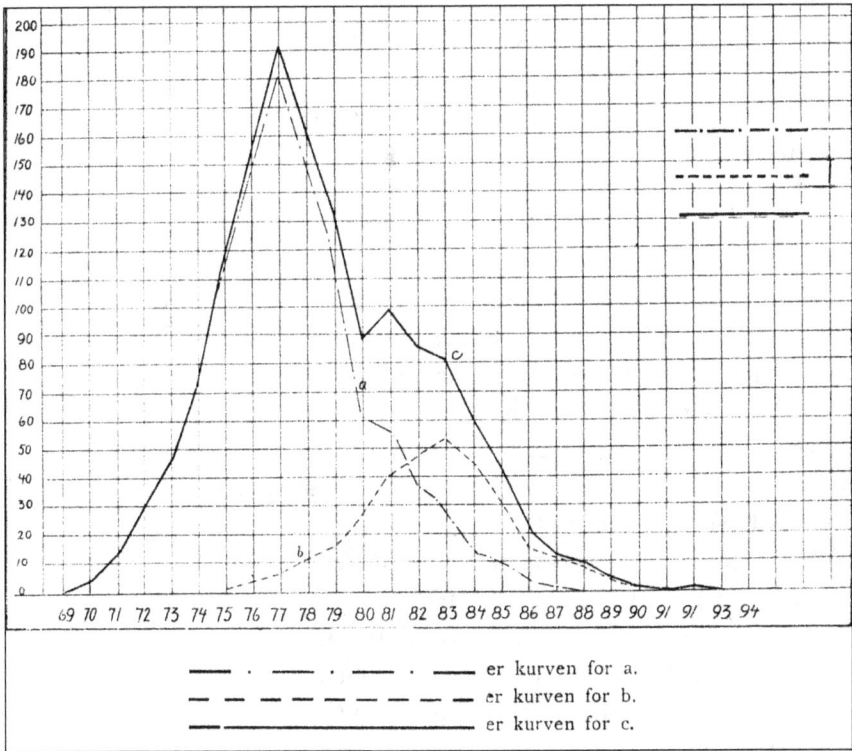

Fig. 11 A graph by Bryn showing the distribution of cephalic indices in an admixed population. Curve A represents Norwegians with an average cephalic index of 77; Curve B represents Sami with an average cephalic index of 83; Curve C represents the sum of the populations.

Bryn and the northern Norwegian bastards

In 1921, Bryn published a work about the racial composition of Troms, Norway's second northernmost county, which had a population of mixed Norwegian, Sami and Kven (Finnish) heritage. He had recorded the frequency of the racial traits corresponding to the Alpine, Nordic and so-called 'Palaearctic' (or Lapp) race in the three groups, and suggested that each group consisted of a mixture of different proportions of the three racial types. Bryn then constructed a taxonomy of 'bastard types', each consisting of a certain ratio of traits derived from the three basic races.[18]

---

18 Halfdan Bryn, *Troms fylkes antropologi*, Skr. D. n. Vidensk. Selsk. MN kl 1921, no. 20 (Kristiania: I kommission hos J. Dybwad, 1922), pp. 72-90.

In defining these bastard types, Bryn placed different emphases on various traits, the cephalic index being the most important and body height the least. He started by sorting the individuals into cephalic index categories and thereafter investigated the correlation between these categories and various eye colour categories. Then he studied how the different combinations of cephalic indices and eye colours correlated to other characteristics, like hair colour, body length and so on. Bryn justified this procedure by claiming that he placed greatest emphasis on the traits that were most directly genetically determined.[19] His main conclusion was that 66 per cent of the ancestry of the Troms population was Nordic, about 30 per cent was Alpine, and 4 per cent or less was Lapp. These findings did not fit well with the official census, in which 9 per cent of the population was classified as Lapp. Bryn overcame this discrepancy by explaining that the 'Lapp racial element' was smaller than the proportion of 'Lapp people' because the latter contained foreign racial elements.[20]

Bryn's conclusions were largely compatible with the theory that Andreas Hansen had put forward in his *Landnåm i Norge* in 1904 (see chapter 4), namely that the Sea Sami population was biologically unrelated to the 'true' Sami, the inland reindeer herders. Bryn argued that the Lapp race had its stronghold in the northeast of the county, an area bordering the principal reindeer herding district of the *Finnmarksvidda* plateau. The Nordic race was overrepresented in scattered agricultural inland communities, while the Alpine race had its stronghold along the coast. Bryn claimed that both the Norwegian and the Sea Sami coastal dwellers were of mixed racial origins and had a large share of dark short-skulled Alpine elements. According to Bryn, the proportion of Lapp racial traits was only slightly higher in the Sea Sami than in the coastal Norwegians.

From social to racial hygiene

Bryn was a politically engaged citizen who belonged to the social-liberal *Venstre* movement and believed in the improvement of society based on science: his political and social engagement went hand in hand with his activities as a scientist and physician. Like many other members of the medical profession, he advocated a set of ideas that is commonly referred to

19 Bryn, *Troms fylkes antropologi*, pp. 73-74.
20 Halfdan Bryn, 'Raceblandingen i Troms fylke', *Norsk Tidsskrift for Militærmedicin*, Vol. 26 (1922), p. 127.

as social hygiene. The social hygiene movement had its heyday in Norway in the years between 1910 and 1940 and focused on the relationship between health and the environment, housing, nutrition, personal hygiene, physical education and the living conditions of children at home and at school. Its two most important aims were the prevention of tuberculosis and other infectious diseases, and the reversal of the quantitative and qualitative consequences of the decline in birth rate. The social hygiene movement, with its measures to improve the living conditions of the population, was related to the racial hygiene movement with its aim of regulating population 'quality' and size. From the early 1920s, Bryn began to combine his ideas about racial hygiene with an increasingly racial-determinist outlook on human nature.

Before moving into the field of anthropology, Bryn had argued against considering race as the cause of differences in the health and biological 'quality' of the population; he had advocated public intervention in the physical and social environment of citizens to improve their health and well-being. However, his views changed as his career in anthropology progressed. By the mid-1920s, he saw racial differences as the main driving force behind variations in human biological quality and was strongly in favour of a racist strand of eugenics. It is important to note, however, that rather than undergoing a fundamental ideological reorientation, many aspects of his paternalist, science-based and progressive worldview remained unchanged.

Let us consider a recurring theme in Bryn's writings on military medicine and anthropology, namely the question of regional differences in the supply of capable army recruits. Around the turn of the twentieth century, Larsen and Arbo had proposed that variations in the quality of recruits from different districts were mainly due to inherent racial differences, and not to local variations in environment and living conditions. In a 1914 article, Bryn countered this argument, claiming instead that the biological quality of the conscripts stemmed from their social background: industrialised urban communities generally produced a lower biological pool of conscripts than rural districts.[21] Bryn pointed to the bad living conditions of the urban working class, their dangerous work, poor nutrition, lack of hygiene and higher incidence of rickets and tuberculosis—environmental risks whose effects were exacerbated by the fact that industrial jobs attracted the poorest members of society, already bearers of biologically disadvantaged children. Towns and cities were caught up in a vicious cycle of poor environments,

---

21 Halfdan Bryn, 'Antropologiske Undersøgelser I. Trøndelagens rekrutteringsevne', *Norsk tidsskrift for Militærmedicin* (1914), p. 21.

poor biological heritage and negative social selection. They became 'incubators of all kinds of spiritual and material infections'.[22]

Bryn's negative views on urbanisation and industrialisation had political implications. As a member of the city council of Trondheim, he worked to improve the living conditions of the poor through housing schemes and the implementation of stricter public controls on urban development.[23] In 1921, he published a book with Ebenezer Howard, the founder of the international garden city movement, in which they argued for state expropriation of slums and tenements in order to replace them with garden cities and fight the property speculators who preyed on the poor.[24] The main goal of Bryn's involvement in politics and the garden city movement was to improve the physical and psychological living conditions of individuals at the bottom of the social ladder, but he also wanted to counter the economic pressures that had created this situation. It is important to note Bryn's strongly paternalist approach to the issue and the fact that he considered the slum-dwellers to be of poor biological quality. However, even while accepting the influence of social selection on the geographical and social distribution of inborn 'biological quality', Bryn rejected the single-cause racial explanation proposed by Arbo and Larsen.

In his first anthropological work, Bryn argued that the only way to substantiate a link between race, health and mental abilities was through a quantitative study. Although Bryn did not believe it was scientifically feasible to measure the psychological characteristics of races or individuals, he argued that it would be possible to elucidate the question by counting the relative proportion of physically and psychologically inferior individuals— those with inheritable diseases or disabilities—in local populations and comparing this number with the relative frequency of cephalic indices, thus correlating the psychological and racial compositions of the local population.[25]

Over the following years, Bryn collected data on chronically ill conscripts from different regions, and at a meeting of army doctors in 1921, he once again addressed the relationship between race, environment

---

22 Bryn, 'Trøndelagens rekrutteringsevne', pp. 20-21.
23 Haakon Odd Christiansen and Wilhelm K. Støren, *Trondheim i går og i dag: 1914-1964* (Trondheim: I kommisjon hos F. Bruns bokhandels forlag, 1973), pp. 117-32.
24 Halfdan Bryn and Ebenezer Howard, *Havebyer og jordbruksbyer i Norge* (Kristiania: Aschehoug, 1921).
25 Bryn, *Trøndelagens antropologi*, pp. 10-11.

and health. This time he did not focus on the army's need for fit soldiers, but on the nation's need for a healthy and able population. Bryn ranked chronic diseases according to their degree of heritability and the level of their negative impact on the individual and society. He then compared this ranking to the regional distribution of the diseases: the resulting data showed the relative burden of chronic disease in different regions, demonstrating a geographical correlation between high levels of the chronically ill and a high incidence of tuberculosis.[26] Tuberculosis was known to be an infectious disease associated with overcrowding, but instead of discussing the evils of the city, as he had done previously, Bryn now suggested that tuberculosis might result from 'genotypic inferiority' caused by racial mixing. His arguments were chiefly based on Herman Lundborg's 1920 work on 'genotypic degeneration' and 'predisposition to tuberculosis'. According to Lundborg, there were two types of 'genotypic inferiority': while a pathological change in a single organ could be caused by a single gene or by a small group of genes, pathological conditions involving several organs could be the result of the abnormal rearrangement of a huge number of genes, leading to a basic weakness in the very 'constitution' of the body. Lundborg suggested that predisposition to tuberculosis was due to a constitutional weakness caused by the genetic chaos arising from bastardisation.[27]

According to Bryn's interpretation of Lundborg's theory, the forces of natural selection had ensured that an individual of a particular race would inherit a combination of genes that were perfectly well adapted to a specific social and natural environment. Racially-mixed individuals, on the other hand, were at great risk of inheriting unusual gene combinations which would lead to an inferior physical and psychological constitution manifesting itself in characteristics such as lack of social adaptability, criminal inclinations and predisposition to diseases like tuberculosis.[28]

Bryn maintained that individual races had different aptitudes for cultural progress as well as varying levels of resistance to disease, mortality rates and predisposition to tuberculosis. He claimed that people were misguided if they believed that environmental preconditions were the main explanation for differences in the cultural level of nations. Instead, he

---

26 Halfdan Bryn, 'Om vort folks kroniske og arvelige sykdomsbelastning', *Norsk Tidsskrift for Militærmedicin*, Vol. 25 (1921), pp. 138-46, Vol. 26 (1922), pp. 1-15.

27 Herman Lundborg, 'Rassen- und Gesellschafts-probleme in Genetischer und Medizinischer Beleuchtung', *Hereditas*, Vol. 1, no. 2 (1920), pp. 135-63.

28 Bryn, 'Om vort folks kroniske' (1922), p. 9.

argued that such differences were determined by the racial composition of the population, which was linked to good or bad configurations of genes.[29] Despite this, in a speech he made in 1921, Bryn nevertheless stressed that scientific insights into the relationship between the environmental and racial causes of disease and inferiority were not yet good enough to justify the use of extensive eugenic interventions such as sterilisation or the detention of genotypically inferior individuals.[30] Three years later, however, Bryn had sufficiently rid himself of these reservations to present himself in a series of newspaper articles as the spokesman for racial hygiene based on the idea of the Nordic master race. The time was now ripe for Gobineau's dogma of fundamental inequality between races, he declared, affirming that the issue of race was firmly rooted in all aspects of human history and that 'only the Nordic race could give rise to a higher civilisation'.[31]

A scientific view of society

As we have seen, Bryn's career as an anthropologist coincided with the development of an increasingly racially-determined worldview. Furthermore, the scientific conceptualisation of race upon which he based his research was intertwined with his view of the social relevance of physical anthropology. Bryn acknowledged that there was no scientifically reliable evidence for the existence of psychological differences between races and declared that, as an anthropologist, he was not qualified to shed scientific light on this question. On the other hand, he claimed that such differences were so well known that further investigation was superfluous.[32] When describing the psychological profiles of various

---

29 Ibid.
30 Ibid., p. 7.
31 Bryn's archive: undated clipping of a newspaper article by Bryn. The article is probably from 1924, since it discusses the U.S. Immigration Act of 1924.
32 In 'Trøndelagens rekrutteringsevne', Bryn argued that no one was yet able to quantify psychological abilities, despite contemporary researchers' repeated attempts to do so. The first standardised intelligence tests—precursors of present-day IQ tests—were developed during World War I. These tests were partly aimed at investigating whether intellectual differences between races existed, research occasionally referred to by Bryn. In 'Raceblandingen i Troms fylke' (p. 130), Bryn claimed that 'new research' had substantiated the existence of such differences: Otto Schläginhaufen, *Rasse, Rassenmischung*

races, he did not refer to scientific research, but invoked instead public opinion, American eugenicists or literature by Gobineau, Lapouge, Ammon, Arbo, the American racial ideologue Madison Grant and the latter's German counterpart, Hans Günther. Even though he admitted that it lacked scientific support, Bryn's belief that psychological and health differences between races did indeed exist shaped his views on the social utility of anthropology. According to Bryn, physical anthropology would be a useless science without such differences. In a 1922 article on the racially-mixed population of Troms County, he stated that the mapping of observable racial traits was only of interest because such traits were correlated to invisible psychological characteristics and health differences.[33] In a lecture given the same year, Bryn claimed that the main task of modern anthropology was 'to identify the conditions for the prosperity and well-being of races and peoples, as well as the causes for their downfall and death': these were determined by the racial composition of the people.

Bryn's perception of the social role of anthropology was closely linked to his conception of race, which in his view meant a group of individuals who inherited a set of traits. The configuration of features specific to each race had arisen in prehistory, when human groups had existed in reproductive isolation. Bounded by geographical barriers for millennia, humankind had divided into distinct groups that had endured different selective forces and become perfectly adapted to their respective habitats (see Fig. 12).[34] This adaptation included the development of specific intellectual and cultural abilities, as well as different moral attitudes, religions and beliefs. The development had taken place undisturbed for thousands of years, and so it had given rise to the 'perfectly cohesive edifice' which was 'the culture of a race'.[35]

---

und *Konstitution* (Bern, 1921), and Eugen Fischer, *Die Rassenunterschiede beim menschen* (München, 1921). However, Bryn generally refrained from claiming that the connection between race and mental abilities had been scientifically proven. When, in the late 1920s, Bryn conducted his own research on this topic, he was eager to emphasise that his research was not 'scientific'. See chapter 9 in this book; Halfdan Bryn, *Der Nordische mensch* (Munchen: J. F. Lehmann, 1929); idem, 'Den nordiske rases sjelelige trekk', *Ymer*, Vol. 49, no. 4 (1929), pp. 347-48.

33 Bryn, 'Raceblandingen i Troms', p. 130.
34 Halfdan Bryn, *Menneskerasene og deres utviklingshistorie* (Oslo: Det Norske studentersamfund, 1925).
35 Bryn's archive: newspaper clipping from *Nidaros lørdagsdagblad*, 18 September

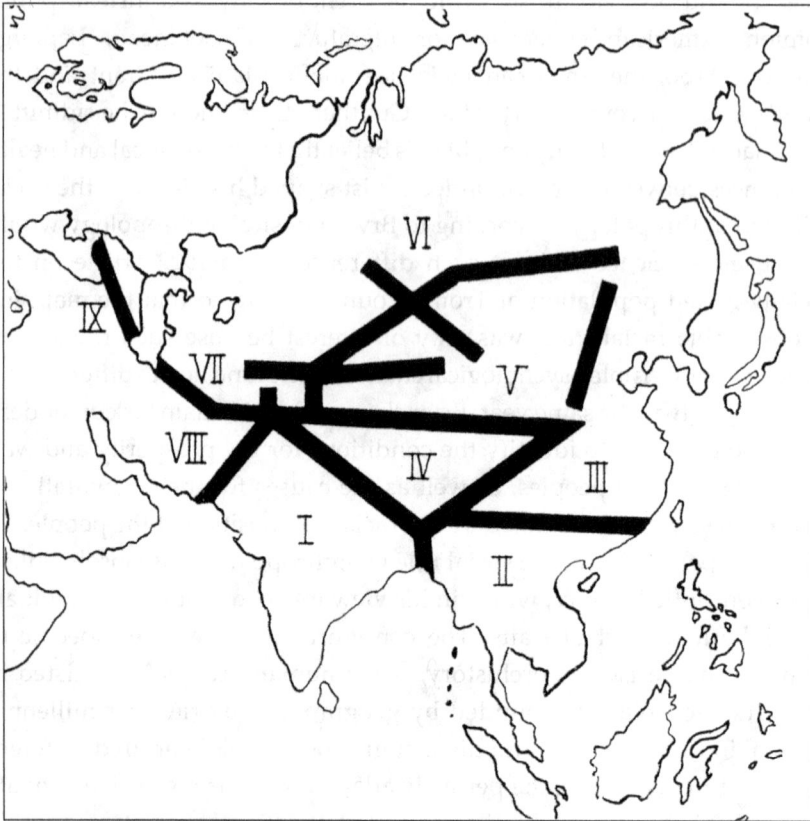

Fig. 12 Bryn's map of areas of anthropological isolation.

Each isolated within its own habitat, different races had developed biological instincts that matched their social and natural environments. After the last Ice Age, however, the barriers separating the isolated habitats had vanished. From that point on, human history had been marked by migration, racial admixture and territorial conflict, eventually giving rise to our present-day populations.

According to Bryn, racial mixing led to two types of problems in the present-day population. At an individual level, mixing could lead to 'genetic chaos', disharmonious individuals and genotypic degeneration; while at the societal level, 'bastardising' led to alienation. Racially-mixed societies resembled bastard individuals: they were ugly and unfit for

---

1926; Halfdan Bryn, 'Befolkningsproblemer, del 2, Raserenhetens betydning'.

intellectual development, since racially heterogeneous societies tended to produce poorly integrated cultures.[36] In a society organised in line with nature, 'race' would coincide with 'nation', and the (racially-determined) psychological drives of individuals would be in harmony with the (racially-determined) culture of the nation. Only in a society like this would it be possible for human beings to lead harmonious, free and wholesome lives.

According to Bryn, the Norwegian people were a mixture of the Nordic and the Alpine races. This blend had been beneficial because of the minor differences between the two races. However, since the Sami were inferior, their blending with Norwegians would lead to the contamination of the Nordic race. The great distance between the two races meant that the hybrids would be of even lower quality than the Sami themselves.[37]

Bryn thought that the crucial difference between superior and inferior races lay in their aptitude for cultural innovation. Superior races, the Nordic race in particular, possessed a great ability to develop culturally, which was lacking in inferior races like the Sami. The latter had been shielded from the struggle for existence by physical isolation, and they had consequently had lost their ability to develop and become 'fossilised'. When such a race was exposed to the rigours of the struggle for existence, it would, and should, disappear. Bryn assumed that the natural relationship between the so-called primitive and the advanced races was mirrored in the relationship between the indigenous peoples and the European colonisers in the age of European empires. Then, the encounter between colonisers and colonised inevitably led to the extinction of inferior races, a mechanism that was the main driving force behind the biological and cultural evolution of humankind.[38]

The Western world had a problem, however, since the theories of the struggle for survival and natural selection had been replaced by the idea of social selection. In this context, bastards and other inferior racial

---

36 Bryn's archive: newspaper clipping from *Nidaros lørdagsdagblad*, 18 September 1926: 'Befolkningsproblemer, del 1, Jordens overbefolkning'. Bryn's archive: undated clipping from unnamed newspaper, article by Halfdan Bryn: 'Amerikanske innvandringsspørsmål'.

37 Bryn's archive: undated newspaper clipping from *Nidaros Lørdagsblad*, interview with Halfdan Bryn: 'Lapper og nordmenn, de fysiske og sjelelige følger av raceblandingen', probably dating around 1922, since the content is very similar to Halfdan Bryn, 'Raceblandingen i Troms'.

38 'Lapper og nordmenn', in *Nidaros Lørdagsblad* (see note above).

elements did not die out, but sank to the bottom of the social hierarchy, while the superior elements rose to the top. It followed that the upper layer of civilised societies had a much greater proportion of people with Nordic racial characteristics such as elongated skulls and blond hair, while the lower layer of the population was characterised by inferior physical features.[39]

Anthropology as applied science

According to Bryn, modern society was unnatural: the struggle for survival had ceased, pure races were being contaminated and the progress of Western civilisation was coming to a halt; political measures were needed to counteract this threat. In a newspaper article about immigration to the U.S., Bryn wrote that American civilisation was threatened by racial admixture and the erosion of the Nordic racial element. To solve this perceived problem, he suggested the introduction of a caste system, even claiming that its basic features were already in place. The policy of racial segregation in many American states relegated blacks to the lowest caste of society, and the U.S. legislation on immigration of 1924, which established quotas for immigrants of different nationalities, limited the entry of inferior elements into the country. However, these measures alone were not adequate to protect the Nordic race. The high fertility of American blacks was a threat to Western civilisation, and so it should be countered by mass sterilisation. Bryn further suggested the deliberate inbreeding of Nordic individuals.[40]

Even in Norway, the Nordic race was under threat, and Bryn held that the Norwegians should learn from the Americans how to deal with the problem.[41] He claimed that inferior elements were migrating to Norway from southern and eastern regions of Europe,[42] and in northern Norway, the Nordic race was being tainted by miscegenation with Lapps. Bryn argued that this situation was comparable to the 'Negro' problem in

---

39 See, for example, Halfdan Bryn, *Norske folketyper*, D. Kgl. n. Videns. selsk. Skr. 6, 1933 (Trondheim: I kommission hos F. Bruns bokhandel, 1934), p. 7.

40 Bryn's archive: undated clipping from unnamed newspaper, article by Halfdan Bryn, 'Amerikanske innvandringsspørsmål'.

41 Ibid.

42 Bryn's archive: newspaper clipping from *Laagen*, 13 March 1931, Halfdan Bryn, 'Det haster'.

the U.S.[43]—though on a lesser scale and therefore requiring less radical measures. Bryn rejected the currently prevailing Norwegian policy of cultural assimilation of the Sami because he believed that although eradicating Sami language and culture would erase the visible traces of the Sami, the Sami racial element itself would persist, gradually blending into the Norwegian people and deteriorating their genetic makeup. Instead, Bryn proposed that the Sami should be encouraged to maintain the nomadic lifestyle which naturally suited their racial instincts, as this would allow the inferior racial element to gradually die out.[44]

Racial determinism and the struggle for survival

In 1914, when Bryn had tried to explain geographical differences in the supply of fit military recruits, he emphasised environmental conditions: differences in material living conditions and socio-cultural environments determined variations in the physical and psychological development of different social groups. This line of scientific reasoning echoed his political attitude. Bryn advocated public intervention in order to improve the cultural and material living conditions of those at the bottom of the social ladder. During the 1920s, however, his academic interests shifted to a racial explanation of cultural and health differences; moreover, his political work to improve living conditions was replaced by a desire to intervene in biological reproduction. Bryn's main goal, however, remained the same: to create happier, abler and socially adjusted citizens by improving their biological makeup.

As we have seen, Bryn's social hygienic and eugenic views were both based on the assumption that human beings belonged to different levels of cultural and psychological development, and that their intellectual abilities determined their position on the social ladder and their physical well-being. He explained this concurrence partly by arguing that social conditions affected the intellectual, physical and psychological development of individuals, and also by claiming that cultural and social differences were products of innate racial disparity. Over the years, however, there was a

43 Bryn, 'Raceblandingen', p. 132.
44 Bryn's archive: undated newspaper clipping from *Nidaros Lørdagsblad*, interview with Halfdan Bryn: 'Lapper og nordmenn, de fysiske og sjelelige følger av raceblandingen'.

shift in his thinking from environmental explanations to racial determinism. Bryn based his reasoning increasingly on the notion of innate biological differences between inferior and superior races.

To put it bluntly, Bryn's engagement with racial hygiene from the mid-1920s onwards had the same goal as his anthropological research, namely to reconstruct an original, natural society in which 'race' was synonymous with 'culture' — a society where the tension between the inner drives of individuals (largely determined by race) and societal mores would be eliminated. Bryn's ideal was a world in which social stratification mirrored racial hierarchy and natural selection could proceed unhindered, so that the strong, dynamic and culturally-advanced Nordic race could propagate at the expense of inferior races and thus advance human civilisation.

7. The Schreiners and the Science of Race

Kristian Emil (1874-1957) and Alette Schreiner (1873-1951) had a lifelong relationship as close scientific collaborators and as a married couple.[1] They were ten years younger than Bryn and came from social backgrounds typical for academics: Kristian Emil's father was a Kristiania merchant with Danish-German roots and his grandfather was a pastor in the Church of Norway; Alette was the daughter of the magistrate of a small town (Eidsvoll) about seventy kilometres north of the capital. As a woman, however, Alette was not at all a typical member of the academic class. In fact, women had only acquired the legal right to pursue university-level studies eight years before she became a student.

The pair met while studying medicine in the 1890s. This was an era of great advances in biology and medicine during which many zoologists and anatomists turned their attention to the inner structure of cells, using laboratory experiments and advanced microscopy techniques to explore the mechanisms behind cell divisions, sexual reproduction and embryo growth. In the 1890s, these researchers began to understand that the chromosomes of the cell nucleus played a role in heredity, and after the rediscovery of

---

1   Biographical information on Alette and Kristian Emil Schreiner is taken from Otto Lous Mohr, 'Kristian Emil Schreiner', in Jan Jansen and Alf Brodal (eds.), *Aspects of Cerebellar Anatomy* (Oslo: Johan Grundt Tanum, 1954); Jan Jansen, 'Alette Schreiner', in *Norsk biografisk leksikon* (Oslo: Aschehoug, 1954), pp. 520-22; Johan Torgersen, 'Minnetale over Kristian Emil Schreiner', *Årbok, Det Norske videnskaps-akademi* (Oslo: I kommisjon hos J. Dybwad, 1958), pp. 59-71; Jan Jansen, 'Minnetale over Alette Schreiner', *Årbok, Det Norske videnskaps-akademi* (Oslo: I kommisjon hos J. Dybwad, 1953), pp. 59-67; Hjalmar Broch, 'Om noen av våre fremste zoologer', *Fauna*, Vol. 21 (1968), pp. 1-6; *Studentene fra 1892* (Kristiania: [n. pub.], 1917); *Studentene fra 1892* (Oslo: [n. pub.], 1942).

http://dx.doi.org/10.11647/OBP.0051.07

Mendelian genetics in 1900, a number of scientists began to scrutinise chromosomes in order to understand the physical mechanisms behind the Mendelian laws of inheritance. The Belgian biologist Edouard Van Beneden was the first to show that sex cells have only half the normal number of chromosomes, and that fertilisation restored the double chromosome sets. This discovery was crucial for the synthesis of chromosome theory and Mendelism and for the rise of modern genetics.

Like Kristine Bonnevie, who was a close friend of Alette Schreiner during their student years, Alette and Kristian Emil Schreiner were pioneers in the introduction of laboratory-based biology in Norway. After obtaining their medical degrees, the couple went abroad, visiting the laboratories of leading embryologists and cell researchers and taking up cytological research. The Schreiners visited Van Beneden's laboratory in Liège, as Bonnevie had, and like her they specialised in the study of chromosome behaviour during the formation of germ cells (a process through which the numbers of chromosomes are reduced). Kristine Bonnevie and Kristian Emil developed competing explanations of this phenomenon, and even though it was Schreiner's theory of 'parallel conjugation' that finally gained currency, they both achieved international recognition for their work, making this an important starting point for their successful scientific careers.[2]

In 1900, Kristine Bonnevie became head of the so-called Zootomic Museum (later renamed the Zoological Laboratory), soon to develop into a core institution for biological research and education. In 1912, Bonnevie became the first female professor in Norway, two years later she took up genetic research and, in 1916, she created the Institute of Genetics as part of the Zoological Laboratory.[3]

In contrast to Kristine Bonnevie, who was unmarried and worked alone, Alette Schreiner conducted her research in close cooperation with her husband. At the beginning of their careers, Alette's research was absorbed into her husband's projects and published under his name. Thereafter, she channelled her scientific work through her husband's career, never holding an academic position, although she managed to carve out an informal role as a member of the Norwegian Academy of Science and Letters and as a writer of textbooks and popular science.

In 1908 Kristian Emil was appointed head of the Department of Anatomy, succeeding Gustav Adolf Guldberg (see Fig. 13). He became

---

2   Inger Nordal, Dag O Hessen and Thore Lie, *Kristine Bonnevie et forskerliv* (Oslo: Cappelen Damm, 2012).

3   Ibid.

head at a time when, after decades of stasis, the department was about to expand as a key centre of medical training. Kristian Emil was soon to play a major role in Norwegian academia as a teacher, textbook author, institutional entrepreneur and scientist. In the memorial address given at the Norwegian Academy of Science and Letters after his death, Kristian Emil was hailed as a 'monumental figure in Norwegian science'.[4] Among his achievements was his contribution to the establishment of genetics as a new research field in the Department of Anatomy. In 1912, he encouraged the medical graduate Otto Lous Mohr to go abroad to study cytology and embryology and to take up the study of chromosomes. As mentioned in chapter 5, Mohr later visited the famous genetics laboratories of Thomas Hunt Morgan in New York (1917-1918), returned with a colony of fruit flies, established a laboratory for genetics in the Department of Anatomy and, in 1919, became Norway's second professor of anatomy.[5]

The Department of Anatomy and racial anthropology

However, in spite of the Schreiners' and Mohr's achievements in embryology, cell research, chromosomal studies and genetics, it was racial anthropology that became the main research field of the Department of Anatomy under Kristian Emil's leadership. But why did he abandon a career in the prestigious fields of cytology and chromosomal research and turn his attention to racial anthropology?

In 1915 Kristian Emil led a major revamping of the Department and assigned ample space for anthropological research. This was, as discussed in chapter 3, the culmination of a process that had begun under his predecessor and was encouraged by, among other things, the rising number of archaeological excavations in the late nineteenth century and the resulting influx of skeletons to the anthropological collection. The expansion of archaeology continued after the turn of the century, and in 1905 (the same year as the dissolution of the union with Sweden) the Norwegian Parliament passed an act that gave archaeologists and archaeological museums legal authority over all physical-cultural remains dated prior to 1536, the year of the Reformation. Menwhile, the University's Collection of Antiquities was relocated to expanded premises in the new Historical Museum.

---

4   Torgersen, 'Minnetale over Kristian Emil Schreiner', p. 61.
5   Lars Walløe, 'Otto Lous Mohr', in *Norsk biografisk leksikon*, http://nbl.snl.no/Otto_Lous_Mohr

Fig. 13 Professor of Anatomy Kristian Emil Schreiner,
painted by Astri Welhaven Heiberg in 1949.

By this time archaeologists were involved in questions about the origins,
migrations and settlements of races, peoples and cultures. Schreiner
himself claimed that his interest in anthropology was first aroused by
archaeologists who sent him skeletons and asked his professional opinion.
In 1912, in a letter to his Swedish colleague Carl Fürst (co-author of
Anthropologia suecica, with Gustav Retzius),[6] Schreiner declared that—as

---

6   Gustav Retzius and Carl M. Fürst, *Anthropologia suecica: beiträge zur Anthropologie
    der Schweden nach den auf Veranstaltung der schwedischen Gesellschaft für
    Anthropologie und Geographie in den Jahren 1897 und 1898 ausgeführten Erhebungen*
    (Stockholm: [n. pub.], 1902).

the only Norwegian professor of anatomy—he saw it as his duty to prevent Norway from lagging behind in this field of research.[7]

During World War I, Kristian Emil began his anthropological research, which he undertook in collaboration with his wife and a number of assistants at the department. Most of the findings, however, were not published until the 1930s, when he issued two accurate and richly-illustrated monographs in which far more space was given to the detailed description of archaeological findings than to any overarching theory (see. Fig. 14). Skulls from 'Norwegian' burial sites were described and analysed in the massive two-volume work *Crania norvegica* (1939-1946), and skeletons from Sami graves were treated in the equally lengthy monograph *Zur Osteologie der Lappen* (1931-1935). These monographs were part of an anthropological tradition of extensive, minutely-illustrated books on the 'craniology' of nations, deriving from research on the collections held at museums and universities, with titles like *Crania helvetica*, *Crania suecica antiqua*, *Crania prussic* and *Crania britannica*. Schreiner's monographs were a late but substantial contribution to these reference works, which were used by anthropologists as an international database for the mapping of the biological history of mankind.

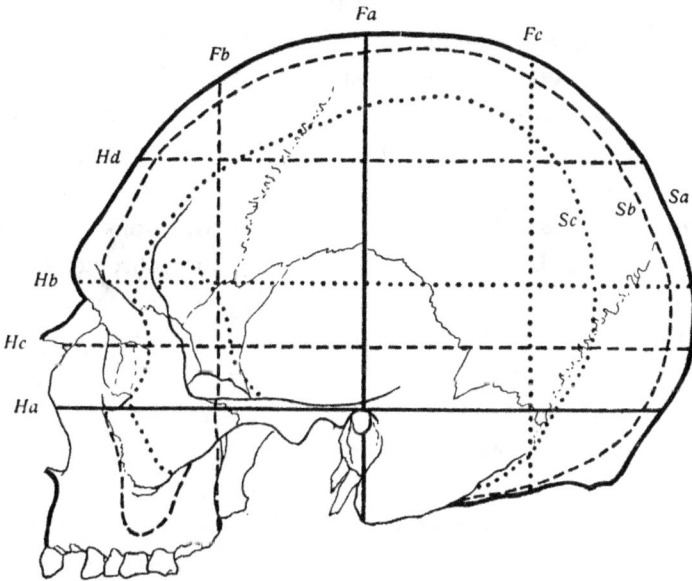

Fig. 14 *Zur Osteologie der Lappen* contains about 300 pages of drawings and photographs of skulls. This image shows the 10 different curves drawn for each skull.

---

7   C. M. Fürst's archive: K. E. Schreiner to Fürst, 2 February 1912.

Schreiner and his assistants at the Department of Anatomy were mainly conducting 'osteological' research on skeletons from ancient burial sites. To compare the racial characteristics of past and present populations, however, Schreiner wanted to combine this archaeological research with anthropological studies of contemporary Norwegians. This is probably the main reason for Schreiner's decision to collaborate with Halfdan Bryn. As we saw in chapter 4, Bryn's first prize-winning anthropological work was in fact written in response to a call from the Faculty of Medicine for papers about the anthropology of Norway's present-day population. Schreiner, who was likely the initiator of the call, assessed Bryn's thesis and recommended it for the award.[8]

The racial history of the Sami

Under Schreiner's leadership, the study of human remains from 'Norwegian' ancestors was supplemented with extensive studies of Sami skulls. However, these remains did not generally come from archaeological excavations because Norwegian archaeologists devoted almost all of their attention to what they considered to be the *national* prehistory, which in their view did not include the Sami. The exploration of Sami cultural heritage sites was not considered a task for archaeology, but for ethnography—a comparatively marginal discipline at the time.[9] This meant that the anatomical collection held at the Department of Anatomy included only a limited number of Sami specimens; in order to explore the racial history of the Sami, researchers had to conduct their own excavations.

There are probably a number of reasons for Schreiner's growing interest in the Sami. Firstly, the racial biology of the Lapps attracted attention from racial hygienists, such as Mjøen and Lundborg, who, like Bryn, were highly concerned about the racial mixing that they imagined was going on in northern Scandinavia. 'Bastardisation' was a major research topic both at Mjøen's private institution, the Vindern Biological Laboratory, and at the Swedish State Institute for Racial Biology, with both Mjøen and Lundborg directing their attention towards the Sami and the mixed offspring of the Sami and Scandinavians. The influential position of Mjøen and Lundborg in the international debates over racial biology

---

8   *Aftenposten*, 3 September 1917.
9   See chapter 4.

meant that the Sami became a topic for discussion, thus stimulating the Schreiners' interest. Secondly, the Sami had been discussed by scientists for many decades within the broader debate about the so-called Arctic peoples, their place in racial taxonomy, their links to other peoples and their origins and prehistoric migrations. As head of the only anatomy department in the country with the largest Sami minority, Kristian Emil was in a strategic position to take up research on such issues.

Thirdly, and most importantly, the interest in the Sami people's biological history stemmed from a specifically Scandinavian political, cultural and academic context. For example, in both Norway and Sweden, disputes about the cultural and territorial rights of the Sami—such as the Norwegian-Swedish conflict over reindeer pastures which arose after the dissolution of the union and was discussed in chapter 2—fuelled academic research on Sami history. Even before beginning his research in the field of physical anthropological, Kristian Emil was drawn into this debate as an expert advisor. Based on comparative studies of skulls from domesticated and wild reindeer, he attempted to elucidate whether the domesticated reindeer populations in Scandinavia had their origins in the local wild strand of reindeer, or whether they were related to the domesticated races used in nomadic reindeer husbandry in Siberia and northern Russia.[10]

The issue of the origin of reindeer husbandry was related to questions concerning the prehistoric migrations of the Sami and thus the debates over the ethnic identity of the prehistoric inhabitants of northern Scandinavia. This was also a key issue in ideological and political struggles over territorial rights and minority policy. As shown in chapter 2, advocates of a harsh ethnic assimilation policy were likely to appreciate Andreas Hansen's theory about a late Sami migration to Scandinavia, whilst those who supported a more liberal minority policy could defend Sami rights by referring to the indigenousness of the Sami population. This political significance, along with a general ethnographic interest in prehistoric migrations and in Arctic peoples, fuelled the academic interest in the prehistory of the Sami.[11]

---

10 *Voldgiftssag mellem Norge og Sverige angaaende renbeite. Første afdeling angaaende tilveiebringelse af oplysninger og bevisligheder. Forhandlinger og beslutninger i Kjøbenhavn 1909-1910* (Kristiania: S. M. Brydes boktrykkeri, 1910), p. 14ff.

11 Jon Røyne Kyllingstad, *'Menneskeåndens universalitet' Instituttet for sammenlignende kulturforskning 1917-1940. Ideene, institusjonen og forskningen*

The founding of the Institute for Comparative Research in Human Culture in 1922 gave new impetus to the study of Sami language, culture and history. This state-funded institution, which had an informal link with the Nobel Peace Prize Committee, gained a key role in financing and coordinating Norwegian research in the humanities. It was established in response to the breakdown of scientific internationalism after World War I and operated on a mix of academic and political agendas.[12] By inviting leading humanities scholars from the belligerent countries to lengthy conferences on neutral Norwegian ground, the Institute helped counteract French, British and Belgian post-war attempts to isolate German academia. Through comparative cultural research, the Institute intended to explore the universal aspect of human cultural development and serve as a counterweight to the aggressive nationalism that was assumed to have paved the way for the war.[13]

The idea of the psychological unity of humankind was a key element in the political campaign for the establishment of the Institute for Comparative Research in Human Culture. This idea was also a core element in the Arctic programme, which was the Institute's main focus in the mid-1920s. The Arctic programme was initiated by the professor of ethnography Ole M. Solberg, who, as mentioned in chapter 4, saw the Arctic as the perfect place to study the basic mechanisms of the evolution of human culture. In the Arctic, he claimed, peoples of different linguistic, ethnic and racial origin had gone through parallel phases of cultural development because they had all been forced to adapt to the same harsh living conditions. All Arctic peoples shared a common 'Arctic way of life', and this demonstrated, according to Solberg, that behind all cultural differences lay one universal human psychology: all 'peoples' respond in the same way to the same environmental challenges.[14] The Arctic programme studied the Sami and their 'Arctic' neighbours to the east from a variety of perspectives— linguistic, folkloristic, ethnographic, archaeological, historical and social-scientific as well as physical and anthropological. Race was relevant to the project, but Solberg saw race as a purely physical concept which could be used as a tool for tracing prehistoric migrations of peoples, but which had no impact upon cultural abilities and cultural differences.

(Ph.D. thesis, University of Oslo, 2008), pp. 3-122

12 Ibid.

13 Ibid.

14 ISKF-archive: Ole M. Solberg, memorandum, 21 October 1923.

For some years, the Arctic programme was led by the socially-engaged natural scientist and explorer Fridtjof Nansen, who had become interested in Arctic ethnography after a lengthy stay among the Greenland Inuit in 1888-1889. In collaboration with Franz Boas, who visited the Institute for Comparative Research in Human Culture in 1925, Nansen made extensive plans for a series of international ethnographic expeditions to northern Russia. The project received financial support from the Laura Spelman Rockefeller Memorial, an American philanthropic foundation, but had to be dropped due to unsuccessful attempts to collaborate with authorities and scientists in the Soviet Union. Instead, the American grant and the scientific staff of the Institute were directed towards a study of the Norwegian Sami. This context is key because Kristian Emil Schreiner's own research into the racial history of the Sami was largely financed and published by the Institute for Comparative Research in Human Culture and the Laura Spelman Rockefeller Memorial.[15]

It is important to note that although the basic ideology of the Institute, and the theoretical foundation of the Arctic programme, were rooted in the idea of the psychological unity of humankind, the attitudes to race among researchers working at the Institute were not always consistent with such an ideology. Some projects financed and published by the Arctic programme were even based on the notion of major inborn psychological differences between races. Two monographs about the Sami population of Kautokeino, a major reindeer herding community in Finnmark, are a case in point. The first of these studies, written by the local state physician (*distriktslegen*) Rolf Gjessing, was a physical and anthropological survey that described the contemporary Sami population as the product of racial mixing between Sami ('*lappiske*') and Finnish ('*kvenske*') elements. These findings were followed up in a work by the local pastor and philologist P. Lorenz Smith, who argued that there was a correlation between the uneven distribution of race-specific Finnish and Sami bodily characteristics in the Kautokeino population and the distribution of typically Finnish and Sami psychological characteristics. Thus, even if the whole population shared a Sami language and lifestyle, a Finnish-looking segment was characterised by psychological features assumed to be typical of the Finns: strength, vigour, introversion, brutality, cunning, ruthlessness and vengefulness. The fraction who ressembled Lapps, meanwhile, were described as

15 Kyllingstad, '*Menneskeåndens universalitet*', pp. 172-76, 190-99, 334-60.

unreflective, simple-minded, peaceful, modest, short-sighted, sensitive and with a nomadic mentality.[16]

This racial psychological 'analysis', which bore similarities to Bryn's approach was however a minor element in Smith's work, which otherwise addressed the history, culture and society of the Kautokeino Sami. The study's elements of racial psychology were also atypical of the Arctic programme, dominated by humanities scholars who directed most of their attention towards the study of Sami culture, language and society. Much of this research involved lengthy field work among the Sami, long-term cooperation with Sami informants and extensive learning of the Sami language and culture. The efforts of the Institute helped preserve knowledge of the Sami culture and language that would otherwise have been lost. Many of the staff were politically opposed to, or critical of, the harsh assimilation policy conducted by the Norwegian government against the Sami.[17]

Centred on the idea of the unity of humankind, the scientific and political programme of the Institute was radically different from the scientific and political programmes of people like Halfdan Bryn, Jon Alfred Mjøen and Herman Lundborg. Based on a review of the correspondence between Franz Boas and the Institute, it is clear that Boas saw the Institute as a potential partner in his campaign against scientific racism, and that he considered Kristian Emil Schreiner (whom he visited at the anatomy department) to have a reasonable attitude as far as racial questions were concerned. As will later become clear, Kristian Emil can hardly be described as an unambiguous anti-racist. However, he did not support the racial ideology espoused by Bryn and Lundborg; moreover, the Institute for Comparative Research in Human Culture provided a context for his racial studies that was very different from the racial hygiene movement to which Bryn's and Lundborg's research was closely tied. The main goal of the Department of Anatomy's anthropological research was not to map the distribution of inferior and superior racial elements, but to help explore the cultural history of the Sami and the Norwegians.

---

16 P. Lorenz Smith, *Kautokeino og Kautokeino-lappene: en historisk og ergologisk regionalstudie* (Oslo: ISKF/Aschehoug, 1938); Rolv R. Gjessing, *Die Kautokeinolappen: eine anthropologische Studie* (Oslo: ISKF/Aschehoug, 1934).

17 Kyllingstad, *'Menneskeåndens universalitet'*, pp. 304-477.

Kristian Emil Schreiner and Sami prehistory

The starting point for Schreiner's research on Sami skeletal remains was the unsettled question of the prehistoric settlement of northern Scandinavia. Of central importance to this discussion was Ole Solberg's 1909 work on the two Iron Age settlements at Kjelmøya Island in eastern Finnmark. While Solberg dated them to approximately 700-1100 AD and claimed they were Sea Sami settlements, Hansen asserted that they had in fact been inhabited by ethnic Norwegian ancestors. Halfdan Bryn supported Hansen's theory and, in his book *Norwegische Samen* (1932), claimed that the Sea Sami on the coast of northern Norway belonged to the same Alpine race as the Norwegian population along the coast of southern Norway, and that they were both unrelated to the newly-arrived, reindeer-herding Sami population of the inland.

It was mainly in order to examine these questions that the Department of Anatomy undertook a series of excavations in Finnmark. In the aftermath of World War I, they dug up a number of presumed Sami pre-Christian burial sites along the fjords, as well as in churchyards in Sea Sami communities, in the typical reindeer-herding districts of the inland and in the district of the Skolt Sami, an ethnic group traditionally belonging to the Russian Orthodox church and inhabiting the borderland of present-day Finland, Russia and Norway. The department also examined an Iron Age site in Tysfjord in Nordland, the southernmost county of northern Norway, where they further undertook a racial survey of the present-day Sea Sami population.[18] This undertaking was extensive and time-consuming. Several individuals were involved in excavating, registering, systematising, measuring, drawing and photographing the bones, calculating ratios, average values and correlation coefficients, and constructing tables and graphs of frequency, etc. In 1927 Kristian Emil published a preliminary work based on some of the material. In it, he claimed to have found remains of Sami progenitors in Iron Age graves along the coast of Finnmark and Nordland. He also argued that there had been close contact between the Sami and Norwegians in the Viking period. In the Tysfjord Iron Age burial mound, he claimed to have

---

18   Kristian E. Schreiner, *Zur Osteologie der Lappen II* (Oslo: ISKF/Aschehoug, 1931), p. 74; Alette Schreiner, *Anthropologische Lokaluntersuchungen in Norge. Hellemo (Tysfjordlappen)* (Oslo: ISKF/Aschehoug, 1932); Audhild Schanche, *Graver i ur og Berg. Samisk gravskikk og religion 1000 f.kr. til 1700 e. kr* (Ph.D. thesis, University of Tromsø, 1997), p. 45.

found a skull of mixed origin (see Fig. 15). According to the archaeologists, the skull came from a person who had belonged to the social elite in a Norwegian community and who Kristian Emil suggested was the offspring of a Norwegian chieftain and a Sami woman.[19]

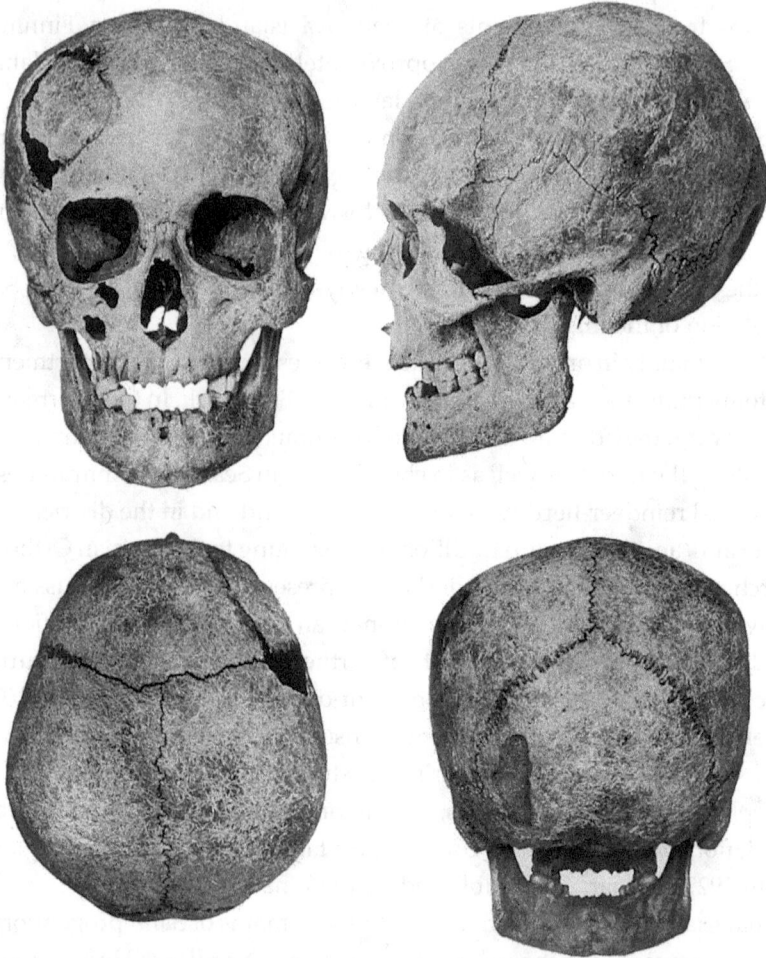

Fig. 15 The Tysfjord skull. According to Kristian Emil Schreiner, both the braincase and the face were very similar to other Sami skulls. In addition, the face had strong Sami features; only the shape of the nose and the relative position of the cheekbone resembled the Nordic Iron Age type.

The main results were published between 1931 and 1935, in the extensive two-volume work *Zur Osteologie der Lappen*. It was based on 582 more-or-less

19 Audhild Schanche, *Graver i Ur og Berg* (Karasjok: Davvi girji, 2000), pp. 45-46.

complete skeletons, and the skulls in particular were described in great detail. For each skull, 63 measurements and angles were measured and 37 indices calculated. On the basis of this large amount of data, Schreiner believed he could dismiss Andreas Hansen and Halfdan Bryn's theory of the Sami as latecomers in Scandinavian history. According to Schreiner, the bones in the pre-Christian graves along the fjords were anatomically similar to the bones from the churchyards of typical Sami communities both along the fjords and in the inland. The Sea Sami on the coast and the reindeer herders in the inland had the same racial identity, Schreiner argued: the Kjelmøya Iron Age site was a Sami settlement.[20]

Schreiner even asserted that the Sami forefathers had been present in Finnmark since at least the Roman Iron Age. This claim was based on a study of human bones from a burial site in Nesseby in eastern Finnmark, excavated by the Sami amateur researcher Isak Saba in 1910-1912. Saba, who died before Schreiner published his work, was a teacher, the first Sami member of the Norwegian Parliament and a leading figure in an ethno-political movement intended to stir ethnic pride among the Sami and to counteract the national policy of cultural assimilation. Saba's excavation was part of an attempt to demonstrate the deep historical roots of the Sami. The grave contained objects of iron and stone that had been typologically dated to the Roman period. It was considered the oldest known burial site in eastern Finnmark, and based on the bones Schreiner declared that it was of Sami origin.[21]

Schreiner's view on 'the Lapp race'

In his study of the racial mixing between the Sami and Norwegians in 1922, Bryn had proclaimed that the mapping of bodily racial traits in the northern Norwegian population was of interest only because such observable traits were correlated to invisible racial differences in the biological quality of the population.[22] His research was aimed at establishing eugenically relevant data to document superior and inferior racial elements in the population. In contrast to Bryn's work, Kristian Emil Schreiner's research did not target issues of racial quality and racial hygiene, and he did not set out to look for evidence of Sami inferiority. It is still evident, however, that even Shreiner

20 K. Schreiner, *Zur Osteologie der Lappen I* (Oslo: ISKF/Aschehoug, 1935), pp. 261-75 (p. 273).
21 K. Schreiner, *Zur Osteologie der Lappen I*, pp. 274.
22 Halfdan Bryn, 'Raceblandingen i Troms fylke', *Norsk Tidsskrift for Militærmedicin*, Vol. 26 (1922), p. 130.

assumed that races could be ranked in a hierarchy of cerebral development; that differences in cultural achievement between nations and 'peoples' were, to a certain extent, the product of such inborn racial differences; and that once upon a time, in some distant prehistoric past, humankind had consisted of racially pure populations.

According to Schreiner, all the Sami findings from both Christian and pre-Christian times were characterised by racial admixture. An ancient 'Lappoid' element was to a varying extent mixed up with 'Nordic' and 'East Baltic' elements—the different Sami populations had had varying degrees of contact with neighbouring Finnish and Norwegian populations. Thus, even though he did not claim to have found any racially pure Sami populations in the past or the present, Kristian Emil still thought it was possible to identify a distinct and ancient 'Lappoid' race that constituted the racial core of the Sami people. His argument was that there were certain statistical patterns of anatomical likeness between the average skull from the Sami churchyards and the average skull from the pre-Christian Sami graves, and that there were certain characteristic differences between all the Sami skulls and the average 'Norwegian' Iron Age skull.[23]

One of the techniques he used for detecting this difference was to construct an average 'Norwegian' Iron Age skull based on a number of quantified anatomical characteristics. He then created a diagram in which the numerical values of the average Norwegian skull were set to zero. Thus, the typical 'Iron Age' skull was represented as a straight horizontal line in the diagram. Corresponding curves representing the skulls from the Finnmark excavations demonstrated their degree of anatomical deviation from the typical 'Norwegian' form. Employing a similar technique, he also constructed an average Sami skull and explored how skulls from different local burial sites deviated or coincided with this Sami type.[24] Those aspects of the Sami skulls which deviated most from the features of the 'Norwegian' Iron Age skull, and which coincided with the skulls from different Sami burials, were characterised by Schreiner as typically 'Lapp'. This was the basis for his claim that it was possible to single out a Lapp racial element within the racially-mixed Sami populations.

There is no reason to doubt that Schreiner detected some statistical differences between the shapes of skulls from Norwegian Iron Age graves and those from Sami graves. But it is a long step from that fact to the claim that ethnic division in northern Scandinavia correlates to ancient biological

---

23 K. Schreiner, *Zur Osteologie der Lappen I*, pp. 276-88.
24 Ibid., pp. 182-96.

divisions between clearly separable races. It is more likely that Schreiner started out by presupposing the existence of a primordial Lapp race and trying to identify it, and that he ended up finding what he was looking for. His approach seems to have been based on the implicit theory of a prehistoric concurrence between the biological entity of 'race' and the linguistic and cultural entity of 'folk' (people/nation), a theory most likely underpinned by belief in inherited racial differences between the primitive Sami and superior Norwegian psychologies.

Zur Osteologie der Lappen was almost exclusively dedicated to an exhaustively detailed description and comparison of the anatomy of bones. The issue of racial psychology was touched upon only once. When Schreiner tried to find a position for the Lapp race in an overall racial typology, it became clear that he envisioned a hierarchy of races in which the superiority or primitiveness of body and mind were interconnected. Summing up his findings, Schreiner claimed that the most racially pure Sami were characterised by traits such as low stature, relatively short legs, long arms, poor beard growth, dark brown eyes, yellow-brown skin and a low, broad face. Schreiner remarked that these typically Sami-looking individuals seemed rather 'alien', even Mongol-like, and suggested that their bodily characteristics implied that they belonged to a primitive ('unspecialised') race.[25]

By comparing average craniological measurements, Schreiner arrived at the conclusion that the primordial Lapp race, the 'Protolapps', had belonged to the same original race as the 'Protoalpines' and 'Protomongols'. This would explain the physical resemblance between the Sami and the dark short-skulled Norwegian coastal dwellers. From their common area of origin, the Protomongols had wandered to the east and the Protoalpines to the west, while the Protolapps had been isolated for a long period south of the Ural Mountains before migrating to Scandinavia.[26] Their isolation had protected them from the forces of evolution, and consequently the Sami had maintained their primitiveness. They belonged to the 'childhood' of humankind, and their infantilism was expressed not only in their bodily appearance but also in their psychology:

> [...] the carefree cheerfulness, that is often encountered among the Lapp, in one moment associated with childlike confidence, the next with great shyness and not infrequently with perfect shyness, corresponds to the somatic typus and points in the direction of the protomorph Eurasian races.[27]

---

25 Ibid., pp. 277.
26 Ibid., pp. 288.
27 Ibid., pp. 286.

Alette Schreiner's philosophy of life

Unlike Bryn, Kristian Emil Schreiner did not see the mapping of inferior and superior racial elements as the goal of anthropology. He did not regard racial anthropology as a tool for racial hygiene, but as an instrument for the exploration of prehistory. Yet it is clear that he still ranked races according to their level of evolutionary development. Did this also imply a normative ranking of their moral worth and, if so, with what consequences for his outlook on society and humanity? It is difficult to answer this question, since most of the texts that Schreiner left behind are factual scientific texts that do not reveal much about his views on these issues. Alette Schreiner, on the other hand, published a number of works in which she discussed the social, cultural and normative relevance of her science (see Fig. 16). She even put forward what she called a scientifically-based 'philosophy of life'. The remainder of this chapter deals with Alette Schreiner's views on human biology, race, society and culture, and compares them to Halfdan Bryn's racial ideology.

Fig. 16 Alette Schreiner showing children an animal skull, ca. 1910.

It is not easy to deduce from the available source material whether Kristian Emil Schreiner shared his wife's views, but it is reasonable to assume that he did. In biographical sketches and obituaries, allusions are frequently made to the particular closeness of their professional and private relationship. According to one obituary written by a co-worker, Alette and Kristian Emil possessed complementary talents. While he was made for relentless, rigorous critique, she was a creative visionary.[28] Besides her scientific work, which included a number of anthropological publications, Alette participated in public debate, wrote popular science books and gave public lectures on a broad range of biological topics. In these texts, scientific facts were often combined with moral, political and social-philosophical thoughts. Like Halfdan Bryn she used scientific theories to legitimate ideas of how people should live their lives; unlike Bryn, who seems never to have reflected on the justification for doing this, Alette explicitly claimed that a 'philosophy of life' could and should be based on exact scientific knowledge about the development of life.[29] The biologically-founded societal theories of Alette Schreiner and Halfdan Bryn had much in common. There were important distinctions, however, and these distinctions coincided to some degree with differences in their attitudes towards basic biological questions.

The following paragraphs discuss Alette's two popular books on biology (1912) and on reproduction and family life among human beings (1916), reports from a series of lectures she held in Trondheim in 1922,[30] and a lecture she gave, entitled 'The Philosophy of Life and the Development of Life' (1929). These texts had a common theme: she criticised Darwin's single-minded followers and argued against the idea of an evolution driven solely by the survival of the fittest. In her opinion the essence of evolution was not blind selection, but what she called *selvutfoldelsesdrift*—the drive towards self-realisation or the tendency towards 'a freer unfolding of spontaneous forces' built into all living organisms.[31] This teleological idea of evolution was a cornerstone in her evolutionary 'philosophy of life'.

---

28 Hjalmar Broch, 'Om noen av våre fremste zoologer', *Fauna*, Vol. 21 (1968), pp. 1-6.

29 Alette Schreiner, 'Livsutvikling og livsanskuelse', *Kirke og kultur*, Vol. 36 (1929), pp. 453-74.

30 Reports on lectures by Alette Schreiner: Nidaros, 2 March 1922; Trondheim Adresseavis, 24 February 1922 and 27 February 1924; Trøndelagen, 4 March 1922. Bryn's archive: letter from Alette Schreiner to Bryn discussing the lectures.

31 Alette Schreiner, *Skapende kræfter i livsformenes historie; utsyn over et centralt omraade av den almindelige biologi med særlig blik paa dyreriket* (Kristiania: Aschehoug, 1912), p. 296.

Some of Alette's arguments came from palaeontology. Nineteenth-century taxonomists had constructed phylogenetic trees in which traced the organic growth of one form of life out of the previous one, all the way back to a single, common root. At the turn of the century, this idea was challenged. It became more common to portray the evolution of species as several parallel trunks that grew side by side and followed a specific direction in their own development. This pattern was explained by the theory of orthogenesis, which claimed that the evolution of a species is determined by certain built-in tendencies to develop in a certain direction.[32] Alette combined this evolutionary theory with a dualist theory of inheritance. Such dualist theories were advocated by many biologists in the German-speaking world in the early twentieth century, and they implied a double genotype. All species-specific properties were thought to be inherited as a cohesive 'building plan', a 'basic type' or 'idea' which had its material basis in the cytoplasm of the cells. Only those properties that varied within a species were located in the chromosomes and were inherited in line with Mendelian rules.[33]

According to Alette, the phylogenies of all life forms ran through the same set of stages from childhood to manhood, old age to death. The phylogenetic 'youth' of a species or lineage was characterised by a simple 'building plan' and then a great number of variable traits inherited according to Mendelian rules. As the life form grew older, these dynamic elements were moulded into the 'building plan' and became tied to the undifferentiated inheritable material of the cytoplasm. An old species had few variable properties left. It was inflexible and less able to adapt to changes in the environment. A disturbance of the environment, which for a younger and more flexible lineage would be an impetus to a stronger unfolding of life, could therefore lead to the death of old lineages.[34] This meant that the struggle for existence ensured the extermination of the old, out-dated forms and the survival of the young, healthy and adaptable species. Alette thus maintained that although natural selection played a key role in species development, it did not determine the direction of

---

32 Niels Bonde, 'Moderne systematik -fylogeni og klassifikation', in Niels Bonde, et.al. (eds.), *Naturens historiefortællere* (København: Gad, 1996), p. 133.

33 Jonathan Harwood, *Styles of Scientific Thought: The German Genetics Community 1900-1933* (Chicago, IL: University of Chicago Press, 1993), pp. 104-28.

34 Schreiner, *Skapende kræfter*, pp. 307, 316.

evolution. The fundamental driving force was not self-preservation, but the 'self-unfolding tendency' which was embodied in all organisms.

In a speech given in 1929, Alette Schreiner discussed the possibility of founding a humane philosophy of life upon the exact science of life. Her conclusion was that this was indeed possible, because science showed that evolution was not random, but rather moved towards a goal. The real machinery of evolution was not the struggle for survival, but a life-drive that strove towards the development of an increasingly advanced brain making possible the human capacity for autonomous reasoning. This implied that the exact natural sciences and the scientific urge for universal knowledge represented the very goal towards which evolution itself was striving. Even if she emphasised that science was unable to study 'the inner meaning of things'—the origin and the final goal of evolution—it is still clear that she considered scientists like herself to be in a very privileged position for expounding the meaning of life and how it should be lived. Not only did science represent the apex of evolution, scientists themselves, by studying the development of life, could reach the highest level of insight into life that any human could possibly achieve.[35]

Biological and cultural evolution

Alette Schreiner made a basic distinction between animals and humans. Animals were totally determined by their inborn drives and were therefore involved in a battle of all against all, with each individual acting alone on behalf of its hereditary material. Only the human species had broken out of this iron cage; by taking the leap out of nature into culture, humankind was no longer determined by its biological drives.[36] Alette defined 'culture' as the ability to understand the laws of nature and to control nature with the help of human tools. Culture was neither determined by hereditary material, nor controlled by individuals; culture was supra-organic and connected all civilised humans in an inseparable whole of which each individual is the instrument of life functions that extended far beyond their own sphere of life. Cultural progress was made possible by the human ability to learn, which meant that knowledge could be transferred and

---

35 Schreiner, 'Livsutvikling og livsanskuelse', pp. 453, 456, 471.
36 Schreiner, *Skapende kræfter*, pp. 319-28; *Slegtslivet*, p. 147.

accumulated across generations. Therefore, cultural evolution — the growth of the supra-organic organism — was to a very great extent detached from the biological evolution of the human species.[37]

Biological evolution and cultural evolution, however, are not totally detached, and Alette's understanding of the relationship between the two was closely related to her view on how culture is (and should be) produced, transferred and accumulated across generations. Alette understood the human capacity for learning as interconnected with the process of individual brain growth. During childhood, humans have a purely receptive mind allowing them to be deeply and unconsciously shaped by culture. In this phase of life, the individual is entitled to all the material and cultural support from society that is needed for the child to realise his/her full potential for cultural growth. According to Alette, it is only in the late teens that an individual develops his/her self-conscious will and ability to think independently. These are the abilities that make cultural creativity and human progress possible, and in this phase of life, society is entitled to make use of the individual for the benefit of the common good.

The relation between the development of the brain and of culture was at the core of Alette's thought on culture and society. To this end, she believed that there are crucial biological differences between individuals, races and the sexes in their ability to create and acquire culture. According to her, the lower human races are offshoots from the main line of human evolution. As with the anthropoid apes, the ontogenetic development of the inferior races is similar to that of the superior races until the age of five or six. At that point, the development of an advanced personality, autonomous reasoning and free will sets in among the superior races, but does not take place to the same degree in the inferior races; from then on, their cerebral development is hampered, and they grow old at a much earlier stage. This implies that their brain growth came to a halt before they developed the capacity for cultural creativity and progress that was typical of civilised man.[38]

Alette Schreiner's ideas about primitive races resemble her husband's notion of the infantile racial psychology of the Sami. It is important to note, however, that this was only a marginal topic in her popular scientific writing. The same goes for Kristian Emil's brief remarks on the

---

37 Schreiner, *Skapende kræfter*, p. 324.
38 Ibid., pp. 322-23.

infantilism of the Sami in *Zur Osteologie der Lappen*. Both Schreiners seem to have taken for granted, as scientific fact, the inferiority and superiority of anthropologically-defined 'races', but there is nothing in the sources to suggest that this was a core idea in their outlook on society.

Eugenics and social reform

Alette Schreiner held that cultural evolution entailed the realisation of certain universal human potentials that were embodied in humanity from 'the beginning', and she argued that society's main task was to provide children and young people with a moral and material environment that enabled them to develop these potentials. 'Learn to know the laws that govern the genesis of the fully-developed human personality', she wrote, 'and build culture and society upon them'.[39] In line with this ideal, she was an advocate for improving the moral environment and material living conditions of children and adolescents. She argued for school reform. Along with her husband, she was involved in research on the diet and growth of schoolchildren. And she was a driving force behind the establishment of *Blindern studenthjem*, a home away from home for students in Kristiania who otherwise would have had to live in cramped and poor lodgings spread around the town.

Alette, however, also used the same type of argument when advocating eugenics: for an individual to become a valuable and happy member of humankind, he/she had to be endowed with the right potentials, and some children did not have these potentials. The forces of culture could nurture potential, but they could not reshape nature, and some human beings were destined from birth to live unhappy and unworthy lives as 'parasites on the social body'.[40] She declared that society had made more progress in the art of keeping young people alive than in the art of enabling them to make the best of their lives. In an ideal world, however, society should be striving towards one major goal: the creation of noble and upright human beings through deliberate interventions in the biological reproduction of members of society.[41]

---

39 Alette Schreiner, *Slegtslivet hos menneskene* (Kristiania: Aschehoug, 1914).
40 Ibid., p. 159.
41 Ibid., pp. 158-85.

According to Alette, some people had inherited mental defects of an intellectual and moral nature that rendered them unable to become productive citizens in an ordered community. She therefore suggested strong measures to prevent the propagation of inferior qualities. Sterilisation was the most humane solution, but compulsory abortion should also be considered.[42] It was nevertheless more important to enhance the propagation of the valuable lineages, through positive eugenics, than it was to weed out inferior elements. Education about sexual reproduction should be liberated from ignorance, prejudice and 'pressure from an unnatural economy'. Birth rates were sinking among the upper social strata, and she feared the growth of the underclass. Even though she did not believe there was a perfect match between social stratification and the distribution of superior and inferior traits, she held that the upper classes were more likely to be of higher biological quality. The conditions for the physical and psychological development of children were also better at the top of the social hierarchy. In order to limit the breeding of the underclass, therefore, she wanted to make contraception and sexual education available to the populace.[43]

To weed out pathological deviations and to safeguard normality and healthiness, were not, however, the final goals of eugenics according to Alette Schreiner. The ultimate goal was to improve mankind on a supposedly objective scale of biological quality. The value of genetic material should be evaluated not according to 'normality', but according to its relatively greater or smaller 'human value'.[44] The evolution of human culture would only continue if the reproduction of superior elements was enhanced and the number of inferiors reduced.

Alette Schreiner versus Halfdan Bryn: the unfolding of life versus racial struggle

Alette Schreiner agreed with Halfdan Bryn that scientific knowledge of human nature should provide guiding principles for the organisation of society, but there were differences in the scientific ideas they advocated and in the moral lessons they took from these ideas. Both Schreiner and Bryn agreed that 'culture' is the defining attribute that distinguishes humans

---

42 Ibid., pp. 164-65.
43 Ibid., pp. 167-70.
44 Ibid., p. 166.

from animals. They both considered 'culture' to be a unified, quantifiable phenomenon. They agreed that some people had little culture while others had more, and that some therefore had lesser human value than others. Both believed that people with a low level of culture could become more human by acquiring more culture, but that different people had different natural aptitudes for cultural development.

Alette and Bryn both wanted a society in harmony with human nature and felt that to achieve this, individuals had to adapt to society and society had to be adapted to humanity. However, society should not be adapted to the average human being, but rather to those at the top of the scale of cultural progress. This implied that individuals should adapt to a society dominated by the norms and values of an elite. Since differences in cultural level were seen as partly inborn, eugenics was an integral means to realising this vision of society. Cultural progress would only happen if the superior, culturally creative elements were allowed to procreate at the expense of the average and pathological elements in society.

The eugenics of Bryn and Alette Schreiner was part of a broader argument for social reform in which biological, social and cultural issues were combined. In the years around World War I, they seem to have advocated views based on a similar understanding of the relationship between biology and culture. First and foremost, they wanted a society in which all people could develop their potential, but both saw the weeding out of lower human elements as a necessary aspect of this main project. In the 1920s, however, Halfdan Bryn moved towards a worldview that was far more biologically deterministic than Alette Schreiner's. He began to describe cultural progress as mainly determined by biological evolution. Central to the racial ideology that Bryn advocated with increasing single-mindedness was the idea of a convergence between the social structure, a cultural hierarchy and the biological quality of the human 'material'. This idea was less important to Alette. She doubted the existence of an exact concurrence between social stratification and genetic quality, but she agreed with Bryn about the existence of genetically inferior 'dregs' at the bottom of society and the threat they posed.

The main difference between Bryn and Alette, however, is the importance they ascribed to anthropological race differences. The idea of racial inequality became more and more the cornerstone of Halfdan Bryn's worldview. Alette Schreiner also believed that the races were unequal, but this was not a leitmotif of her outlook on society; above all, the superiority of the Nordic race was not an important building block of her worldview. She assumed that the superior individuals were those who propelled progress. These people were the result of happy genetic combinations, and Alette often spoke positively about great genetic variation, in contrast to Bryn's premium on racial purity.

The 'primitives'—'peoples without culture'—played a paradoxical role in the worldviews of both Bryn and Alette Schreiner. The two scientists depicted 'primitives' as backward and stagnant, but idealised them at the same time. Both positive and negative notions derived from the same theory: the 'peoples without culture' existed in equilibrium with their environment. They were perfectly adapted to a certain way of life in which psychological drives, cultural demands, social structure and natural environment all matched. This was the reason, the theory goes, why their cultural development had stopped, and it was also the reason why the primitives lived harmonious lives. Both Alette and Bryn idealised this supposedly harmonious state which they felt was lacking in modern society. Since Bryn presumed that people's psychological dispositions were determined by their race, this meant that he idealised a racially pure society. Human beings could only live in harmony with their biological instincts in a society in which 'the people' coincided with the 'race'. Alette perceived human psychology more as the product of cultural learning. According to her view, human beings lived in a divided world, but this division was caused not just by a tension between social structures and individual biological dispositions, but by tensions within culture itself.

To sum up, both Halfdan Bryn and Alette Schreiner embraced an 'evolutionary' worldview in which different human groups were ranked according to their level of development and in which eugenic measures were necessary to maintain the biological evolution of the human species. However, there were clear distinctions between their approaches: Bryn was preoccupied with the idea of racial differences and racial mixing, and he advocated eugenic measures to uphold the purity of the Nordic race. Alette supported a racial hygiene focused not on 'races', but on individuals with 'inferior' and 'superior' genetic traits. Bryn and Alette owed their differences partly to the distinct biological theories that underpinned each of their worldviews. Alette had a less deterministic view of race and biology, and held that the essence of human evolution was not the struggle for survival between races, but the gradual unfolding of certain universal human potentials. Bryn, on the other hand, argued that culture was determined by race and that cultural progress was driven by the gradual victory of the superior races over the inferior races in the struggle for existence. The difference in their respective approaches did not, however, prevent Bryn and the Schreiners from joining forces in a huge collaborative undertaking to map the racial character of the Norwegian nation.

8. From Collaboration to Conflict: The Racial Survey of 1923-1929

In 1920, Halfdan Bryn and the Schreiners began to collaborate on a large, state-funded anthropological survey of the Norwegian population. The project highlighted many of the scientific and ideological differences between them, and after an initial period of amicable cooperation, their joint undertaking ended in deep and insoluble conflict. This chapter charts the path their relationship took from collaboration to conflict: their initial accord, the causes of their disagreements and the factors that led to the eventual breakdown in their working partnership.

Launching the project

As mentioned in chapter 3, Guldberg had already floated the idea of a national racial survey in 1904. Kristian Emil Schreiner and Bryn, together with the head of the Army Medical Service, General Hans Daae, took up the idea again during World War I. On 17 May 1919, Bryn received a letter from Herman Lundborg suggesting that a joint Scandinavian survey be launched. Bryn seized this opportunity to finally bring the Norwegian plans to fruition and contacted Kristian Emil, who welcomed the idea and

http://dx.doi.org/10.11647/OBP.0051.08

convinced the Norwegian Academy of Science and Letters to help with organisation and funding.[1]

In his application to the Academy, Schreiner argued that the project was important 'by virtue of its significance and Scandinavian nature',[2] and he used the opportunity to give an account of Bryn's recent anthropological investigations. Schreiner later reported to Bryn that this report had aroused positive interest at the meeting.[3] Beyond this, there is nothing in the minutes of the Academy or in the correspondence between Bryn and Schreiner to suggest that the project provoked much discussion at the Academy meeting. It is likely that the Academy's unanimous decision to support it was taken without any questioning of the project's legitimacy or fruitfulness. The racial survey was added to the Academy's budget for the next year and was later approved by the Norwegian Parliament without discussion.[4] Judging from Schreiner's and Bryn's arguments, and the response from the Academy and Parliament, we may conclude that a significant amount of money was granted to this ambituous and costly project because of its 'Scandinavian character' and 'its significance'. There is no precise explanation, however, of why the project was considered significant.

By the time the funds were made available, everything was in place to begin the collection of data. The plans had been approved by the Defence Department, measuring tools had been purchased and data sheets had been printed. Dr Johan Brun and the Anatomy Demonstrator Georg Wåler had been trained in anthropometric techniques so that they could assist Bryn and Schreiner. The measurements were conducted during the summers of 1920 and 1921, and those surveyed included all Norwegian recruits turning 21 in the designated year. The data were organised geographically according to where the recruits' parents were born. Thus, according to Schreiner, the survey showed the distribution of the population in the year 1869, not 1920, and permitted extrapolation to the population distribution before industrialisation

---

1   Vitak (Vitak: The National Archives in Oslo/Riksarkivet): Protokoll, 1 October 1919.
2   Vitak, no. 218, 27 October 1919. Letter from K. E. Schreiner to the Norwegian Academy of Science and Letters.
3   Bryn's archive: Schreiner to Bryn, 4 October 1919.
4   St forh. 6A: Indst. S. XXVI, 1920 and Inst. S. XXVI, 1921.

and mass migration had disrupted the traditional patterns of settlement. In addition to the survey of army recruits, more detailed studies were carried out in selected districts. The populations of Hålandsdal and Eidfjord in Hordaland, as well as Valle in Setesdal were surveyed, as these places were thought to be the ancestral homelands of the long-skulled blond race. Likewise, Luster and Hafslo in Sogn were studied since they were considered to be the core areas of inhabitation by the dark short skulls.[5] Lastly, the Sea Sami population of Hellemo in the community of Tysfjord in Nordland was investigated (see Figs. 17 and 18). These regional studies were meant to supplement the data from the survey of the recruits, for they also recorded family relationships and included children, youths and women.[6]

The collection of data seems to have unfolded according to plan, and collaboration on the analysis of the data worked well until the middle of the decade. Although disagreements arose during the project on a number of methodological and theoretical questions, both Halfdan Bryn and the Schreiners recognised the need to respect each other's professional position. They regarded each other's points of view as scientifically valid and agreed that potential areas of conflict could be resolved through scientific research.

Towards the end of the 1920s, however, it became clear that research alone would not suffice to resolve their disagreements. Professional and political debates on the question of race had become progressively more polarised, and it was increasingly evident that methodological and theoretical divisions were tied to ideological oppositions. The final result was the breakdown of collaboration between the Norwegian anthropologists; a conflict over scientific legitimacy replaced their scholarly conversation.

---

5   The data from Sogn was not published in a monograph, but was used in Alette Schreiner's genetic study 'Zur erblichkeit der Kopfform', *Genetica*, Vol. 5, nos. 5-6 (1923), pp. 385-454, and in K. E. Schreiner, *Anthropological Studies in Sogn*, Skr. D. n. Vidensk. Akad. MN kl. 19 (Oslo: I kommisjon hos Jacob Dybwad, 1951). K. E. Schreiner, *Anthropological Studies in Sogn*, pp. 6, 9.

6   Alette Schreiner, *Anthropologische Lokaluntersuchungen in Norge, Valle, Hålandsdal und Eidfjord*, Skr. D. n. Vidensk. Akad. MN kl. 1929 (Oslo : I kommisjon hos Dybwad, 1930), p. 7; idem, *Anthropologische Lokaluntersuchungen in Norge, Hellemo (Tysfjordlappen)*, Skr. D. n. Vidensk. Akad. MN kl. Oslo 1932 (Oslo: I kommisjon hos Dybwad, 1932).

Fig. 17 A family from the Sami community of Tysfjord. Both the survey of recruits and the studies of localities made use of portraits and anthropological measurements.

Fig. 18 'East Baltic' women from Norway. Although the community of Valle was studied extensively because it was regarded as the untouched heartland of the Nordic race, it turned out that a large number of its women displayed anthropological traits characteristic of the so-called East Baltic race.

Descriptive anthropometry?

Before the survey began, Halfdan Bryn raised the issue of mapping psychological characteristics. He discussed the issue with Lundborg, who had previously dealt with the heritability of traits such as 'endowment, temperament and character' in his research. Lundborg replied that he would not advise the recording of psychological traits, as such data would be unreliable unless long-term observations could be carried out. If one was to collect information on psychological characteristics, he argued, one should limit it to clear cases of psychological superiority or inferiority.[7] Bryn also brought the idea to Kristian Emil Schreiner, who categorically refused to consider it. According to Schreiner, Lundborg's use of concepts such as 'endowment' was a scam; such descriptions of psychological characteristics were only of interest to the researcher himself.[8] Schreiner got his way: the survey was restricted to the measurement of somatic characteristics.

Following the model applied by Gustav Retzius and Carl Fürst in their *Anthropologia suecica,*[9] the scientists prepared a printed form for recording each recruit's somatic data (see Fig. 20). Their discussion of which elements to include in the form and how to make the measurements mainly revolved around the practical feasibility of the undertaking. In addition, they agreed upon the importance of sticking to international standards that would render the data compatible with, and therefore comparable to, data from similar studies elsewhere. The anthropological 'relevance' of certain traits was repeatedly discussed, but the premises of such 'relevance' were never explicitly formulated. It seems that Bryn and the Schreiners designed the project without explicitly considering the underlying theories upon which it was to be based.[10]

---

7   Bryn's archive: Lundborg to Bryn, 25 May 1918.

8   Bryn's archive: K. E. Schreiner to Bryn, 6 March 1918.

9   Gustav Retzius and Carl M. Fürst, *Anthropologia suecica: beiträge zur Anthropologie der Schweden nach den auf Veranstaltung der schwedischen Gesellschaft für Anthropologie und Geographie in den Jahren 1897 und 1898 ausgeführten Erhebungen* (Stockholm: [n. pub.], 1902).

10   Bryn's archive: K. E. Schreiner to Bryn, 29 February 1920, 23 March 1920, 10 April 1920, 17 April 1920, 6 May 1920.

No.	**Somatologisches Beobachtungsblatt**	Untersucher:
Photo. no.		Ort u. Datum:

Name (Vor- u. Familienname):	Alter:	Beruf:

Geburtsort (Gemeinde):	Geb.ort des Vaters	Geb.ort der Mutter

1. Irisfarbe	2. Haarfarbe	3. Körperhöhe	4. Spannweite	5. Sitzhöhe	6. Beinlänge $(3 \div 5)$
7. Größte Länge des Kopfes	8. Größte Breite des Kopfes	9. Jochbogen-breite	10. Unterkiefer-winkelbreite	11. Ohrhöhe des Kopfes	12. Morpholog. Gesichtshöhe
13. $\dfrac{\text{Spannweite}}{\text{Körperhöhe}}$ $\left(\dfrac{4 \times 100}{3}\right)$	14. $\dfrac{\text{Sitzhöhe}}{\text{Körperhöhe}}$ $\left(\dfrac{5 \times 100}{3}\right)$	15. $\dfrac{\text{Spannweite}}{\text{Sitzhöhe}}$ $\left(\dfrac{4 \times 100}{5}\right)$	16. $\dfrac{\text{Beinlänge}}{\text{Sitzhöhe}}$ $\left(\dfrac{6 \times 100}{5}\right)$	17. $\dfrac{\text{Kopfbreite}}{\text{Kopflänge}}$ $\left(\dfrac{8 \times 100}{7}\right)$	18. $\dfrac{\text{Ohrhöhe}}{\text{Kopflänge}}$ $\left(\dfrac{11 \times 100}{7}\right)$
19. $\dfrac{\text{Ohrhöhe}}{\text{Kopfbreite}}$ $\left(\dfrac{11 \times 100}{8}\right)$	20. $\dfrac{\text{Gesichtshöhe}}{\text{Jochbogenbr.}}$ $\left(\dfrac{12 \times 100}{9}\right)$	21. $\dfrac{\text{Unterk. w. br.}}{\text{Jochbogenbr.}}$ $\left(\dfrac{10 \times 100}{9}\right)$			

Fig. 19 The form used to survey recruits.

The final list of characteristics to be covered in the survey included body height, arm span, leg length, angle of the lower jaw, length and width of the head, face length, eye colour, hair colour and ear position (see Fig. 19). These measurements would then be used to calculate size ratios; for example, the length and width of the head was used to calculate the cephalic index, according to which the material was classified into seven further categories ranging from ultrabrachycephalic (extremely short skull) to ultradolichocephalic (extremely long skull). The length of the face and the width of the chin would be employed to calculate the so-called morphologic face index. This, in turn, formed the basis of five groups in a scale from hyperuryprosopy (extremely short face) to hyperleptoprosopy (extremely long face).[11]

Rudolf Martin's *Lehrbuch der Anthropologie* was the main point of reference for the discussion of which traits to include in the study.[12] In his textbook, Martin emphasised that the classificatory relevance of the various traits was unknown and that the collection of data should have a purely descriptive aim. It is reasonable to argue, however, that the apparatus of measuring techniques that Martin prescribed in his *Lehrbuch* was mainly defined by the anthropological research tradition, and was thus the product of the theoretical debates and assumptions that had influenced the discipline throughout its history. A key example is the cephalic index. Invented by Anders Retzius in the 1840s and grounded in specific theories of brain anatomy, it later became a standard tool in the anthropometric toolbox of anthropologists, although the rationale for using it shifted over the years and remained a controversial topic.

The 'traits' that Bryn and the Schreiners chose to scrutinise in their survey were largely determined by the anthropological research tradition as it was expounded in Martin's textbook. A long history of theoretical reasoning and debate lay behind the use of these traits as racial markers, but Kristian Emil and Bryn did not initially discuss the implications: data gathering was considered a simple descriptive undertaking. However, when the statistical processing of the data began, theoretical and methodological problems arose that gave rise to heated discussions.

---

11 Halfdan Bryn and Kristian E. Schreiner, *Die Somatologie der Norweger*, Skr. D. n. Vidensk. Akad. MN kl (Oslo: I kommisjon hos Dybwad, 1929), pp. 2-6.

12 Rudolf Martin, *Lehrbuch der Anthropologie in systematischer Darstellung mit besonderer Berücksichtigung der anthropologischen Methoden* (Jena: Gustav Fischer, 1914).

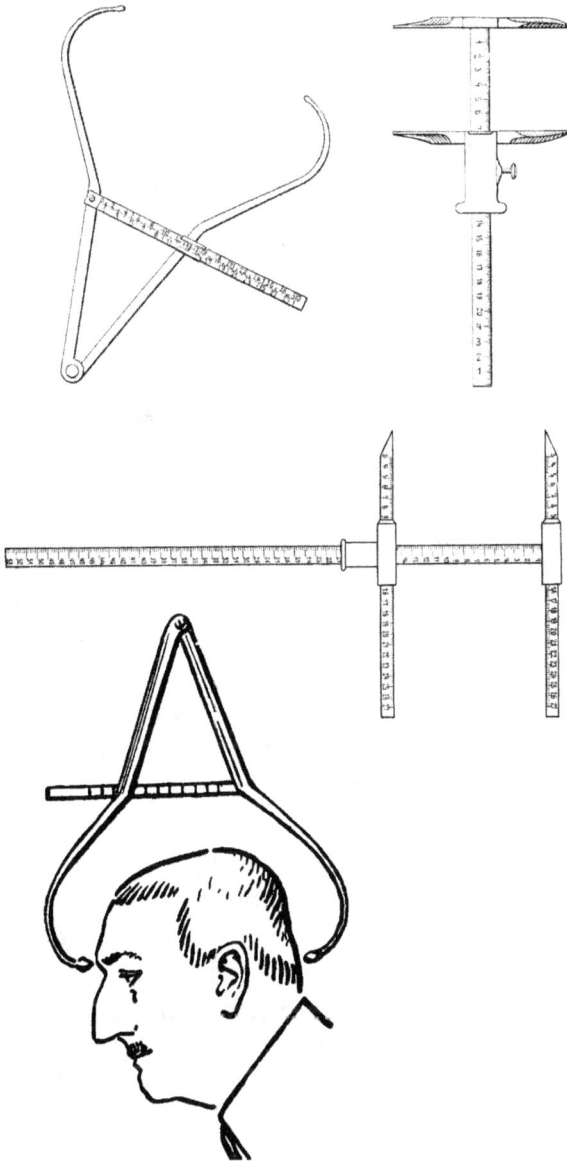

Fig. 20 Various kinds of calipers for the measurement of various parts of the body.

A scholarly debate on the hereditability of the cephalic index

The debate had already begun by the end of the first summer of fieldwork. In 1920-1921, Bryn performed a Mendelian analysis of the heritability of skull shape and eye colour based on data collected from the local communities of Selbu and Tydalen, in the southeastern region of Trøndelag. He concluded that these peoples consisted of three original racial types, each characterised by a typical skull shape: the Alpine were dolichocephalic, the Nordic mesodolichocephalic and the Cro-Magnon brachycephalic. According to Bryn, each skull shape was inherited in Mendelian fashion. It was not the cephalic indices themselves that were inherited, however, but rather their tendency to vary around a central value. Therefore, one of the key premises of Bryn's analysis was that there was a great degree of variability within each inheritable skull form.[13]

In a letter to Bryn dated 2nd December 1920, Alette Schreiner praised his study as the best that had ever been conducted on the inheritability of skull shapes. However, she also pointed out that certain questions remained unanswered, and she doubted the existence of three inheritable skull shapes with such high variability as proposed by Bryn. She suggested that the relationship between inherited Mendelian traits and measurable characteristics was more complex than Bryn had shown: what appeared to be a simple morphological trait might derive from a complicated interaction of numerous Mendelian factors.[14] In a letter to Bryn two weeks later, she wrote that it was not only likely that head shape was 'controlled by several wholly or partly independent [Mendelian] factors', but that it could be influenced by environmental and cultural conditions as well. She argued that the shape of the skull could be related to a number of factors including body height, sex, the overall size of the brain, the relative size of the different parts of the brain, intellectual capacity and individual psychological development in childhood and youth.[15]

---

13 Halfdan Bryn, 'Researches into Anthropological Heredity', *Hereditas*, 1 (1920), pp. 186-212; idem, 'Arvelighetsundersøkelser vedrørende index cephalicus', *Tidsskrift for den Norske Lægeforening*, Vol. 41, no. 10 (1921), pp. 431-52.
14 Bryn's archive: A. Schreiner to H. Bryn, 2 December 1920.
15 Bryn's archive: A. Schreiner to H. Bryn, 19 December 1920.

Alette's arguments touched on the basic premise of Halfdan Bryn's research. He believed he had demonstrated that certain racial characteristics, say dolicocephaly and height, tended to coincide among present-day Norwegians. Bryn took this observation as proof of the past existence of a race of tall, long-skulled inhabitants in the country. Such a conclusion was predicated on the independent heritability of specific racial characteristics. However, if traits such as dolichocephaly were genetically or physiologically related to tallness, Bryn's conclusions would be invalidated. This was precisely what Alette hinted at in her letter.

She went a step further and suggested that perhaps the individual's psychological development in childhood might also affect the size of the brain and thus, indirectly, the shape of the skull. Alette concluded her letter with a postscript asking Bryn to imagine the possibility that a cultured environment and education could affect the brain's development and lead to a more brachycephalic skull shape.[16] Thus, her letter criticised not only Bryn's genetic study of the shape of the head, but the very foundation upon which his anthropological investigations were based. Her concluding remark turned the entire theory of a superior, long-skulled race on its head. Could it be possible that the short-skulled, and not the long-skulled, peoples represented the high point of evolution?

In 1923, the first publication based on the national survey appeared in the Dutch journal *Genetica*. It was a study, by Alette Schreiner, of the heritability of skull shapes and was based on the local case studies that had been carried out as supplements to the survey of conscripts. In the article Alette systematically criticised the use of the cephalic index as a genetic marker. She reviewed the few existing studies on the subject, including the one by Halfdan Bryn, and launched a devastating attack against Bryn's conclusion that brachycephaly, mesocephaly and dolichocephaly were simple traits inherited in a Mendelian fashion.[17] Alette argued that Bryn had oversimplified the issue by attributing a range of variability to the three heritable head types so wide as to make it impossible to distinguish between extreme variants of each type. Bryn's data, she continued, instead pointed to the same conclusion as hers, namely that head shape was controlled by a larger number of Mendelian factors. In addition, she suggested that these

---

16   Bryn's archive: A. Schreiner to H. Bryn, 19 December 1920.
17   Alette Schreiner, 'Zur erblichkeit', pp. 411-13.

factors should not be considered as absolutely determinative, but rather as inherited tendencies that were modified by external and internal conditions during the bodily development of the individual.

In Alette Schreiner's opinion, Broca and other nineteenth-century anthropologists had overestimated the importance of living conditions and lifestyle on skull development. Contemporary anthropology, however, had gone too far in the opposite direction, and a thorough analysis of skull-shape heritability could not be made until all the complex issues concerning the ontogenesis of the brain and skull had been explored.[18] Furthermore, she claimed that the causes of skull length and width were so complex that the cephalic index, the most important trait studied by anthropologists, was useless as a tool to explore the issues of heritability and race. The popularity of the cephalic index was due not to its scientific value, but to the fact that it had engendered a classification system of seductive simplicity. People had forgotten that it was actually an artificially constructed concept.[19]

At the end of the article, she raised the question of why the European population had become increasingly short-skulled since the Iron Age. This question had first been asked and discussed in the latter part of the nineteenth century, when anthropologists became aware of a discrepancy between the overwhelmingly dolichocephalic skulls from South-German Iron Age burial mounds and the overwhelmingly brachycephalic character of the present-day South-German population. There were two main and competing explanations for the phenomenon. Some argued that Central Europe had been the home of an original, short-skulled Slavic population that had survived when the Germanics invaded. They had adopted a Germanic language and mixed with the invaders. Over the centuries, the brachycephalic part of the population had procreated at a higher rate than the dolichocephalics and ended up as the dominant element. Lapouge was among those who advocated this view. The other explanation was that the cephalic index of the original dolichocephalic population had changed as the populaton became more civilised. The growth of the brain led to a more globular skull shape, and thus to a higher cephalic index.[20] It may not be

---

18 Schreiner, 'Zur erblichkeit', p. 449 and passim.

19 Ibid., pp. 444-45.

20 There are many references to this debate in Norwegian anthropological literature. My account is mainly based on Gustav Retzius, 'Blick på den fysiska

surprising that Bryn was in favour of the former explanation, while Alette supported the latter. Cultural development had led to a rounder skull shape, she argued, adding that there was certainly no reason to interpret this trend towards brachycephalisation as a sign of 'degeneration'.[21]

Alette disagreed with Bryn on key scientific questions and criticised his methodology, but this does not mean she questioned his scientific credentials or regarded him as a pseudo-scientist. In the letter of 1921 in which she suggested that brachycephaly could be sign of intellectual superiority, she also wrote that Norwegian anthropology would benefit if Bryn moved to the capital. 'We are getting nothing done, and Kristian is sick and tired at the moment. It would be helpful for us to talk to you in peace sometime'. Elsewhere in the same letter she wrote in general terms about the need for scientists to work together and talk with each other: '[...] one should make use of each other as much as possible; that is what can help us reach the truth'.[22]

She went on to write of their common acquaintance Andreas Hansen, about whom she had ambivalent feelings. 'Though he may be the most gifted of all of us', she still considered him to be 'rather superficial and dogmatic'. She admitted to being somewhat impressed by him, but she also referred to Ole Solberg's criticism of Hansen for holding 'muddled ideas', for lacking 'thorough expertise and education' and for having no respect for educated experts. The message of Alette's letter seems to be that scientific progress depends upon collaboration and open debate based on mutual respect between people with the proper 'expertise and education'. Her confident and friendly tone suggests that despite their differences, she considered Bryn among those with 'knowledge and education'. On the other hand, her sceptical attitude to Hansen's scientific credibility could be taken as an indirect critique of Bryn, since Hansen was Bryn's collaborator and the original source of many of Bryn's scientific ideas.

The relationship between Kristian Emil Schreiner and Halfdan Bryn seems to have been good until the mid-1920s. All evidence suggests that

antropologiens historia', *Ymer*, Vol. 16, no. 4 (1896), pp. 240-41; Gaston Backman, 'Den Europeiska rasfrågen ur antropologisk och sociala synspunkter', *Ymer*, Vol. 35, no. 4 (1915), p. 345.

21 Schreiner, 'Zur erblichkeit', p. 449.

22 Bryn's archive: Alette Schreiner to Bryn, 19 December 1920.

the Kristiania professor considered the Trondheim army doctor a valuable colleague. Following World War I, Schreiner used his academic network and influence in the capital to provide research funding for the provincial Bryn, helping him to obtain a grant from the Nansen Foundation and supporting the publication of his articles in the journal of the Norwegian Academy of Science and Letters. He even let Bryn use the Department of Anatomy's anthropometric measuring tools. As late as 1924, Bryn still received letters signed, 'your devoted Kristian Emil Schreiner, with best regards from my wife'.[23]

From collaboration to conflict

The clear scientific and ideological differences between Bryn and the two Schreiners had direct implications for their project. Alette Schreiner used data from the studies to support her critique of Bryn's ideas on the heritability of skull shapes and to refute key elements of the theory upon which Bryn based both his research methods and his racial ideology. Nevertheless, these differences do not appear to have been an obstacle to fruitful collaboration until the mid-1920s. Both parties considered their disagreements to be scientific matters that could and should be solved with the help of scientific research and scholarly debate. The project was severely delayed, however, and only completed in 1929. By then, their scholarly communication had come to a halt, and the efforts to analyse and publish the data of the conscript survey had led to an intense quarrel, both professional and personal, in which the scientific credibility of the participants was at stake.

During the 1920s, the Department of Anatomy was reorganised and the number of students increased. Kristian Emil Schreiner began to feel burdened by his duties as head of the department. In 1921 he suffered a bout of depression that required hospitalisation, and in 1924 Georg Wåler, Schreiner's co-worker at the department, fell ill as well. This meant that their analysis of the survey data had to be temporarily abandoned.[24]

---

23 Bryn's archive: Schreiner to Bryn, 11 December 1917, 6 February 1917, 6 March 1918, 25 September 1918, 4 October 1919, 10 October 1920, 12 April 1920, 5 April 1922, 15 October 1922 and 31 March 1924. Quotation from Schreiner's letter to Bryn, 18 January 1924.
24 C.M. Fürst's archive: K. E. Schreiner to Fürst, 13 June 21; Bryn's archive: Alette

Not only was Schreiner's research set back, he was also slow to respond to letters from Bryn, who was in Trondheim working on his part of the project. Despite this, Bryn managed to complete the analysis of data from eastern Norway and to publish it in 1925 as part of the proceedings of the Norwegian Academy of Sciences and Letters in a volume entitled *Antropologia Norvegica I*. Moreover, the Swedish survey was also completed long before Schreiner had finished his part of the project. Bryn was in fact hired by the Institute for Racial Biology in Uppsala to help conclude *The Racial Character of the Swedish Nation*, which was published in 1926.[25] This work received international attention as one of the most comprehensive studies of its kind and was published a year later in German as well as in a Swedish-language short version.[26]

Following the Swedish publication, Schreiner wrote to his Swedish friend and colleague Carl M. Fürst: 'Hopefully it will not be long before our survey will see the light of day. It will not be anything as grand as Lundborg's, but just a modest affair that can provide a basis for further research'.[27] Schreiner had toned down his expectations because the data analysis had run into a number of time-consuming problems. Additional money had to be requested from a government research fund to complete the statistical analyses.[28] The technical problems that caused the delay resulted partly from Halfdan Bryn's sloppy work and partly from scientific disagreements between Schreiner and Bryn. This finally resulted in open conflict. Early in 1928, Schreiner wrote a letter to Bryn arguing that the figures on arm span had to be omitted from the final publication as he had discovered systematic differences between the figures from the regions surveyed by Bryn and the rest of the study. He pointed out further technical errors in Bryn's work, including trivial mathematical errors in several tables. The errors had multiplied throughout the analyses and

Schreiner to Bryn, 1 February 1921; K. E. Schreiner to Bryn, 31 January 1923, 18 January 1924, letter no. 43, 1924 [partly undated].

25 Among the letters from Schreiner there is also a list of questions concerning the project that Bryn had sent to Schreiner in the period 1923-1925; he received no reply. C. M. Fürst's archive: Schreiner to Fürst, 20 December 1926; Bryn's archive: sections of *The Racial Character of the Swedish Nation* with a note by Bryn indicating that he is the author of part of the manuscript.

26 Gunnar Broberg and Mattias Tydén, *Oönskade i folkhemmet. Rashygien och Steriliseringar i Sverige* (Stockholm: Gidlund, 1991), p. 42.

27 C. M. Fürst's archive: Schreiner to Fürst, 4 April 1927.

28 Bryn's archive: K. E. Schreiner to Bryn, 11 September 1925, 14 September 1926 and 21 September 1926.

led to a lot of extra work. Schreiner suggested that the scope of the project should be reduced, but he still hoped that 'despite all its imperfections,' it would present an interesting overview and stimulate further research. He also suggested replacing the planned concluding chapter with a summary written by himself.[29]

Bryn was highly provoked by Schreiner's proposal and drafted two replies. In one of them, he wrote: 'To be honest, I find it hard to reply to your last letter, as I believe you deliberately tried to offend me'. In the second, he wrote: 'When we started this huge undertaking at my suggestion in 1919, it was on the explicit assumption that we would stand on an equal footing. There would not be a superior and a subordinate'.[30] Schreiner replied that he had not intended to deprive Bryn of any credit, and said he would withdraw the suggestion if Bryn felt that he was being bullied. He wrote that he had made the suggestion because he 'considered collaboration—in the full sense of the word—as not practicable, both because we lack the opportunity to meet to talk things over, and because we have very different views on many issues'.[31]

The dispute ended with the work being published with neither a summary nor a conclusion as a final chapter, and with a title altered from *Antropologia Norvegica* to the less ambitious *Die Somatologie der Norweger* (see Figs. 21 and 22). The additional work had overrun the budget, which meant that Bryn and Schreiner had to exclude some of the data as well as cover some of the additional costs out of their own pockets.

Bryn and Schreiner assessed the conflict quite differently. Bryn, who had already published his conclusions in *Antropologia Norvegica I*, was both aggrieved and angered by his colleague's criticism. A barrage of letters followed in which Schreiner—in polite terms—accused Bryn of negligence and professional incompetence, while Bryn—in less diplomatic terms—accused Schreiner of bullying him and of trying to take control of the project and steal credit for the work. Both interpretations of the dispute seem reasonable, but the fundamental explaination for the breakdown of their cooperation was that, technical errors apart, they did not agree on the interpretation of the data and the conclusion of the study.

---

29 Bryn's archive: K. E. Schreiner to Bryn, 2 January 1928 and 2 February 1928.
30 Bryn's archive: Bryn's drafts of two replies, 6 February 1928 and 11 February 1928.
31 Bryn's archive: Schreiner to Bryn, 19 February 1928.

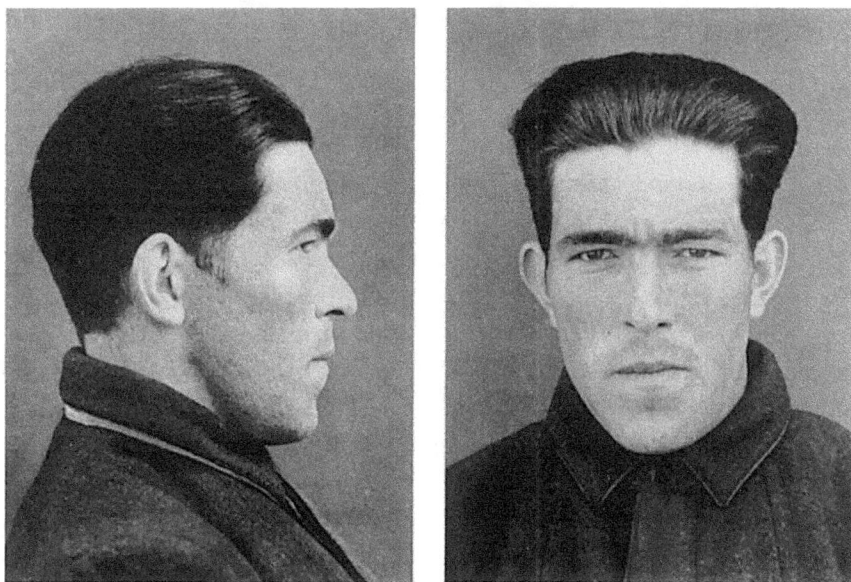

Fig. 21 Alpine racial type depicted in Kristian Emil Schreiner, *Bidrag til Rogalands Antropologi* (1941). According to Schreiner, this man from Ryfylke was a textbook example of a dark short skull belonging to the Alpine race.

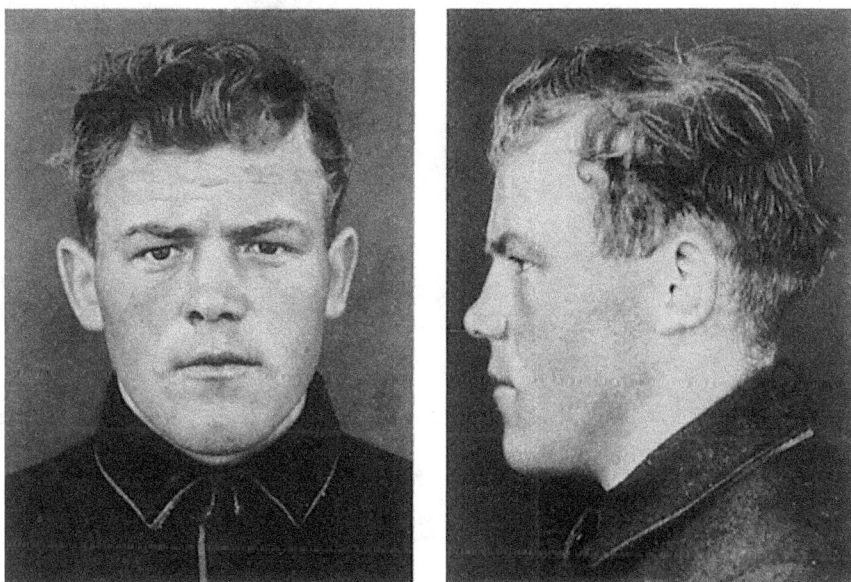

Fig. 22 A pure or mixed racial type? According to Kristian Emil Schreiner, this recruit was a typical representative of the blond brachycephalic population of southwestern Norway. Schreiner dismissed Hansen's description of these people as mixed-race, proposing instead that they represented a local instance of the 'East Baltic race', an ethnicity otherwise dominant in Russia and Finland.

A dispute over the classification of eye colour and hair colour

During the years of collaboration, two themes increasingly marked the correspondence between Bryn and Schreiner: the question of the classification of eye colour and hair colour, and the applicability of arm span as a criterion for classification. Hair colour was recorded by comparing the recruit's hair with a set of hair samples that had been developed by Eugen Fischer and were referred to as the 'Fischer *Haarfarbentafel*'. This tool consisted of 26 bundles of cellulose fibres that had been coated with non-fading colours and fitted together like a handy little 'palette' (see Fig. 23b). The colours were supposed to be representative of every hair colour that existed within humankind. In Fischer's system, each of the 26 colours had a number, the light colours taking high numbers and the dark low ones. The hair colour of the recruit was classified by correspondence with the different hair samples, and the numbers were noted on the registration form. Eye colour was classified in a similar way using a similar tool developed by Rudolf Martin, a 'palette' consisting of sixteen glass eyes (see Fig. 23a).

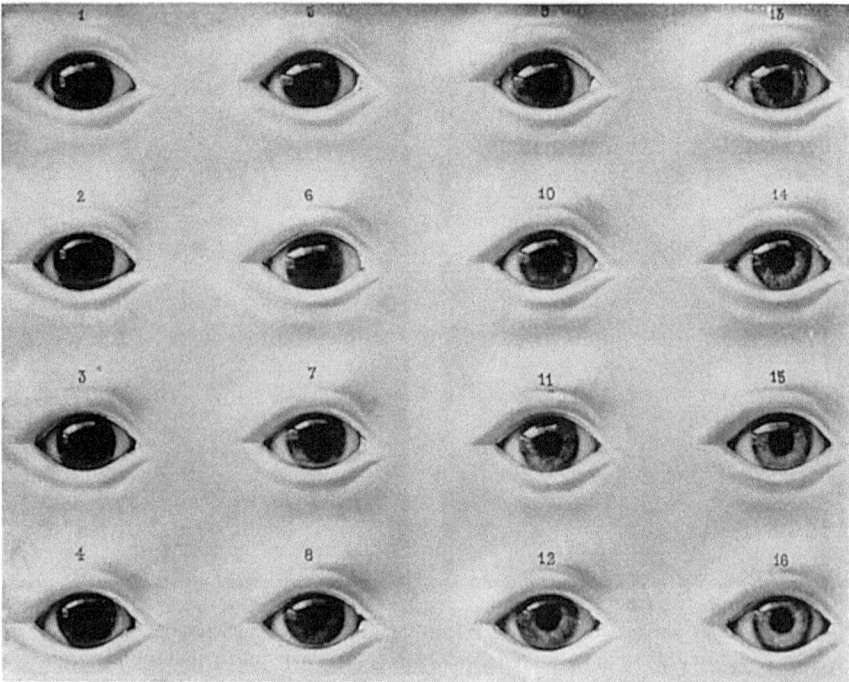

Fig. 23a Martin's eye colour chart.

Fig. 23b Fischer's hair colour palette.

But when the data were collected and ready to be analysed, it proved impossible to use the large number of categories that Martin and Fischer's systems encompassed. The question was which categories should be merged. Eye colour was a major topic. Where was the boundary between brown and mottled eyes? In 1923 Schreiner wrote to Bryn: 'I am not very fond of placing the distinction between 5 and 6, because many 6-eyes in my material from northern Norway undoubtedly contain more pigment than many 5-eyes from the west coast; it is only the concentration of the pupil in 6-eyes that gives them a lighter colour. For these reasons, I would prefer to set the limit for brown eyes at 6 (like Martin does)'.[32]

A similar problem appeared when the hair colours were to be grouped. The question was where the boundary should be drawn between brown and blond. According to Fischer, 7 was 'light brown' and 8 'dark blond',[33] and Schreiner argued in favour of this measurement. Bryn wanted to set the border between 6 and 7, however, defining 'blond' more broadly and brown more narrowly than Schreiner.[34]

This discussion continued until the book went to press. While preparations for printing were in full swing, Schreiner wrote to Bryn: 'I am very surprised to see that you denote Martin 13 and 14 as dark blue. Martin himself describes 13 as light grey, which it actually is. Both Wåler

---

32 Bryn's archive: Schreiner to Bryn, 9 March 1923.
33 Rudolf Martin, *Lehrbuch der Anthropologie*, p. 212.
34 Bryn's archive: Schreiner to Bryn, 17 May 22.

and I have in our records classified the dark blue colour as 15'.[35] The matter ended, however, with the adoption of Bryn's definition of blue eyes.[36]

Homo cæsius nidarosiensis

Bryn was internationally acknowledged for his research on the classification and inheritance of Norwegian eye types. By 1920, he had already published his first work on the topic in the journal of the Norwegian Medical Association and in the Swedish-based international journal *Hereditas*.[37] Between 1923 and 1925 he did further research in this field, resulting in the extensive treatise *On eye types in Norway and their heredity* (*Über die Augentypen in Norwegen und ihre Vererbungsverhältnisse*). This was published by the Norwegian Academy of Science and Letters in Oslo in 1926 and extensively cited in the second edition of Rudolf Martin's textbook on anthropology, issued the same year.[38]

Why was Bryn so passionate about this subject? In his 1930 thesis *Homo cæsius*, he showed that the type of eyes which Martin had identified as nos. 13-14 appeared with particularly high frequency in the central Norwegian counties of Møre and Trøndelag, whereas there was a higher frequency of Martin-type nos. 15-16 in the southern Telemark and Agder counties. He also claimed that there was a strong correlation between Martin-type nos. 13-14 eye colour and Fischer-type nos. 6-19 hair colour, on the one hand, and between Martin-type nos. 15-16 eye colour and Fischer-type nos. 20-24 hair colour on the other.[39] He argued that these correlations, taken together

---

35 Bryn's archive: Schreiner to Bryn, 26 February 1929: 'Jeg har med den største overraskelse sett at De betegner Martin 13 og 14 som dunkelblau. Martin selv betegner 13 som hellgrau, hvilket den jo også er. Både Wåler og jeg har i våre bestemmelser angitt den mørkeblå farge som 15'.

36 Bryn and Schreiner, *Die Somatologie der Norweger*, p. 6.

37 Halfdan Bryn, 'Arvelighetsundersøkelser. Om arv av øienfarven hos mennesker', *Tidsskrift for den Norske Lægeforening*, Vol. 40, no. 10 (1920), pp. 329-42; idem, 'Researches into Anthropological Heredity. On the Inheritance of Eye Colour in Man. II. The Genetic of Index Cephalicus', *Hereditas*, Vol. 1, no. 2 (1920), pp. 186-212.

38 Halfdan Bryn, *Über die Augentypen in Norwegen und ihre Vererbungsverhältnisse*, Skr. D. n. Vidensk. Akad. MN kl. 1926, no. 9 (Oslo: I kommisjon hos Dybwad, 1926); Rudolf Martin, *Lehrbuch der Anthropologie*, pp. 511-12.

39 Halfdan Bryn, *Homo cæsius*, Skr. D. Kgl. no. Vid. Selsk. (Nidaros: F. Brun 1930), p. 110.

with some other evidence, indicated the existence of two variants of the Nordic race.

Bryn's theory was based on Carl F. Larsen's old claim that the typical inhabitants of Trøndelag had a slightly shorter skull shape and face than was typical for the Nordic race. Bryn had previously explained away Larsen's Trønder type as the product of racial admixture. Now Bryn reinvented the Trønder type, not as a separate race, but as a variety of the Nordic race which he named *Homo cæsius nidarosiensis*, after Nidaros, the old Norse name for Trondheim. In light of this theory, Trøndelag no longer appeared to be the homeland of a 'bastard population', as Bryn had deemed it in his first anthropological thesis, but rather the centre of a separate branch of the Nordic race.

In the book *Der nordische Mensch* (*The Nordic Man*) and in articles in the German and Swedish journals *Volk und Rasse* (*People and Race*) and *Ymer*, Bryn described the presumed mental characteristics of the two variants of the Nordic race.[40] This was based on input from people with local knowledge who had been asked to submit their descriptions of the mentality of people in the North-Trøndelag communities.

He compared their statements with Arbo's descriptions of the typical mindset of the population in those eastern Norwegian districts dominated by the Nordic race. Bryn stressed that this survey was not scientific, but rather a representation of subjective assessments. He concluded nevertheless that the Trøndelag variety was just as intelligent as the eastern Norwegian variety, though they had a different temperament. The Trøndelag type, *Homo cæsius nidarosiensis*, might be a little bit slow, but he was also independent, upright and stubborn, as well as frugal, enlightened, politically interested, righteous, honest, sturdy and steady.[41]

Kristian Emil and Alette Schreiner put forward a different interpretation of the distinctive Trøndelag combination of racial traits. In her analysis of the data from northern Norway, Alette Schreiner maintained that the population in northern Trøndelag and the three northernmost counties was dominated by a specific phenotype, one characterised by a more spherically-shaped head and a longer body than those of the ordinary Nordic race.[42]

40 Halfdan Bryn, 'Den Nordiske rases sjelelige trekk', *Ymer*, Vol. 49, no. 4 (1929), pp. 340-50; idem, 'Seelische Unterschiede zweier Spielformen der nordischen Rasse', *Volk und Rasse*, Vol. 4 (1929), pp. 158-64.
41 Halfdan Bryn, 'Den nordiske rases sjelelige', p. 348.
42 Alette Schreiner, *Die Nord-norweger*, Skr. D. n. Vidensk. Akad. MN kl. (Oslo: i

Alette Schreiner explained this deviation from the Nordic norm as the result both of racial mixing and of the influence of the environment, living conditions and cultural development: the more globular shape of the skull had to do with increased brain size. The base of the skull had not been able to expand to accommodate the growing brain, but the more flexible top of the skull could. Therefore, the classic Nordic long skull had over time developed a rounder shape, thereby altering the cephalic index. This process of change was partly due to the large body size of the population in northern Trøndelag, which called for a greater brain capacity. However, Alette also suggested that it was due to extensive brain growth during adolescence, which was stimulated by a high level of civilisation among the farmers around Trondheimsfjord, possessors of a high social standing since ancient times.[43]

Alette and Kristian Emil Schreiner also reintroduced the blond brachycephal in order to explain the 'somatological' peculiarity of the population of Trøndelag. In his contribution to *Die Somatologie der Norweger*, Kristian Emil described a blond, mesocephalic Trøndelag type with a high, vaulted cranium. He claimed that this combination of traits could not be explained as a mixture of dark, short-skulled and blond, long-skulled races. There also had to be an element of the blond, short-skulled East Baltic race in the population of Trøndelag.[44]

Race or environment?

When discussing the material from Trøndelag, Alette Schreiner and Halfdan Bryn drew on different sets of theories. Both partners based their reasoning on theoretical assumptions that were considered scientifically sound within their discipline. Nevertheless, it is clear that the different choices they made when attempting to explain the bodily characteristics of the Trønder population coincided with differences in their professional and ideological attitudes. Something similar was revealed in the discussions between Bryn and Kristian Emil about urban populations. When planning their survey of recruits, they saw the big towns differently than the rural districts. Since the main goal of the survey was to map a traditional settlement pattern, Bryn

kommisjon hos Dybwad, 1929), pp. 172-74.

43   Ibid.

44   Bryn and Schreiner, *Die somatologie*, pp. 551, 561.

suggested that they concentrate on the countryside and let the populations of Oslo and Bergen be represented by a small sample of individuals with deep historical roots in the towns. Schreiner agreed that it was most important to study the rural areas, but maintained that contemporary data from Oslo and Bergen would be useful, since ongoing processes could be elucidated by comparing immigrants with native townspeople.[45]

Kristian Emil Schreiner's idea may have originated less from his interest in racial classification than from his interest in how the social and material environment affected physical growth. During World War I, he and Alette cooperated with the municipal medical officer Carl Schiøtz on an extensive survey of height and weight among schoolchildren in Oslo.[46] The goal was to study how nutrition and living conditions influenced their physical development. Schreiner's survey resembles similar German projects led by Rudolf Martin to study the effect of wartime food shortages on the physical development of children. Schreiner's idea of comparing immigrants with established townspeople may have had to do with his interest in the health effects of differences in living conditions and lifestyles between urban and rural areas. If so, he shared this interest with Halfdan Bryn, who, as already noted, had a very pessimistic view of the effects of urban living.

Concern about the deteriorating effects of city life was widespread among contemporaries of Bryn and the Schreiners. This was rooted in an often harsh reality: overcrowding, disease and malnutrition among the urban poor were major problems. In public debates, however, these problems were often related to a general criticism of 'modern' society and a fear of cultural and biological degeneration. Conservative nationalism was frequently coupled with anti-urbanism. In addition, many eugenicists saw the city as an arena of racial decline. Eugen Fischer's previously-quoted speech on anthropology and eugenics exemplifies this view. He maintained that the city tore apart families and social ties and led to racial mixing and degeneration. This type of thinking is an important background factor in the dispute that arose between Bryn and Kristian Emil Schreiner when they began analysing the data from Bergen and Oslo.

In both *Antropologia Norvegica I* and *Die Somatologie der Norweger*, Bryn claimed that the distribution of racial traits in the population of Oslo confirmed Otto Ammon's law stating that the dynamic Nordic race had

---

45   Bryn's archive: K. E. Schreiner to Bryn, 17 April 1920.
46   Ola T. Alsvik, *'Friskere, sterkere, større, renere': Om Carl Schiøtz og helsearbeidet for norske skolebarn* (Master's thesis, University of Oslo, 1991).

a nature-given tendency to migrate to the city.[47] Bryn once again based his arguments on an analysis of the distribution of eye and hair colour, in addition to arm span, and on the assumed existence of a *Homo cæsius nidarosiensis*. Bryn's theory of a Trøndelag variety of the Nordic race implied a correlation between dark blue eyes and short arm span. This combination of traits had its centre of radiation in Trøndelag, he maintained, and it could be followed like a broad stream through the eastern Norwegian valley of Gudbrandsdalen and all the way down to Oslo. Dark blue eyes and short arm span were also more common in Oslo than among the average national population, a fact Bryn explained by pointing to a great influx of Nordic racial elements into Oslo. The migration to the capital was a process of social selection, according to Bryn.[48]

Bryn ran into a major problem, however. The survey showed that the population of Oslo had a shorter average body height than the total national population. This did not fit well with the notion of Oslo as a stronghold of the tall Nordic race. Bryn resolved the difficulty by claiming that the high frequency of short-statured people was the product of bad living conditions in the capital, conditions which prevented inhabitants from fulfilling their racial potential. He pointed to the fact that newly-settled residents were taller than the native city-dwellers, and to a strong statistical relationship between social status and body length. Members of the higher social strata were in general taller than average, both because the Nordic race was overrepresented due to social selection and because good living conditions had allowed them to develop their full potential for bodily growth. Short body height among the lower strata, on the other hand, was due to bad living conditions.[49] Bryn's analysis implied that Oslo attracted the best racial elements, but offered unfavourable living conditions for its immigrants.

In his treatment of the data from Bergen, Kristian Emil argued against Bryn's hypothesis. He asserted that the claim of a correlation between short arm span and dark blue eyes was unfounded, and pointed to the fact that the Bergen population also had a short average arm span, despite its racial

47 Halfdan Bryn and Kristian E. Schreiner, *Die Somatologie der Norweger*, Skr. D. n. Vidensk. Akad. MN kl (Oslo: I kommisjon hos Dybwad, 1929), p. 334: '[...] und diese psychischen Eigentûmlichheiten äussern sich bald in Zufriedenheit mit den bestehenden Lebensbedingungen, bald in unzufriedenheit mit ihnen, und dies führt dann das Bedürfnis mit sich, sich anderswo zu versuchen'.

48 Bryn and Schreiner, *Die Somatologie der Norweger*, p. 342.

49 Ibid., pp. 337-38.

composition being very different to Oslo's. Therefore, he reasoned, racial composition could not explain low average arm span. The explanation had to lie in the influence of the urban environment. An urban lifestyle led to weakened growth in muscles of the back and shoulders. Urban dwellers had narrow shoulders and therefore relatively short arm spans.[50] Thus, while Bryn interpreted short arm span as indicative of short arms and as a characteristic racial trait of the Nordic race, Schreiner saw short arm span as indicative of narrow shoulders resulting from an urban lifestyle. Both these interpretations were based on data from the same survey, and they were published in different chapters of the same book. It is not surprising, then, that their authors had difficulty agreeing on the content of the concluding chapter.

Was Bryn an imposter?

Bryn's interpretations of the data from the survey confirmed many of his preconceived ideas. Both his theory of *Homo cæsius nidarosiensis* and his analysis of the racial composition of the population of Oslo seem to have strengthened his growing faith in the gospel of the Nordic race. Moreover, Kristian Emil Schreiner was correct in accusing Bryn of inconsistency, calculation errors, inaccuracies and weak reasoning.[51] Does this mean that Bryn consciously manipulated the figures in order to confirm his ideological convictions?

It is easy to find examples of sloppiness in Bryn's work, both in his overall analysis and in its particulars. His lack of attention to detail may partly explain the impressive rate at which he published scientific results. The treatise *The Anthropology of Troms County* (*Troms fylkes antropologi*) demonstrates his carelessness. Some of the correlations he claimed to have discovered between racial traits were simply wrong, and his graphical representations of the findings did not always match the figures that they were supposed to represent, though they often fit Bryn's theories well.[52] This does not

---

50 Ibid., pp. 478-84.

51 An example of Schreiner's critique: on p. 521 in *Die Somatologie der Norweger*, Kristian Emil Schreiner dismisses Bryn's description and analysis of the racial composition of the population of Møre county, claiming that Bryn's previous research on the distribution of eye and hair colour deviates significantly from the findings in the conscript survey.

52 Bryn, *Troms fylkes antropologi*, p. 75, table 44: compare 'bastards' nos. 7-10 with nos. 17-18.

necessarily mean that Bryn deliberately manipulated his data. The errors in the diagrams on bastard types in *The Anthropology of Troms County* served to confirm Bryn's preconceived ideas. On the other hand, the overall analysis in the same thesis was fundamentally flawed in a way that served to undermine Bryn's own arguments. As was explained in chapter 6, Bryn claimed that the population of the county was comprised of three parental races: the Alpine, the Nordic and the Paleoarctic/Lapp. He assembled a series of 'bastard types' which he claimed to have identified in the contemporary population. Then he attempted to estimate the contribution of each of the three original races to the current populace. By calculating the relative frequency of the racial traits of the parental races within the present population, Bryn thought he could reconstruct a prehistoric situation of racially pure populations and estimate their relative size.[53]

He did not stop there, however. Having calculated the contribution from each primordial race to the original population of the country, he also tried to go from the past to the present and recalculate the size of each racial element in the contemporary population. Then, however, he took as his premise the notion that racial traits were inherited according to Mendelian mechanisms. He assumed that certain traits were dominant and others recessive. The results of Bryn's calculation did not match the findings in his survey of the contemporary population. Without being aware of it, Bryn had made a circular argument, though he changed its terms along the way. When moving from the contemporary mixed population back to the pure ancient races, he had not questioned the assumption that some traits were inherited recessively and others dominantly.

The reasoning was flawed, but instead of discovering and correcting his mistakes, Bryn constructed a variety of ad hoc hypotheses to explain the discrepancies he thought he had identified. Among other things, he dismissed the conclusions in his own previous studies of the inheritance of eye colour and skull shape.[54] In *The Anthropology of Troms County*, Bryn criticised himself when making new (erroneous) findings that contradicted his own previous findings.[55] The same torturous reasoning was used to reconcile the calculation errors he made when analysing the figures from the great conscript survey. In *Antropologia Norvegica I*, Bryn himself claimed

---

53   This is a somewhat simplified account of Bryn's method; see Bryn, *Troms fylkes antropologi*, chapters 9 and 10.

54   Halfdan Bryn, *Troms fylkes antropologi*, pp. 97-116.

55   Ibid., p. 107.

that it was difficult to explain some of his figures, which Schreiner later regonised as errors.[56] If Bryn had not made the mistakes, it would have been easier for him to interpret the data. The flaws and errors in Bryn's works should primarily be seen as indicative of inaccuracy, sloppiness and hastiness. His rough working methods, combined with an inclination for high-flown hypothesising and a strong faith in the Nordic dogma, led to the strong one-sidedness in his research. Nevertheless, this does not imply that Bryn was consciously disseminating fraudulent findings.

Dismissing the Nordic idea

In 1929, the year *Die Somatologie der Norweger* was published, Alette Schreiner gave a speech on 'The Philosophy of Life and the Development of Life' (*'Livssyn og livsutvikling'*). This is the earliest source I have found in which she or her husband explicitly discussed the idea of the superiority of the Nordic race.[57] In the speech, she advocated the same kind of evolutionary ideas that had previously been outlined in her popular scientific works. For the first time, however, Alette portrayed Nordicism as a prime example of the kind of evolutionary thinking she dismissed. According to Alette, the essential driving force of evolution was not self-preservation and the struggle for survival, but the *drive towards self-realisation* (*selvutfoldelsesdrift*): there is a general tendency in all biological development, she claimed, towards the emergence of the civilised human being with its 'beautifully vaulted cranium'. If the struggle for life becomes too brutal, the development of life forms lead to evolutionary dead ends; the selective pressure produces species that are increasingly specialised and inflexible and that finally become incapable of adapting to environmental changes. She pointed to the dinosaurs as a prime example; their success in the struggle for survival had turned them into 'monsters of technical perfection', but they had also developed low and narrow braincases that hindered the evolution of their brains. That is why these 'wonderful [...] war machines' finally became extinct.[58]

Alette summed up her line of reasoning by comparing those extinct 'master animals' with the contemporary master race of man:

---

56 Bryns archive: Schreiner to Bryn, 2 February 1928. Schreiner remarks that Bryn himself on page 6 of his book noted that the average figures seemed suspiciously low.

57 Alette Schreiner, 'Livsutvikling og livsanskuelse', *Kirke og kultur* (1929).

58 Ibid., pp. 460-61.

> And we should erect a monument to them [the dinosaurs], we the Nordic
> peoples, who are imbued with so much of their spirit. Maybe it is the Nordic
> race—the master race of the blue Viking and of warrior blood, praised by
> poets and others as the most glorious product of the struggle against a harsh
> environment and the proof of this struggle as the only fruitful means of
> development—who will be the next to run our head against the wall! [59]

Instead of attacking the notion of a warrior-like Nordic race, Alette
Schreiner criticised the very idea of a biological and cultural evolution
driven by the struggle for survival and favouring the kinds of human
abilities that the Nordic race embodied. She compared the Nordic warrior
race to the dinosaurs: perfectly equipped for the struggle for life, but still
an evolutionary dead end. In short, she portrayed the idea of the Nordic
master race as the very negation of the teleological evolutionism upon which
she based her 'philosophy of life'. Three years later, in the popular-scientific
radio-lecture *The Races of Europe*, Kristian Emil Schreiner dismissed the idea
of 'the Nordic man as the sole creator of the highest intellectual culture'. He
also criticised the 'many so-called racial hygienists' who held that 'the real
task of racial hygiene' was to 'cultivate and favour the Nordic race at the
expense of all other types of human beings'. He declared that from a 'scientific
viewpoint', the Nordic race clearly belonged among the superior races, but
that its 'superiority over all other races' had not been 'historically proven'.
The Nordic race was a 'race of warriors and explorers, hardy, enterprising,
independent and adventurous men', but as creators of culture, they lacked
persistence. With regard to such properties, 'the Mediterranean race and the
Oriental races were clearly equivalent to the Nordic'. The 'stabilising and
unifying element' in Western Europe, however, was not these but 'the often
belittled Alpine race', whose strengths were 'unwavering stamina', 'love of
the earth' and 'austerity'.[60]

Nevertheless, according to Kristian Emil, Europe's leadership in the world
was not the product of the mental characteristics of a single race, but of the
'happy interaction of races that had complemented and mutually stimulated
each other. To glorify one race at the expense of others must therefore be
regarded as unscientific'. A scientifically-based racial hygiene should not be

---

59   A. Schreiner, 'Livsutvikling og livsanskuelse', p. 461.
60   Kristian Emil Schreiner, 'Europas menneskeraser', *Universitetets radioforedrag.
     Mennesket som ledd i naturen* (Oslo: [n. pub.], 1932), pp. 143-45.

associated with 'one or the other anthropological race, but with more or less superior and inferior genetic properties that are present in all races'.[61]

Anti-racists?

There is nothing to suggest that in the early 1920s Alette and Kristian Emil Schreiner took a clear stance against the notion of the Nordic master race, nor is there any evidence that they supported the idea. It is more likely that they thought of the racial ideology that Halfdan Bryn advocated as a set of theories and hypotheses that could and should be proved or disproved with the help of science. It is certain, however, that from the late 1920s they took a clear stance against Bryn's racial worldview, which they now regarded and rebutted as unscientific.

It is nevertheless important to note that their position did not amount to a general rejection of the idea of racial hierarchies. In her speech on 'The Philosophy of Life', Alette used arguments predicated upon a hierarchy of races. She claimed that there was a gradual transition between animals and humans with regard to intellectual qualities, and that the brains of white men were more advanced than the brains of 'inferior' human types.[62] In her husband's radio lecture there was also no rejection of the notion of superior and inferior races. Kristian Emil simply said that the Nordic race had to share the top of the racial hierarchy with other equally superior European races.

Alette and Kristian Emil Schreiner were opposed to an ideology that saw racial difference as the central driving force of human history. They also rejected the notion that European races could be placed in a hierarchy. However, neither of them rejected the basic idea of superior and inferior races, and this basic idea continued to influence their research even after their dismissal of Nordicism. *Zur Osteologie der Lappen* was published in the 1930s and, as we saw in the previous chapter, this work was influenced by the idea of Sami racial inferiority. In accepting racial hierarchy as an unproblematic presupposition for their own scientific research, the Schreiners also contributed to its reproduction and legitimisation.

Kristian Emil Schreiner delivered the traditional eulogy in the Norwegian Academy of Science and Letters after Halfdan Bryn's death

---

61 Ibid., pp. 143-45.
62 A. Schreiner, 'Livsutvikling og livsanskuelse', p. 469.

in 1933. In his address Schreiner praised Bryn for his enthusiasm and energy, but noted that his work was not free from the weaknesses of a self-taught man and spoke ironically about Bryn's 'research' on the mental characteristics of the races. Still, there was no great principal difference between their attitudes on this question. Schreiner, like Bryn, referred to traditional assumptions about the mental properties of the races, and even though he often emphasised that these beliefs had not been scientifically tested, he nevertheless implied, on other occasions, that there was scientific evidence for his conception of equally valuable, but still mentally distinct European races.[63]

Like Bryn, both Alette and Kristian Emil accepted the idea of psychological differences between races, and they maintained a set of traditionally-established ideas about the mental characteristics of the various ranked races. It can also be argued that even if they did not support an all-embracing racial ideology based upon the notion of racial inequality, their notions of racial superiority had a real impact on their view of humankind and on their way of acting towards their fellow human beings.

In the preface to the local study undertaken in Tysfjord in Nordland as part of the great racial survey, Alette Schreiner commented on practical problems in the study of the local Sami population (see Fig. 24). She wrote: 'As is often the case with primitive people, most of our Lapps, despite their childlike curiosity and friendliness, were reluctant to submit themselves to an accurate examination, especially when it came to undressing the body'.[64] The problem was mainly that they did not understand the purpose of the survey and therefore did not consider it worthwhile. She continues: 'Using small gifts, it was possible to get most of them to submit themselves to a more or less thorough examination; not infrequently, it was necessary to resort to mild force'.[65] It was probably her notion of the primitiveness of

---

63 K. E. Schreiner, 'Minnetale over divisjonslæge Halfdan Bryn', *Avhandlinger, Det Norske videnskaps-akademi. I MN kl.* 1933; idem, 'Europas menneskeraser', pp. 143-45.

64 Alette Schreiner, *Anthropologische Lokaluntersuchungen in Norge, Hellemo (Tysfjordlappen)*, Skr. D. n. Vidensk. Akad. MN kl. 1932 (Oslo: I kommisjon hos Dybwad, 1932), p. 13: 'Wie es wohl im allgemeinen mit primitiven Menchen der Falle ist, waren unsere Lappen, trotz ihrer kindlichen Neugierde und Freundlichkeit, meistens recht unwillig, sich einer kindlichen Neugierde und Freundlichkeit, meistens recht unwillig, sich einer genauen Untersuchung zu unterwerfen, vor allem insofern dieselbe eine Entblössung des Körpers'.

65 Alette Schreiner, *Anthropologische Lokaluntersuchungen*, p. 13: '[...] nicht selten

the Sami that made her think it was legitimate to use 'mild force' when conducting her investigations. It is difficult to imagine that she would have found it equally legitimate to use 'small gifts' or 'mild force' when she measured nursing students in Oslo for her anthropological thesis on Norwegian women.[66]

Fig. 24 According to Alette Schreiner it was uncommon for the Sami to regard themselves as 'Norwegians'. She maintained that the intellectually superior among them had the most developed Sami ethnic identity. For example, she claimed that the man on the right in this picture (from the Sami community of Tysfjord) 'undoubtedly' had huge amounts of 'Nordic' blood in his veins and that he also had a strong sense of Sami national consciousness. This implies that Alette Schreiner considered ethnic consciousness to be a sign of intellectual superiority, which was in turn associated with racial superiority.

Notions of Sami primitiveness also influenced the way the anatomical institute responded to local protests against the excavations of Sami burial sites. After having excavated the churchyard at Angsnes in Varanger, the excavator, a

---

war es notwendig, zu santter Gewalt zu greifen'. Concerning the Tysfjord survey and Schreiner's attitudes to the Sami, see also Bjørg Evjen, 'Measuring Heads: Physical Anthropological Research in North Norway', in *Acta Borealia* (1997), pp. 3-30.

66 Alette Schreiner, *Anthropologische studien an Norwegische Frauen*, Skr D. n. Vidensk. Selsk. MN kl 1924 (Kristiania: I Kommission bei Jacob Dybwad, 1924).

student named Bjarne Skogsholm, wrote to Schreiner that the Sami were 'ridiculously superstitious' and very dissatisfied with the disturbance of their ancestors' graves. Still, the excavations went ahead.[67]

It is clear that Alette and Kristian Emil Schreiner were not what we would today call 'anti-racists'. Nevertheless, they were opposed to a certain racist ideology which drew its legitimacy from science and which, from the end of the 1920s, became increasingly important politically, first and foremost because of the affinity between the Nordic idea and Nazism.

The breakdown of communication

When the great racial survey was initiated in the early 1920s, Bryn and the two Schreiners had differing views on a number of scientific and ideological questions. Nevertheless, all three seem to have agreed that these types of questions could and should be solved through scientific research. However, when the 'descriptive' data from the survey was about to be analysed, their interpretations were revealed to be in conflict. Contradictory views of the racial composition of the Norwegian people were justified using the same empirical material; their different scientific perspectives were based on, and helped to legitimise, different evolutionary beliefs and worldviews. This does not mean that either Bryn or the Schreiners were consciously manipulating the data to fit their preconceived ideas. The fact is rather that the research they undertook could not provide unambiguous answers to the questions which increasingly divided them. When Bryn and Kristian Emil Schreiner interpreted their data, they chose to draw on different aspects of the range of established theories and knowledge within the physical anthropological tradition of research. The choices they made were influenced by the ideological and cultural implications of the various possible explanatory strategies. Therefore, both parties could use the same 'raw data' to produce dissimilar and internally contradictory scientific knowledge, and they could use this knowledge to legitimise significantly different worldviews.

Despite analysing the same empirical reality using theories, methods and concepts developed within the same physical anthropological tradition,

---

67 Skogsholm's letter cited in Audhild Schanche, *Graver i Ur og Berg: Samisk gravskikk og religion fra forhistorisk til nyere tid* (Karasjok: Davvi Girji, 2001), p. 50.

they still reached contradictory conclusions. The tensions that had existed in the discipline of physical anthropology since the nineteenth century had not subsided, and they continued to exist within the framework of Martin's 'descriptive' anthropology. The great racial survey rekindled many of these divisions. When Bryn and Schreiner began to analyse the collected data, they could draw on different strands of the research tradition. Each could defend his viewpoint using arguments taken from the physical anthropological armoury of methods, theories and already established scientific 'facts'. Thus, both parties confirmed their own worldview using the same empirical material and the same scientific method.

9. Science and Ideology, 1925-1945

The rising tensions between Alette and Kristian Emil Schreiner and Halfdan Bryn were related to changes in their political and scientific surroundings. From the end of the 1920s, the idea of the superior blond race became the object of an increasingly polarised debate in the international scientific world. Dogmatic racial ideas gained support within German anthropology, and advocates of racial inequality and the fear of 'bastardisation' began to dominate the International Federation of Eugenics Organizations (IFEO). Meanwhile, a growing number of geneticists, physical anthropologists, social scientists and humanities scholars in the English-speaking world and in Scandinavia began to question the scientific legitimacy of such ideas. During the 1930s, these tensions were reinforced by the reactions to Nazi-German racism. This chapter shows how the rising conflict between Bryn and the Schreiners was intertwined with the increasingly divisive and politicised debate on race within the scientific world, the racial hygiene movement and society at large.

As we have seen, there is nothing to suggest that the Schreiners actively supported or distanced themselves from the idea of the superior Nordic race in the early 1920s. By the end of the decade, however, they took a clear stance against it and began to brand it as unscientific. Their altered attitude was probably symptomatic of a general change of mood in the Norwegian academic community. The kind of racial thinking that Bryn represented did not encounter very strong opposition in the early 1920s, but it became far more controversial in the early 1930s. Accordingly, Bryn

http://dx.doi.org/10.11647/OBP.0051.09

suffered a loss of scientific prestige in his home country. In Germany, on the other hand, he was more in tune with the prevailing political and academic trends, and there his academic status rose markedly during the same period. The reason was the same in both cases: Bryn's career as a scientist was closely linked to the shifting fortunes of the idea of the Nordic master race. This had a major impact on his relationships with his German and Scandinavian colleagues, as well as on his connection to the international eugenics movement.

Bryn and the conflict over Mjøen's racial hygiene

As we saw in chapter 5, there was no unified eugenics movement in Norway. Jon Alfred Mjøen was in conflict with the University-based experts in genetics and anthropology. Schreiner, Mohr, Vogt and Bonnevie considered Mjøen to be an amateur, and his leading position in the international eugenic movement caused them to abstain from entering the IFEO. Although he shared many of Mjøen's ideas, Halfdan Bryn, unlike Mjøen, was an acknowledged member of the Norwegian academic establishment. Four years after the 'attack' on Mjøen's book on *Racial Hygiene*, Bryn received the University's gold medal for his first anthropological treatise, and, in 1919, he was asked to join the newly founded Norwegian Association for Genetics, an organisation to which Mjøen was denied access.[1] Around the time Bryn accepted this invitation, he also visited Mjøen's private 'laboratory' and broached the subject of collaboration. Mjøen reacted positively and made sure that his friends Alfred Ploetz and Fritz Lenz were aware of Bryn's research.[2] Nevertheless, he also made it clear that Bryn would have to distance himself from Otto Lous Mohr and the two Schreiners before any professional cooperation could begin.

Kristian Emil Schreiner had been involved in the 'attack' on Mjøen's book in 1915. In a newspaper article, he had described Mjøen as a pseudo-scientist who claimed scientific authority to which he was not entitled.[3] In

1   Bryn's archive: letter from the secretary of the Association, Aslaug Sverdrup, to Bryn, 1 December 1919 (letterhead of the University's Zoological Laboratory).
2   Bryn's archive: Mjøen to Bryn, 5 December 1920 and 29 December 1920.
3   Gunnar Broberg and Nils Roll-Hansen (eds.), *Eugenics and the Welfare State* (East Lansing, MI: Michigan State University Press, 1996), p. 156.

a letter to Bryn, Mjøen bemoaned this critique which, in his view, was not scientifically motivated: 'the attack was characteristic of the personalities of those who planned, organised, and carried it out [and] if anything can be characterised as malice and callousness, it is these people's attempt at ruining my life'.[4] Mjøen was convinced that Alette Schreiner was still 'spreading lies' behind his back, and he did not feel able to enter into a trusting relationship with Bryn if he was also collaborating with the Schreiners.[5]

Bryn received two more letters from Mjøen in 1920.[6] Then the correspondence appears to have dried up for many years, which may suggest that Bryn felt pressured into choosing the Schreiners' side in the conflict and dropping his proposed collaboration with Mjøen. If so, this was a strategically wise decision, as working with Mjøen could have disrupted a relationship with the Schreiners that was fundamental to Bryn's professional success; Kristian Emil Schreiner used both his contacts and his prestige to help Bryn with funding and publication.[7]

Rising tensions beneath the surface

In the mid-1920s, it had become clear that Bryn and Kristian Emil were in disagreement on a number of questions related to the great racial survey, but this did not for the moment lead to deeper conflict or open argument. In late August 1925, a conference was arranged in Uppsala and Stockholm with the aim of strengthening Nordic cooperation on racial research. In addition to Halfdan Bryn and the Schreiners, Jon Alfred Mjøen and his wife were invited from Norway. The Schreiners declined to attend, in their own words, due to the heavy workload at the anatomy department. By not attending the conference, however, they also kept their distance from an academic setting in which Mjøen was accepted as a legitimate participant. They furthermore avoided discussions on topics about which they would probably have had fundamentally different opinions to those of Bryn and Lundborg.

---

4 Bryn's archive: Mjøen to Bryn, 10 April 1920.
5 Ibid.
6 Bryn's archive: Mjøen to Bryn, 5 December 1920 and 29 December 1920.
7 See chapter 6.

Two of the thirteen presentations made at the conference were given by Halfdan Bryn. One was on the inheritance of eye colour, a topic that was a source of disagreement between Bryn and Kristian Emil. The other was about the anthropology of eastern Norway and was probably based on *Antropologia Norvegica I*, published that same year. Bryn's papers won great acclaim from Lundborg, who was particularly intrigued by Bryn's analysis of the data from Oslo, an analysis which, as previously noted, would later be criticised by Kristian Emil.

Two items on the programme were aimed at bringing about closer Nordic cooperation. One was a preliminary discussion regarding a proposed organisation of Nordic racial researchers. The other was a speech by the Icelandic professor Gustaf Hannesson, on 'Nordic Measuring Techniques and Nomenclature for Anthropologists'. Hannesson was making anthropological studies of the Icelandic population and had cooperated with Bryn and Lundborg since the early 1920s. He spoke strongly in favour of establishing a common Nordic standard for anthropological measurement and of introducing a shared Nordic terminology.

Hannesson was highly sceptical of Kristian Emil's approach to anthropology, which he found excessively empirical and descriptive. In 1922, he wrote to Bryn that he preferred Bryn's modus operandi to 'Schreiner's method', which was like 'driving out one devil, and letting seven others in'.[8] In a letter written five years later, Hannesson once again expressed doubts about the usefulness of Schreiner's 'meticulous survey of bones'. 'Anthropology must aim at living human beings and their future', he claimed. The discipline should not remain content with measuring only outward physical characteristics; one way or another, psychological properties had to be considered.[9]

The year after the Scandinavian race conference, Mjøen resumed his correspondence with Bryn and informed him that he had been 'attacked' by the American academic William Castle, author of a paper strongly criticising Mjøen's theories on racial mixing (see Fig. 25). Mjøen believed that this incident would usher in a 'permanent' struggle over the issue. Professor Charles Davenport had told Mjøen that 'professor Castle is pugnacious' and that 'he had also attacked Davenport'.[10] Mjøen contacted Bryn because he wanted to refer to Bryn's research in his reply to Castle.

---

8   Bryn's archive: Hannesson to Bryn, 15 February 1922.
9   Bryn's archive: Hannesson to Bryn, 4 December 1927.
10   Bryn's archive: Mjøen to Bryn, 1926 [partly undated].

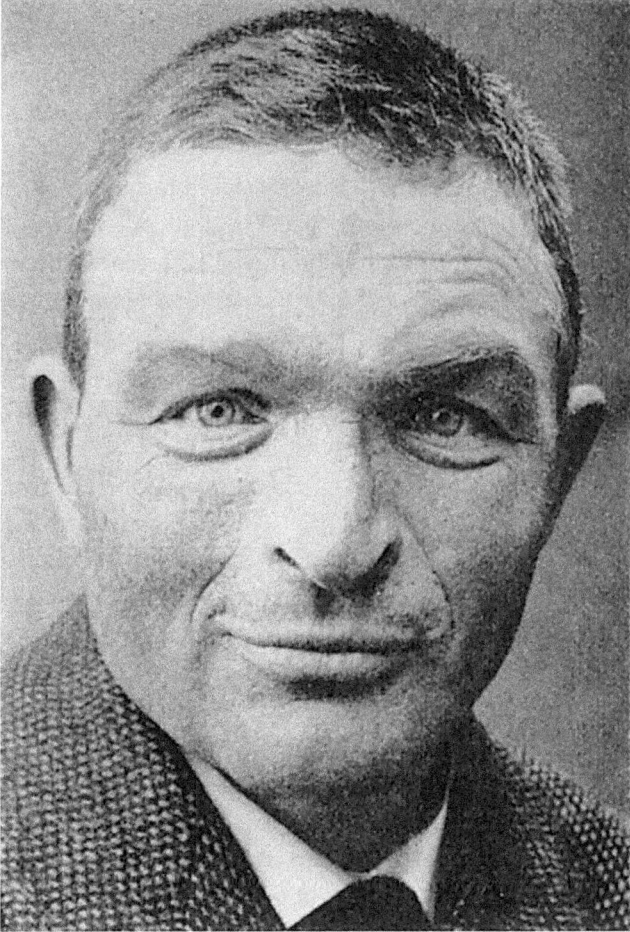

Fig. 25 Racial mixing. Photo from the 1938 edition of Mjøen's book *Racial Hygiene*. The subject is supposed to exemplify a 'Nordic-Lapp mixed type' possessing typical 'bastard' features, such as 'a discordant mentality' and 'poorly developed mental faculties'.

Mjøen's prediction proved to be correct and the struggle became protracted. His adversary had an influential position in American genetics. In 1916, Castle had written the book *Genetics and Eugenics*, which was the most commonly used textbook on the topic at American colleges in the 1920s. He had been one of Davenport's students, but became by the mid-1920s an engaged and profiled critic of the orthodox type of eugenics that Davenport represented. Castle's critique along with those of certain other prominent scientists helped to set the agenda for intensive debates about psychological differences between races and the degenerative effects of racial mixing (see Fig. 26).[11]

In autumn 1927, the IFEO arranged an international congress in Amsterdam at which Davenport was elected president. Under his leadership, racial mixing and psychological differences between races became prioritised fields of study. At the same time, other topics in the field of human genetics and anthropology, which until then had been discussed under the auspices of the IFEO, were taken up by competing institutions. In subsequent years, therefore, the IFEO became increasingly dominated by an explicitly racist style of eugenics.[12]

25 countries were represented at the Amsterdam congress. Kristine Bonnevie, Kristian Emil Schreiner, Jon Alfred Mjøen and his wife came from Norway. This time Bryn cancelled his participation, despite the fact that he was supposed to make a presentation. After the congress, Schreiner reported to Bryn that Mjøen had given a 'terrible' speech on racial mixing. It had been strongly criticised by everyone with whom Schreiner had spoken. Mjøen had invoked Bryn's support and Schreiner thought it was unfortunate the Bryn had not been there to denounce him.[13] However, there is nothing in the letters between Mjøen and Bryn to suggest that Mjøen would have met with any criticism from Bryn if he had indeed attended the congress. Quite the opposite, for Mjøen had the backing he wanted from Bryn in his polemics against Castle.[14]

---

11 Stefan Kühl, *Die Internationale der Rassisten* (Frankfurt am Main: Campus, 1997), p. 75, Daniel J. Kevles, *In the Name of Eugenics* (Berkeley, CA: University of California Press, 1986), p. 68; Elazar Barkan, *The Retreat of Scientific Racism: Changing Concepts of Race in Britain and the United States between the World Wars* (Cambridge: Cambridge University Press, 1992), pp. 143-46, 166, 204.

12 Kühl, *Die Internationale der Rassisten*, pp. 76f., 103-20.

13 Bryn's archive: K. E. Schreiner to Bryn, 7 October 1927.

14 Bryn's archive: Mjøen to Bryn, undated letter, written after 1930.

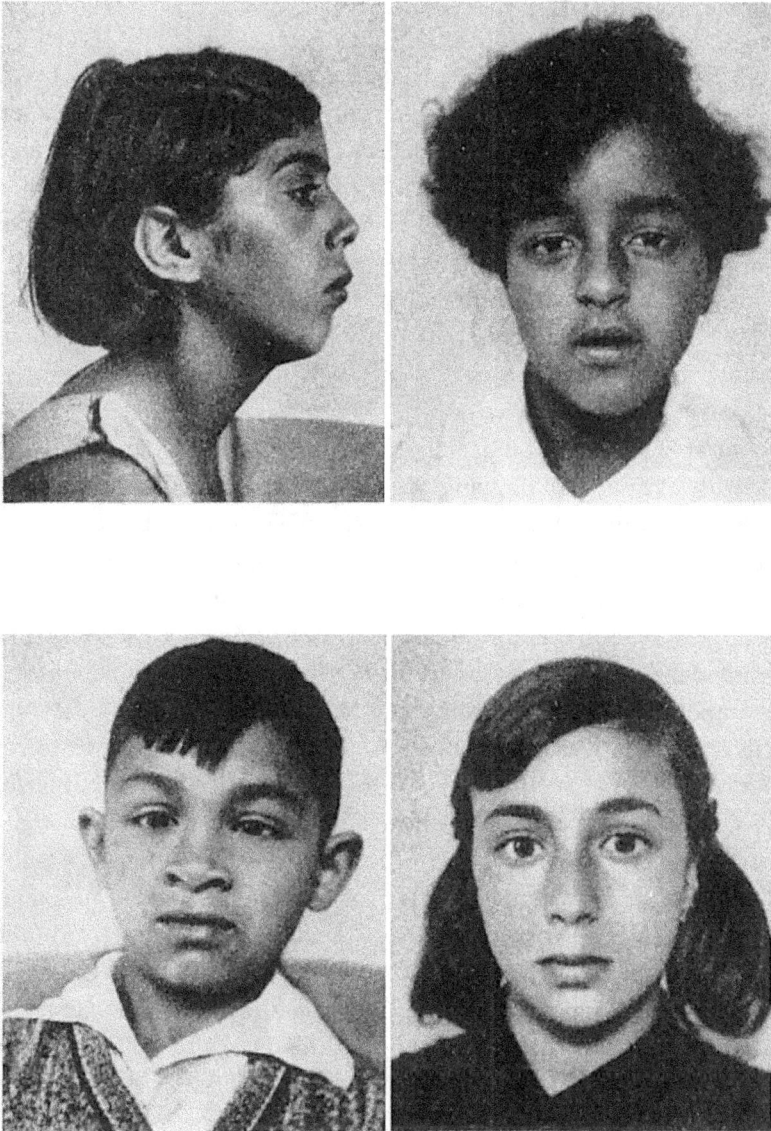

Fig. 26 Racial mixing. The children of German women and the African soldiers who participated in the French occupation of the Rhineland in 1923. Mjøen used them as examples of 'bastards' in his book *Race Hygiene*.[15] At that point, in 1938, the so-called 'Rhineland bastards' had already been sterilised through a campaign led by Eugen Fischer, Hans Günther, Fritz Lenz and Wolfgang Abel.

15   Jon Alfred Mjøen, *Racehygiene* (Oslo: Dybwad, 1914; 2nd ed. 1938).

Tensions reach the surface

Only a few months after the Amsterdam congress the tensions between Bryn and Schreiner moved into open conflict, and soon after Bryn became a public ally of Mjøen. February 1928 saw the total collapse of cooperation on the analysis of the data from the great Norwegian racial survey. Five months later Bryn accepted Mjøen's nomination to become a member of the IFEO,[16] and he was soon a member both of the IFEO and of Mjøen's Consultative Eugenics Commission of Norway.[17] Formally, Bryn entered the IFEO as a representative of the Royal Society of Science in Trondheim. In reality, he was never a particularly active member, and Mjøen paid his membership fees. Bryne nevertheless received a number of requests from the IFEO. Among other things, the organisation tried to establish a worldwide overview of ongoing processes of racial mixing, and asked for an account of Bryn's research on the northern Norwegian 'bastards'. Bryn's response to these inquiries was rather lukewarm.[18]

Mjøen had the largest interest in bringing Bryn into the IFEO. The IFEO was supposed to be a coalition of the foremost organisations and institutions relevant to the field of eugenics. Its leaders saw Mjøen's membership as the most important factor preventing key Norwegian scientists from joining. In this situation, it must have been an advantage for Mjøen to recruit a recognised scientist such as Bryn to the organisation, even though Bryn was a poor substitute for Kristine Bonnevie, who had already turned down a series of offers. The irony is that, by all accounts, Bryn's entry into the IFEO and the Consultative Eugenics Commission of Norway weakened his academic prestige in Norway and made him a less valuable asset for Mjøen.

Kristian Emil Schreiner was also invited to collaborate with the IFEO under Davenport's leadership. In 1930, he received an invitation to an IFEO conference which aimed at establishing a better methodology for research on racial differences in intelligence. At the conference, a committee of psychiatrists and psychologists tried to establish an international standard for the

---

16 Bryn's archive: Mjøen to Bryn, 7 July 1928 and 30 July 1928; a copy of a letter from Mjøen to C. B. Hodson, 11 July 1929.

17 Bryn's archive: Mjøen to Bryn, 7 July 1928, 30 July 1928 and 24 December 1928.

18 Bryn's archive: IFEO-file: a number of letters in which the organisation's secretary complains about Bryn's failure to follow up on the IFEO's initiatives. See: 1 October 1929 and 16 June 1930. Davenport-file: Davenport to Bryn, 28 March 1930 and 26 February 1929. American Philosophical Society Library, B D27 Charles Davenport Papers: IFEO's adm. secr. C. B. S. Hodson to Mjøen, 9 July 1931 and 22 July 1931; Hodson to Bryn, 23 July 1931; Hodson to Davenport, 26 February 1931.

measurement of intelligence, while a committee of physical anthropologists suggested a set of international standards for anthropometric measurements that could then be proposed at an international anthropology conference in Lisbon the same year. In contrast to Lundborg, who was involved in this undertaking, Schreiner refused to participate.[19]

Around the same time as the IFEO conference, Lundborg attempted to persuade Schreiner to organise the planned second Scandinavian conference on racial science in Oslo, but Schreiner had by then lost all interest in efforts at Scandinavian cooperation. One of the reasons was that 'Lundborg's studies and interests', as Schreiner saw them, had become 'more and more distanced from what we normally think of as anthropology'.[20] The Oslo conference was never held, and permanent Nordic cooperation on racial science ended before it began. At this point, Lundborg's academic prestige began to decline in Sweden. His activities received negative reviews in Swedish newspapers. He was about to reach the age of retirement and the struggle over who was to succeed him at the Institute for Racial Biology had started. In 1936 the social democrat, geneticist and anti-racist Gunnar Dahlberg assumed the position, signalling the end of the Nordic race's heyday at the Institute.[21]

Nazism and the Nordic idea

The increasingly polarised scientific debate on race was partly a response to the rise of the Nazi movement in Germany. However, the relationship between National Socialism, racial hygiene, anthropology and 'the Nordic idea' was complex. The critique against dogmatic racism was already on the rise before Nazism became a powerful movement, and ideas that resemble Nazi racial ideology gained a strong foothold in German anthropology well before the Nazi takeover of 1933.

The reorientation of German anthropology was the work of a new generation of scholars who brought new ideas into the discipline. A key representative of this generation was Hans Günther. He had a background as a *völkish* writer. During the 1920s, he became the chief ideologue of the Nordic movement, which combined racial science with right-wing romantic

---

19 American Philosophical Library, B D27 Charles Davenport Papers: Davenport to the General Secretaries, the International Congress of Anthropological and Ethnological Sciences, 22 March 1934; Davenport to K. E. Schreiner, 4 June 1930, 26 June 1930 and 14 July 1930. The IFEO conference was held in Farnham, UK.
20 C. M. Fürst's archive: Schreiner to Fürst, 13 February 1931.
21 Broberg and Roll-Hansen (eds.), *Eugenics*, pp. 91-95.

nationalism and the idolisation of the Nordic race. In the 1930s, he became a professor of anthropology, a member of the Nazi Party and an influential race ideologue of the Third Reich.[22] Günther had strong ties to Scandinavia, and in the early 1920s he cooperated with Bryn, Kristian Emil Schreiner and Lundborg. A closer look at Günther's activities as an ideologue and populariser of science may illuminate the relationship between the Nazi movement, the Nordic idea and physical anthropology in Germany and Scandinavia.

In the 1920s, Günther became well known among the German public for his popular-scientific writings. In 1922, he published the book *Racial Science of the German People (Rassenkunde des deutschen Volkes)*, which soon became a best-seller. It was followed by a series of similar books, such as *Racial Science of the Jewish People (Rassenkunde des judischen Volkes)* and *Racial Science in Europe (Rassenkunde Europas)*. Before 1930, *Racial Science of the German People* had been reprinted in its tenth edition and Günther was so well-known to the German public that the publisher could, in an advertisement from 1929, describe the abridged version of his book as '*Der billige Volks-Günther* (The Affordable Günther For All)'. During the Third Reich, Günther's books on *Rassenkunde* became even more popular.[23]

Publisher J. F. Lehmann had taken the initiative for *Racial Science of the German People*. Allied to Adolf Hitler from the early 1920s, and specialising in popular-scientific literature on race,[24] Lehmann had first tried to persuade Rudolf Martin to write the book, but Martin rejected the proposal because he thought that anthropology was too young and immature a science and the data too insufficient for such a book.[25] Günther did not have a professional background in anthropology when Lehmann approached him. He was a young humanist scholar, a *völkisch* nationalist and author. When he accepted the assignment, Günther began travelling to European anthropological institutions to do research for the book. He thus established an extensive network of anthropologists, and even if Günther's books on *Rassenkunde* were written by an outsider and meant for the general public, they were also read by professionals. This was the first

---

22 George L. Mosse, *The Crisis of German Ideology: Intellectual Origins of the Third Reich* (London: Weidenfeld and Nicolson, 1964), pp. 302ff.

23 Proctor, Robert, 'From *Anthropologie* to *Rassenkunde* in the German Anthropological Tradition', in George W. Stocking, Jr. (ed.), *Bones, Bodies, Behavior* (Madison, WI: University of Wisconsin Press, 1988), pp. 149; Hans F. K. Günther, *Rassenkunde Europas* (München: Lehmanns Verlag, 1929), pp. 344. Mosse, *The Crisis of German Ideology*, pp. 302ff.

24 Mosse, p. 224.

25 Robert Proctor, 'From *Anthropologie* to *Rassenkunde*', p. 149.

systematic attempt at giving an overview of the races of Europe since the publication of Denniker's and Ripley's books at the turn of the century.[26]

Scandinavia held a key position in Günther's worldview: he believed the peninsula to be inhabited by the purest Nordic population in world. Günther had strong personal ties to Scandinavia as well. In 1923, he married a Norwegian woman, Magda ('Maggen') Blom, and settled with her in Norway for a couple of years. In 1925, he moved to Sweden where he worked for Herman Lundborg at the State Institute for Racial Biology and as a freelance researcher and author, before returning to Germany in 1929.[27]

In 1923, the year after the publication of *Racial Science of the German People*, Günther asked Kristian Emil Schreiner for access to research data from Norway. According to letters from Günther to Bryn, Schreiner had given him this data. Günther also claimed that Schreiner, when sending the material, had taken the opportunity to praise Günther's book.[28]

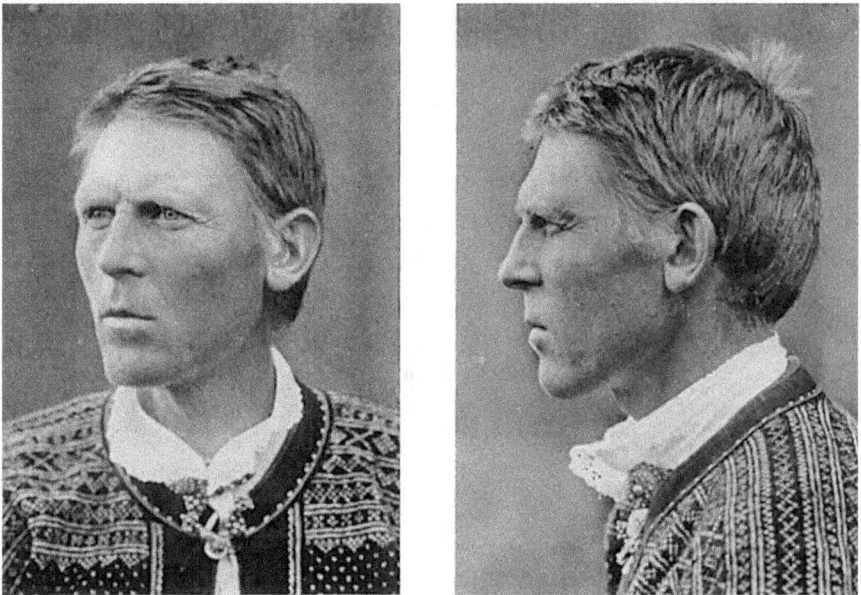

Fig. 27 The Nordic race. When after their survey of recruits, Günther requested a portrait of a purebred Nordic man, neither Schreiner nor Bryn could help him. In 1929, however, Alette Schreiner described this man from the Setesdal valley as a prototypical 'Viking'.

---

26 Ibid.; Mosse, *The Crisis of German ideology*, p. 224.

27 Hans Fredrik Dahl, *En fører blir til* (Oslo: Aschehoug, 1991), pp. 156-57.

28 Bryn's archive: Günther to Bryn, 2 December 1923: '[...] der mir bei Übersendung sehr gütig über mein Buch geschrieben hat [...] den er nach Weihnachten besprechen will'. Günther's *Racial Science of the German People* was published in 1922 and was his first book on anthropology. He was, therefore, most likely referring to this work.

On a later occasion, Günther visited the anatomy department in search for photos of racially pure members of the Nordic race, images he wanted to use in his book (see Fig. 27). After the visit, he commented in a letter to Bryn that he was very pleased to have become acquainted with Schreiner, who had welcomed him at a 'very gracious manner'. The next year, Günther met Bryn in person for the first time, and this was the beginning of a lasting personal friendship.[29] That same year Bryn wrote a positive review of *Racial Science of the German People*.[30]

There is much to suggest that Günther got along well with both Schreiner and Bryn when he met them for the first time in 1923-1924. This changed, however. Early in the 1930s, Mjøen wrote to Bryn that the same people who had once 'organised the attack on me and my laboratory' had now attempted to prevent the publication of a Norwegian version of Günther's book. Mjøen warned Bryn that he should expect opposition from similar quarters.[31] Judging from the context, it is likely that Mjøen believed that Alette and Kristian Emil Schreiner were among those who had obstructed the publication of Günther's book. At the time when Mjøen wrote this letter, Günther was receiving a lot of public attention because of his relationship with the Nazis. In 1931, he accepted a professorship at the University of Jena. His opponents considered this to be a political appointment engineered by the Nazis, winners of the recent local elections. Günther thus became the object of a heated debate in Germany questioning his scientific credentials. This conflict was also reported in the Norwegian newspapers and must have been noted by the Schreiners and the others who had 'organised the attack' on Mjøen. The year after his appointment, in 1932, Günther joined the Nazi Party.[32]

Bryn's German friends

Bryn and Günther, who met often during their summer holidays by the Oslo Fjord, developed a long-lasting, mutually-beneficial friendship. Since

---

29 Bryn's archive: Günther to Bryn, 11 February 1924. Günther describes a visit to Schreiner in Kristiania: 'Der uns sehr liebenswürdig aufgenimen hat und mir sehr Wichtige Dinge geseigt und berichttet hat, Ich freue mich sehr ihn kennen gelernt zu haben'; Günther to Bryn: postcards, 1924.
30 Bryn's archive: Bryn's review of Günther's *Racial Science of the German People*; newspaper clippings of *Trondhjems adresseavis*, 22 March 1924.
31 Bryn's archive: Mjøen to Bryn, undated letter, written after 1930.
32 Bryn's archive: Günther to Bryn, 16 January 1932.

Bryn was already a recognised scientist in the early 1920s, his friendship was an asset to Günther in his attempts to gain academic credibility upon first venturing into the field of racial science. Later on, Günther opened doors for Bryn, providing him with access to the Nordic movement in Germany and even to the German anthropological community.

Günther furthermore saw Bryn as a key collaborator in the quest to spread the gospel of the Nordic race throughout Scandinavia. Günther was a leading member of the *Nordischer Ring*, which was founded in 1926 and which soon became the most important umbrella organisation for the Nordic movement. The organisation had many scientists among its members and was inspired by authors such as the founders of anthroposociology Vacher de Lapouge and Otto Ammon, the *völkisch* racial philosophers Ludwig Schemann and Ludwig Woltmann, the American race thinkers Madison Grant and Lothrop Stoddard, as well as Hans Günther and not least Walter Darré, whose *völkisch* ideas about *Blut und Boden* and Nordic racial purity had a great impact on the Nazis and were instrumental in winning for Darré the post of Minister of Agriculture after Hitler's seizure of power.[33]

The *Nordischer Ring* was part of the *völkisch* movement but had no particular relationship with the Nazis before 1930; at that point, the leaders of the organisation acknowledged that the Nazi Party had become so powerful that any future attempt at propagating the Nordic idea would have to be made in alliance with them. In the following years, Günther, like many other leading members, joined the Party. After 1933, the organisation was incorporated into the Nazi movement, and many of its leading members gained prominent positions in the new regime.[34] Scandinavia, as a place of Nordic racial origin and purity, played an important part in the organisation's ideology, and an effort was made to recruit Scandinavian allies. Günther was the main point of contact with Scandinavia, and his alliance with Bryn was an important asset. Bryn joined the *Nordischer Ring* in 1926 and soon developed an extensive social network of likeminded Germans.[35]

---

33 Nicola Karcher, 'Schirmorganisation der Nordischen Bewegung: Der Nordische Ring und seine Repräsentanten in Norwegen', *NORDEUROPAforum*, Vol. 19, no. 1 (2009), p. 15.

34 Ibid., pp. 19-21.

35 Bryn's archive: Konopacki-Konopath to Bryn, 22 December 1926. This was a standard letter from Hanno Konopacki-Konopath urging the recipient to join the newly-established *Nordischer Ring*. In Bryn's archive there is also a confidential circular to members, from which one can assume that he most likely became a member. See also Karcher, 'Schirmorganisation der Nordischen Bewegung'.

Many of Bryn's German acquaintances belonged to the new generation of anthropologists who took the lead in redefining the discipline from '*Anthropologie*' to '*Rassenkunde*'. One of them was the young anthropologist Egon Freiherr von Eickstedt, a friend of Günther's. In 1925, he began publishing the journal *Archiv für Rassenbilder* with Bryn as one of his contributors. Later von Eickstedt was appointed to a professorship in anthropology in Breslau and became a leading figure in the discipline.[36] Another friend of Bryn's was Bruno Kurt Schultz, an anthropologist, editor at J. F. Lehmann's publishing house and also editor of *Volk und Rasse,* a popular-scientific journal established by Lehmann in 1925 and later incorporated into the Nazi-German propaganda machine. At the end of the Weimar period, Bruno Kurt Schultz was also editing the journals *Verhandlungen der Gesellschaft für physische Anthropologie* and *Anthropologischer Anzeiger.* The year before Hitler's takeover, Schultz became a member of the Nazi Party. During the Third Reich he worked for the *Rassenamt der SS*—the SS Race Office—and was involved in formulating the so-called 'settlement policy' in occupied Eastern Europe, which entailed the ethnic cleansing of local Slavic populations and the settlement of members of the Germanic race.[37]

The rise of Nazism and the destiny of the Nordic idea in Norway

Bruno Kurt Schultz's career is typical of how the relationship between the Nordic idea, German physical anthropology and the Nazi regime developed. The destiny of the scientific idea of the Nordic race became strongly intertwined with its success as a political idea. After the Nazi takeover, *völkisch* and right-wing journals and organisations were integrated into the Nazi movement, and the superior Nordic/Germanic/ Aryan master race became a key element of the ideology of the new regime. The Germanics were seen as the origin and the core of the German nation. This nation had to be purged of all contamination from alien races, and it had a right and a duty to expand, settle new territories and subdue or displace other races. This ideology was combined with an intense hatred of the Jews, the alleged eternal enemy of the Germanics.

---

36 Wilhelm E. Mühlmann, *Geschichte der Anthropologie* (Frankfurt am Main: Athenäum Verlag, 1968), p. 189.

37 Proctor, 'From *Anthropologie* to *Rassenkunde*', pp. 149, 158-61.

Nazi ideology was strongly inspired by Pan-Germanism, by Gustaf Kossinna's archaeological theories, by the idea of the Germanic Aryans, by a racist style of eugenics and by Günther's *Rassenkunde*. Leading Nazis wanted to establish a Great Germania, which was to include all peoples of Germanic origin. This Germanic empire was meant to expand at the expense of inferior peoples, primarily the Jews and Slavic peoples of Eastern Europe. During World War II, these ideas were applied with brutal consistency. The extermination of the Jews was construed as a war against an internal enemy and an effort to preserve the racial purity of the nation. The war on the Eastern Front was framed as a racial war to ensure 'Lebensraum' for the Germanics by killing, displacing or enslaving the native population.

Scandinavia played an important part in the Nazi worldview. Scandinavian peoples were assigned a specific place in the Great Germanic Empire along with other Germanic peoples, such as the Dutch, the Flemish and the Germans themselves. The Scandinavians even had a special position in the historical myths of the Nazis, as the Nordic/Aryan/Germanic race was thought to have its historical roots in northern Germany and southern Scandinavia, and since it was believed that the Scandinavians had maintained an especially high degree of racial purity. Leading Nazis, such as Heinrich Himmler and Walter Darré, held that the Norwegian allodial freeholders, the 'Odal' peasants, had kept their race particularly pure and maintained that traditional Norwegian rural culture embodied the racial psychology of the Nordic race.[38]

Even Scandinavia saw the rise of right-wing organisations inspired by German *völkish* nationalism, by the Nazis and by the idea of the Nordic race. In 1932, the Norwegian National-Socialist Labour Party (NNSAP) was established. It was based on the blueprint of the German National-Socialist Party (NSDAP), and its members had organisational and personal connections to the NSDAP and the SS. It was, however, a tiny party that never had more than a thousand members and never had any political impact on the national scene.[39] The nationalist and fascist party National Gathering (*Nasjonal samling*, NS), established in 1933, was of greater significance. Its main goal was to overcome class tensions and unite the

---

38 Terje Emberland and Matthew Kott, *Himmlers Norge. Nordmenn i det storgermanske prosjekt* (Oslo: Aschehoug, 2012), pp. 56-90.

39 Terje Emberland, *Religion og rase, Nyhedenskap og nazisme i Norge 1933-1945* (Oslo: Humanist, 2003), pp. 122-33.

nation around a set of values and symbols, to establish a corporatist system of governance and to combat Bolshevism. The idea of a superior Nordic race played an important role in the ideology of the NS. It is likely that their racial ideas were partly inspired by Hans Günther; the party leader Vidkun Quisling was a close friend of Günther's Norwegian sister-in-law, Cecilie Blom.[40]

Although more influential than NNSAP, even Vidkun Quisling's NS was rather marginal in the Norwegian political landscape prior to World War II. The party was not even represented in the Norwegian Parliament. However, on 1 February 1942, less than a year after the German invasion of Norway, Vidkun Quisling established a puppet government that ruled the country until the end of the German occupation on 9 May 1945. During these years, when NS membership peaked at 43,000, the party was more unambiguously inspired by Nazi-German role models and tried to reorganise the country according to National-Socialist principles. This effort included participation in the deportation of Norwegian Jews to death camps on the continent.

National Socialism did not become a topic in the correspondence between Bryn and Günther until January 1932, when Günther urged Bryn to contact the Norwegian Nazis. He mentioned Adolf Egeberg Jr., the leader of the NNSAP, and a group of Nazi-sympathising military officers in Oslo; he also referred to Vidkun Quisling and the organisation Nordic Uprising in Norway (*Nordisk Folkereisning i Norge*). This organisation had been founded the year before and was incorporated into the establishment of the NS in 1933. Günther, however, was particularly concerned with a man called Carl Lie. Lie was the editor of the newspaper *Ekstrabladet*, which for a couple of years in the early 1930s existed as the Norwegian mouthpiece for German-inspired National Socialism. Günther suggested that Bryn begin writing for *Ekstrabladet*,[41] though Bryn does not seem to have followed up on the proposal. After receiving Günther's letter, he contributed no signed articles to *Ekstrabladet*, and there is nothing in the style and content of the unsigned articles to suggest that Bryn was their author.[42]

---

40 Hans Fredrik Dahl, *En fører blir til* (Oslo: Aschehoug, 1991), p. 156.
41 Bryn's archive: Günther to Bryn, 16 January 1932.
42 The *Ekstrabladet* of 3 November 1931 contained an editorial entitled '*Ekstrabladet* Will from Now on Be an Organ for *Norsk Folkereisning* (*Ekstrabladet vil nu bli organ for Norsk Folkereisning*)'. The statute of the organisation was published in the same issue. The newspaper came out once a week and printed, among

Bryn's racial ideas were similar to, and had the same origin as, the racial ideology of the Nazis, and it is clear that Bryn, through his scientific activities in the 1920s, was involved in developing the conceptual foundation and academic legitimacy of racial ideas that later became key elements of that ideology. There is nothing in the letters between Günther and Bryn to suggest that Bryn was actively opposed to his friend's political views. Many of the Germans and non-Germans who shared Bryn's racial ideas ended up supporting the Nazi movement. These included Mjøen and Lundborg: both were members of the *Nordischer Ring* and both became Nazi sympathisers. However, I have not found any evidence to show that Bryn actively supported the National Socialist movement. Bryn died in 1933, the same year that Hitler seized power in Germany and the NS was established in Norway. After Bryn's death, Günther put his trust in Quisling as the *Nordischer Ring*'s main Norwegian contact. While it is unclear to what extent Quisling allied himself with the *Nordischer Ring*, it is a fact that Günther was convinced he had found in Quisling a prominent Norwegian advocate of the Nordic spirit.[43]

Sinking scientific credibility in Norway, rising scientific star in Germany

In 1929, Bryn received a letter from Günther, who had read *Die Somatologie der Norweger*, noted Kristian Emil Schreiner's criticism and claimed that Bryn had good reason to be upset by the Schreiner couple's ambush.[44] Günther praised Bryn for having finally decided to choose Mjøen's side and join the IFEO, but he pointed out that, a conflict with someone of Schreiner's high academic standing was likely to weaken Bryn's scientific prestige.[45] Günther's judgment appears to have been correct: the break with Schreiner and the collaboration with Mjøen were both bad for Bryn's academic standing in Norway. On the other hand, Günther noted that Bryn still enjoyed a high reputation outside Norway, especially in

---

other things, a number of articles signed by Adolf Hitler.

43 Karcher, 'Schirmorganisation der Nordischen Bewegung', pp. 15, 28.
44 Bryn's archive: Günther to Bryn, 24 October 1929. Günther commented on Kristian Emil Schreiner's behaviour towards Bryn: 'Dass doch so oft die Universitätsmenschen sich so hinterhältig benehmen'.
45 Bryn's archive: Günther to Bryn, 24 October 1929.

Germany where his name was acknowledged beyond the small realm of specialists.

There is much to suggest that Günther's assessment of the situation was correct. During the first years of Bryn's career as an anthropologist, Kristian Emil Schreiner acted as his advocate and helped to get his works published by the Norwegian Academy of Science and Letters in Oslo. Until 1926, most of Bryn's larger works were published by the Oslo Academy; none were published in Trondheim. After 1926, however, only *Die Somatologie der Norweger* among his works was published by the Oslo Academy. The three substantial works that he published between 1926 and his death in 1933 were issued by the less prestigious Royal Society of Science in Trondheim, where Bryn himself was highly influential by virtue of his position as president of the Society.

Bryn's reception in Germany was very different. Prior to 1926, Bryn had not published anything in Germany. In 1926 he published two titles there; in 1929 and 1930, he published eight. Most of them were printed in anthropological journals like *Anthropologischer Anzeiger* and *Verhandlungen der Gesellschaft für physische Anthropologie* in Stuttgart, *Mitteilungen die Anthropopologische Gesellschaft* in Vienna, *Archiv für Rassenbilder* and the ethnographic journal *Anthropos*, as well as in the *völkisch*, popular-scientific journal *Volk und Rasse* in Munich.[46] With the exception of *Anthropos*, all these publications were edited by Bryn's friends Bruno Kurt Schultz and Egon Freiherr von Eickstedt, both of whom were rising stars in German anthropology in the late 1920s and early 1930s.

Der nordische Mensch

According to Günther, it was the book *Der nordische Mensch* that made Bryn's name well-known to Germans interested in the issue of race. This was the first general account in German of Bryn's research, and it was Günther himself who had initiated the project. It was first titled *Kleine Rassenkunde Norwegens* and was thus supposed to offer a parallel to Günther's bestselling books on *Rassenkunde*, a standard, popular-scientific account of the racial

---

46 Per Holck, *Den fysiske antropologi i Norge. Fra anatomisk institutts historie 1815-1990* (Oslo: Anatomisk institutt, University of Oslo, 1990), p. 95ff.: 'Bibliography of the Works of Norwegian Physical Anthropologists'.

composition of the Norwegian population—the heartland of the Nordic race—written by a leading authority on the subject.

The quality of the final manuscript fell below the publisher's expectations, as Bryn took the opportunity to put forward his unorthodox theory about the two variants of the Nordic race. In spite of this, the *Der nordische Mensch* received positive reviews. Journals like *Volk und Rasse* and *Die Sonne*, a journal propagating the '*nordische Weltanschauung*', were laudatory. Even the American scientific journal *The Quarterly Review of Biology* praised it as an 'excellent treatise' and hailed Bryn as 'one of the most distinguished Norwegian anthropologists'.[47]

During the summer of 1929, Bryn received a letter from von Eickstedt, who had just become a professor at the University of Breslau and was developing a new department of anthropology and ethnography there.[48] He wanted to hang portraits of the discipline's leading figures on the wall of the department's reading room, and he asked Bryn to send him a signed portrait. A couple of months later he wrote that the picture was now in place and had begun to interest students in Bryn's publications.[49] In other words, von Eickstedt considered Bryn to be a key contributor to the anthropological research tradition, and the letters between them reveal that this was largely due to Bryn's theory about the two variants of the Nordic race. Von Eickstedt informed Bryn that he had produced slides based on *Der nordische Mensch* and was using them in lectures.[50] In addition, the anthropologist Josef Weininger assured Bryn that the book was eagerly studied in his department, the reason being that the question of the Nordic race was at the core of all debates on the issue of race.[51]

Thus the interest in Bryn's book arose mainly its relevance to the ongoing debate about the existence of the Nordic race,[52] for some influential German

---

47 Bryn's archive: clipping from *The Quarterly Review of Biology* [n. d.].
48 Bryn's archive: Egon von Eickstedt to Bryn, 25 June 1929.
49 Bryn's archive: Egon von Eickstedt to Bryn, 24 September 1929.
50 Bryn's archive: Egon von Eickstedt til Bryn, 25 December 1929.
51 Bryn's archive: Josef Weininger to Bryn, 16 February 1931.
52 The debate led to an extensive correspondence between Bryn and his adversaries and allies. Bryn's archive: Günther to Bryn, 1 October 1929, 16 March 1931, 3 January 1932, 16 Janaury 1932; K. Saller to Bryn, 27 October 1930; Bryn to W. Scheidt, 28 February 1931; W. Scheidt to Bryn, 5 March 1931, 19 November 1931; H. K. Konnopath to Bryn, 3 March 1932; B. K. Schultz to Bryn, 1 January 1932, etc.

212 Measuring the Master Race

anthropologists argued that the Nordic race was a theoretical construction based on a weak empirical foundation.[53] These anthropologists took as their starting point a theory which was commonly held among German anthropologists, namely that the Nordic race descended from the prehistoric Cro-Magnon's. The craniological difference between the Nordic and the Cro-Magnon races, however, was so great that some archaeologists and prehistoric anthropologists held that the two races could not be related. They had the same cephalic index, but differing facial indices. The Nordic race had a long face (it was 'leptoprosopic'), while the Cro-Magnon race had a broad face (it was 'hypereuryprosopic').[54]

The critics held that these anatomical differences meant that 'the Nordic race' should be split into two different taxonomic categories, and that only one of these could be related to the Cro-Magnon race. This biological argument was also underpinned by archaeological studies connecting the two races to two different prehistoric cultures.[55]

The anthropologist Karl Saller was among those who wanted to abolish the concept of the Nordic race. Many of Saller's critics belonged to Bryn's circle of friends, and when they discussed the question in letters to Bryn in the early 1930s, they made no secret of their belief that Saller was politically motivated. After 1933, Saller was among the very few anthropologists who distanced themselves from the racial policy of the new German regime.[56] In addition to Saller, Walter Scheidt was singled out as one of the architects behind attempts to deny the existence of the Nordic race.[57] Scheidt was a leading racial hygienist and anthropologist. He did not deny that a 'Nordic race' might be a useful scientific concept to describe and explore the racial character history of northern European populations, but he dismissed the established delineation and definition of the race, suggesting it could be

---

53 Karl Saller, 'Die entstehung der "nordischen Rasse"', *Zeitschrift für die gesamte anatomie/Zeitschrift für anatomie und entwicklungsgeschichte*, Vol. 83, no. 4 (1927), pp. 411-590. Bryn's archive: Prof. Schroller (editor of *Antropos*) to Halfdan Bryn, 20 January 1926.
54 Bryn's archive: Prof. Schroller to Bryn, 20 January 1926.
55 Ibid.
56 Proctor, 'From *Anthropologie* to *Rassenkunde*', p. 165.
57 Bryn's archive: Ministerialrat Hanno Konopacki-Konopath to Bryn, 3 March 1932; Bruno Kurt Schultz to Bryn, 29 January 1932; Günther to Bryn, 3 January 1932, 16 January 1932, 16 March 1931, 1 October 1929.

split into two sub-races.[58] Karl Saller took a more radical stance. According to him, 'the Nordic race' was a theoretical construct based on a dubious scientific foundation. He used skull measurements and archaeological theories to justify this claim. He even pointed out that the craniologists of the nineteenth century had had different perceptions of the typical Nordic/Germanic skull-shape, and he claimed that evidence casting doubt on the idea of a uniform Nordic/Germanic race had been illegitimately barred from the discipline.[59]

On this issue, much weight was given to Scandinavian racial anthropology, and the data from *Die Somatologie der Norweger* were drawn into the debate as soon as they were published.[60] Saller's theory did have some similarities to Halfdan Bryn's notion of the two types of the Nordic race. Nevertheless, there was one crucial difference. Bryn did not argue for the existence of two races, but for two branches of the same race. According to Bryn, the Nordic race had its roots in Asia, and the two branches had arisen because the Nordics had migrated to Europe in two separate groups. The two groups were slightly different in their genetic composition, and through genetic drift they had developed in distinct directions. This meant that Bryn agreed with the criticism of a Nordic ideal type; the established notion of a Nordic race was not scientifically well-founded. Like Saller and Scheidt, he criticised the way Lundborg, Günther and Fischer characterised the Nordic race.[61] But Bryn's conclusion was different from Saller's: by defining the characteristics of the Nordic race in a new way, he thought he could prove not only its existence, but also that it was actually more widespread than commonly assumed.

58 Walter Scheidt, 'Die rassischen Verhältnisse in Nordeuropa nach dem gegenwärtigen Stand der Forschung', *Zeitschrift für Morphologie und Anthropologie*, Vol. 28, nos. 1/2 (1930), pp. 1-197.
59 Saller, 'Die Entstehung der "nordischen Rasse"'.
60 The data were published in Walter Scheidt's *Die rassischen verhältnisse in Nordeuropa* (Stuttgart: Schweizerbart, 1930) to support his argument against the existing notion of the Nordic race. The book is referred to extensively in the correspondance between Bryn and Günther, and between Bryn and Scheidt. Bryn's archive: Bryn to Scheidt 28 February 1932, 5 March 1931, 19 November 1931; Günther to Bryn, 3 January 1932, 16 January 1932, 16 March 1931, 1 October 1929. My account is based on these letters.
61 Halfdan Bryn, *Norske folketyper*, Det kgl.n.Vid.selsk. Skr. 1933 (Trondheim: Brun, 1934).

The decline of the idea of the superior Nordic race

The idea of a blond, long-skulled elite race had been part of Norwegian anthropology since Arbo began his research in the late nineteenth century. There is a direct line from Arbo's assessments of the psychological character of the short skulls and long skulls, via Hansen's *folkepsykologi*, to Halfdan Bryn's racial ideas. Bryn appears extreme, but it can be claimed that he only drew logical conclusions from ideas that had had scientific legitimacy within the Norwegian academic community for several decades.

Bryn died in 1933, and he was the last Norwegian anthropologist to embrace the idea of the blond master race. After his death, there was widespread public criticism of the ideas he represented. Because of political developments in Germany, such notions had become strongly associated with the Nazi movement. In contrast to Germany, this movement had limited political success in Norway. While 37 per cent of German voters supported Adolf Hitler and the Nazi Party in the election of 1932, their Norwegian counterpart (NNSAP) remained completely marginal, and even Quisling and the NS never got more than 2 per cent of the vote in any election.

1933 saw the establishment of Nazi rule in Germany, but the same year marked the breakthrough of the Labour movement as the dominant political force in Norway. The 1933 election was a landslide victory for the Labour Party, which had recently disavowed its revolutionary past and embraced more pragmatic policies. In 1935, it entered into an agreement with the Farmers' Party (*Bondepartiet*), which until then had been the most vociferously anti-socialist party and more open to right-wing ideas than had any other large party in Norway. The agreement between Labour and the Farmers' Party was aimed at counteracting the economic crisis. It led to a less polarised political landscape and ushered in a long period of Labour Party dominance. From 1935 to 1963, Norway had an uninterrupted series of Labour majority governments. This political development did not provide a fertile climate in Norway for racial ideas now strongly associated with Nazi Germany.

In October 1940, the Norwegian Nazi writer Sigurd Saxlund complained about the political climate that had characterised Norway in the years before the war. In 1919, he had published a series of articles on race in *The Norwegian Journal of Pedagogy* (*Norsk pedagogisk tidsskrift*), but when he reworked those articles into a book manuscript in 1933, it was no longer possible to get them published because—according to the author—they were not politically correct in the new environment. Saxlund claimed that Norway was backward in racial science, and that Marxists and liberals dominated the Norwegian University. It was only after the German invasion and the installation of Quisling's puppet government that Saxlund was able to publish his *Race and Culture: The Results of Racial Mixing* (*Rase og kultur: Raseblandingens følger*).[62] Saxlund pointed to Halfdan Bryn as a lonely prophet in the Norwegian desert, one who had not received the attention he deserved until he was introduced to a German audience through the publication of *Der nordische Mensch.*[63]

The notion of a Nordic race refuses to die

Even if Bryn was the last Norwegian anthropologist to advocate the superiority of the Nordic race, the concept of a Nordic race did not disappear from Norwegian science with his death. Although Alette and Kristian Emil Schreiner rejected racial ideology in the spirit of Ammon, Lapouge and Günther, they continued to believe in the existence of a Nordic race. Thus 'the Nordic race' even survived the war, albeit in a somewhat reduced version. No longer a master race, it became a purely descriptive category.

Volume I of Kristian Emil Schreiner's great work *Crania norvegica* was published in 1939. It was a study of the more than 2,000 medieval skulls deposited in the Department of Anatomy. The study showed that in the Middle Ages, the eastern Norwegian population was already more long skulled than the western Norwegian population. However, Schreiner also pointed out that there were huge local differences among the eastern Norwegian long skulls. Most local types belonged to the Nordic long-skulls, but there were also some that could be characterised as Cro-Magnon skulls. Between these, moreover, there were a number of transitional types. Schreiner concluded that a comprehensive discussion of the causes behind his findings could not be undertaken before he had also analysed the small amount of Norwegian prehistoric bones. This task would be addressed in Volume II, which was in progress.[64]

---

62 Bryn's archive: Saxlund to Bryn, 3 December 1925 and 5 January 1926.
63 Sigurd Saxlund, *Rase og kultur. Raseblandingens følger* (Oslo: Stenersen, 1940).
64 K. E. Schreiner, *Crania norvegica I* (Oslo: ISKF/Aschehoug, 1939), pp. 1, 196-97.

Then the war broke out. The German occupation of Norway had major consequences for Schreiner and his workplace, the University of Oslo. At the outbreak of war, only three professors were members of the NS or had publicly voiced support for the party. Both the Norwegian NS regime and the German occupation authorities, however, wanted to make the University a tool for their political agenda. This policy aroused opposition from the vast majority of professors and students, and turned the university into an ideological war zone. A large number of lecturers were arrested, and the University was finally closed in 1943; 644 students were deported to prison camps in Germany, where an unsuccessful attempt was made to raise their racial consciousness and mould them into SS men.

In 1942, as part of its Nazification campaign, the NS government established a new University Institute of Racial Biology under the leadership of the geneticist Tordar Quelprud. This institute was given the task of conducting research, providing the government with advice on population and teaching racial biology. The subject was given high priority in the NS's plans for the University. It was part of the planned curricula for medicine, law and theology and other disciplines. If Quelprud had fulfilled his mission, the idea of a Nordic master race would likely have made a strong comeback in Norwegian academia, but after a year as director he resigned his position, citing a less than hospitable social environment.

Quelprud's closest neighbour at the University was the already extant Institute of Genetics, which happened to be the workplace of Kristine Bonnevie, Quelprud's former supervisor who was now involved in the resistance movement. The Institute of Genetics was also the workplace of the outspoken anti-Nazi Otto Lous Mohr; just across the yard was the Department of Anatomy, led by Kristian Emil Schreiner, who, along with Mohr, was among the professors imprisoned for their resistance to the Nazification of the University.[65]

The second volume of *Crania norvegica* was published right after the war. While Volume 1 had been written in German, the second volume was in English. In the first part of the book, Schreiner compared the small number of Norwegian Stone Age skeletal remains with similar material from other parts of northern and central Europe. The physical anthropological evidence was analysed in light of archaeological theories about cultural

---

65 Jorunn Sem Fure, *Universitetet i kamp: 1940-1945* (Oslo: Vidarforlaget, 2007), pp. 151f. and 176f.

areas and cultural diffusion. He found that the Nordic skull shape that was typical of the Iron Age and later medieval findings was prevalent in the Stone Age material as well. When discussing this discovery, Schreiner began by dismissing a theory that had been considered scientifically valid within 'certain circles' in 'recent years', namely that a 'pure' Nordic race existed and had its origins in the north of Europe. It had then wandered southward and along the way had become 'contaminated' through intermixing with inferior short-skulled peoples, or so the theory went. Schreiner argued instead for the opposite view: that the Nordic skull type had been from the beginning a product of racial mixing. There were so many causal factors involved in the shaping of these skulls that they could 'by no means be regarded as a genetic entity'.[66] 'It seems obvious', he claimed, 'that the term "Nordic race" designates only a particular phenotype within the populations which have developed in the north [of Europe] during and after the Neolithic'.[67] This means that in his *magnum opus* on ancient Norwegian skulls, Schreiner established a purely descriptive definition of the Nordic 'type' and implied that craniology was not a very useful tool for the investigation of the biological origins and migrations of northern European populations.

In a lecture the same year, he summarised his view in the following way: the 'Nordic race' is the name for a certain body type which occurred with relative frequency among a bastard population in which, for thousands of years, mixing had taken place between different lineages, and in which the mechanisms of isolation and selection had produced a number of more or less distinctive types.[68] Furthermore, according to Schreiner, the experts could only agree on one thing concerning the typical Nordic skull shape — its low cephalic index. However, it can be argued that had Kristian Emil taken his wife's previous research seriously, he would have dismissed even the cephalic index as a relevant classification tool. The conclusion of her 1923 work on the inheritance of skull shapes was that the shape of the head, as measured by the cephalic index, was not a genetic entity but rather the product of a huge number of genetic and environmental factors.[69]

---

66 K. E. Schreiner, *Crania norvegica II* (Oslo: ISKF/Aschehoug 1946), p. 63.
67 Ibid., p. 169.
68 K. E. Schreiner, 'Hva er nordisk rase?', *Forhandlinger, Det norske vitenskapsakademi* (Oslo: [n. pub.], 1946), and *Crania norvegica II*.
69 Alette Schreiner, 'Zur erblichkeit der Kopfform', *Genetica*, Vol. 5, nos. 5-6 (1923), p. 445.

Despite this, neither Schreiner nor his successor at the Department of Anatomy stopped using the category 'Nordic' for the classification of skeletal remains from archaeological findings. When Schreiner withdrew from his position after the war, the golden age of Norwegian physical anthropology came to a close. His successor, Johan Torgersen, continued the tradition of physical anthropological research, but on a very modest scale. The department no longer initiated its own excavations and anthropology was mainly reduced to an ancillary role, subordinate to archaeology. There was a dwindling interest in general theories about the racial composition of the Norwegian people, but there was still an interest in issues relating to the Sami or Norwegian identity of archaeological findings.[70] To answer such questions, ancient bones continued to be classified according to established racial categories.

Internationally, the aftermath of World War II saw a decline in scientific racism and the growth of a prevailingly anti-racist attitude within the scientific world. Two UNESCO-initiated declarations on race in the early 1950s constituted an important turning point. Leading psychologists, sociologists, and cultural and physical anthropologists were deeply involved in drafting these statements, which dismissed the idea of large, inborn psychological inequality between races and claimed that it was scientifically unsound to explain cultural differences as the product of unequal racial endowments. After an intense international debate, especially among anthropologists and geneticists, it was agreed that the concept of race should not be abandoned. Instead, race was defined as the equivalent of biological populations or 'isolates' that were genetically different due to two kinds of processes. On the one hand, the genetic composition of isolated populations is constantly being altered by natural selection and mutation, by fortuitous changes in gene frequency and by marriage customs. On the other hand, crossings are constantly breaking down these differentiations. The new mixed populations are in turn subjected to the same processes. Existing races are merely the result, considered at a particular moment in time, of the total effect of such processes.[71]

---

70 Audhild Schancke, 'Samiske hodeskaller og den antropologiske raseforskningen i Norge', appendix to I. Lønnig, M. Guttor, J. Holme, et al. (eds.), *Innstilling fra Utvalg for vurdering av retningslinjer for bruk og forvalting av skjelettmateriale ved Anatomisk institutt* (Oslo: University of Oslo, 1998), p. 6.

71 UNESCO, *Statement on the Nature of Race and Race Differences* (Paris: UNESCO,

The UNESCO declarations became important reference points for the scientific debates on race in Scandinavia. When Johan Torgersen discussed race in a popular-science book in 1956, his conceptualisation seemed to echo the UNESCO declarations. He thought that race was a matter of the different frequency of genes in populations. He maintained that there were no clear boundaries between races, that race was a statistical abstraction, that intermixing between populations was common and that the racial history of humankind was characterised by changing periods of isolation and gene flow between populations, by population boundaries that were constantly coming into being and disappearing.[72] In a similar vein, in an article written in 1968 on 'The Origin of the Lapps', Torgersen criticised the idea of a primordial Sami type. He argued that the range of variability among Sami both past and present indicated that Sami culture had arisen within biologically heterogeneous populations, and that the concept of race was problematic due to the complex relations and histories of the biological populations.

Despite these views, however, Torgersen continued to base his own anthropological investigations on established racial typologies. In a 1972 article on prehistoric races in northern Norway, he used terms such as East Baltic, Nordic and Sami, but argued that these were purely descriptive designations for skull types which could not be related to particular ethnic groups.[73] It can still be asked whether these ethnically-coloured categories had an impact upon Torgersen's historical interpretation of skeletal remains. The archaeologist Audhild Schanche has pointed out that when Torgersen classified bones into categories such as Nordic and Sami, he did not usually make it explicit that these were purely descriptive categories with no relevance to ethnicity.[74] Thus, even though racial anthropology was marginalised after the war, and pre-war concepts of race were criticised, racial classifications based on pre-war typologies continued at least until the 1970s. Notwithstanding the loss of scientific credibility for the notion of a superior blond race, the Nordic type survived as a scientific concept into the post-war era.

1951), http://unesdoc.unesco.org/images/0015/001577/157730eb.pdf

72 Johan Torgersen, *Mennesket. Vidunder og problembarn i livets historie* (Oslo: Aschehoug, 1956), pp. 130-36.

73 Schancke, 'Samiske hodeskaller', p. 7.

74 Ibid., p. 8.

10. The Fall of the Nordic Master Race

It was Carl Oscar Eugen Arbo who, with his anthropological surveys of Norwegian soldiers of the late 1880s, laid the foundation for physical anthropological research in Norway. Arbo also helped reinvigorate the notion of Norwegian nationhood centred upon the idea of a Nordic or Germanic master race and turned himself into a spokesperson for racist views on hisotry and society. Inspired by Otto Ammon, Arbo explained social and cultural differences in Norwegian society as the product of social selection resulting from the struggle for survival between inferior and superior races. These ideas remained highly controversial among scholars both in Norway and abroad, but they were still accepted within Norwegian academia as scientifically valid. The Norwegian government funded Arbo's racial research, as well as Andreas M. Hansen's work towards a grand synthesis of national history based on Ammon and Georges Vacher de Lapouge's racial ideas. These ideas were also discussed at meetings of the Norwegian Academy of Science and Letters, and Arbo and Hansen's works were published through recognised academic channels.

The concept of the superior Nordic race maintained its scientific legitimacy well into the interwar years, influencing discussions about national identity and becoming a key issue in the Norwegian debate over eugenics. Even though Halfdan Bryn may seem like an academic with extreme ideas, he was arguably nothing more than a very consistent advocate of theories that had circulated within Norwegian academia for decades. It was only in the aftermath of the conflict between Kristian Emil Schreiner and Bryn in the late 1920s that the notion of the superior Nordic race was seriously contested and finally downgraded to an unscientific idea. But how do we explain the demise of such an established scientific concept?

http://dx.doi.org/10.11647/OBP.0051.10

Racism in science has often been portrayed as the influence of commonly-held prejudices, prejudices that in the long run have been unmasked through growing scientific insights. The history of physical anthropology bears witness to a more complex relationship between prejudice and scientific knowledge. Scientists were not simply influenced by commonly-held racist attitudes. The reverse was also true; racism had an impact on society because it was legitimised by science. Such interdependence was to some extent implicit and subliminal. Scholars, like anyone else, were influenced by ubiquitous racial ideas, and the dominant scientific 'truths' helped shape ordinary notions of race. However, there was also a very explicit and direct interconnection between science and ideology: political ideologies, such as 'the Nordic idea', could be directly legitimised with the help of scientific knowledge.

In the anthropological study of race, ideological and scientific issues were often interwoven. Many of the scientists presented in this book offered scientific arguments to public debate and political life. Most of them did not merely use such arguments as rhetorical tools for achieving political goals; they also felt it was their duty to enlighten the public, and that natural science was to guide people's lives and society's structure. Central to their worldview was the idea of a naturally-progressing social, cultural and biological evolution. Everything that was in line with evolution was see as positive, and everything that deviated from evolution was considered negative. They thus had a double justification for claiming a privileged position for scientists in setting the agenda for the development of society. Scientist had privileged insights into the nature of human evolution and its driving forces, and at the same time positioned themselves at the top of the evolutionary hierarchyand at the forefront of human progress.

The idea of the superior Nordic race was one version of this worldview. It presupposed that Europeans could be ranked in a hierarchy of races, with the Nordics at its pinnacle. According to this worldview, Western civilisation was the product of the inheritable qualities of the Nordic race, and the future evolution of civilisation depended upon the expansion of this race. Throughout the period we have studied, some anthropologists embraced these ideas and claimed that they were based on science, while others dismissed them as unscientific. Both sides felt that it was their professional responsibility to enlighten the public as they believed that society should be organised on scientific knowledge about human nature.

However, this was a two-way relationship: their scientific worldview influenced their ideals and outlook on society, while their engagement in cultural, societal and political struggles shaped their research.

In order to understand the relationship between racial science and society, this book has examined the shifting ways in which the boundary between science and non-science was constructed. Who had the authority to define scientific truths about 'race' and on what grounds? In order to speak about race with scientific authority, scientists would first had to be well-versed in the physical-anthropological research tradition; in order to gain scientific acceptance for specific racial ideas, a scientist had to ensure that these were based on empirical data obtained by acknowledged methods and interpreted in accordance with existing anthropological theories.

Physical anthropology was an arena for scientific debates on human biology, evolution and race, and these debates were often charged with political and ideological meaning. Despite their differing theoretical orientations and ideological stances, however, physical anthropologists still shared a frame of reference. They had a mutual scientific interest in the classification of human races and the mapping of the biological history of humankind, and they often used a common set of methods. Of particular importance for the discipline was the development of an increasing range of methods for measuring and quantifying characteristics, leading to an ever-expanding store of meticulously gathered empirical data. Anthropologists were involved in the mapping of human variation, and each new piece of research added fresh data to this collective undertaking.

By the time Halfdan Bryn and the two Schreiners began their racial studies of the Norwegian population, anthropologists had been piling up huge numbers of descriptions of human bodies for almost half a century. Bryn and Kristian Emil Schreiner saw it as part of their task to add to this stock of data, and their collaboration was based on the belief that these data were merely descriptive entities. Rudolf Martin's textbook represented their starting point. According to Martin, anthropology's main goal was to produce neutral descriptions of the variations in bodily characteristics between different human groups. The notion that anthropology was a descriptive science, however, was largely a delusion, since the very selection of the 'traits' listed in anthropologists' typologies was based on the fact that there existed techniques to describe them. These techniques had been created as part of changing and often incompatible theories on heritability, brain anatomy and evolution. They amassed over the years like archaeological layers in the discipline's warehouse of methods. Progressively their original meaning was lost: a criterion for racial classification that had been established on the grounds of one set of biological theories might later acquire new meaning in the light of new scientific beliefs, or be regarded as an objective description of an existing trait.

The cephalic index provides the best example of this phenomenon. It was invented by Anders Retzius in the 1840s and remained in use until World War II. After the war, the dominant theories of heredity and evolution underwent a complete transformation and criticism of both the cephalic index and the racial typologies that were based on it was increasingly voiced within the scientific community. Despite all this, the cephalic index continued to be used within ever-changing theoretical frameworks. The long survival of the cephalic index can be, at least in part, explained by a reverence for the existing anthropological research tradition. Over the years, huge amounts of work, money and prestige were invested in amassing extensive data on variations in the cephalic index between populations. To abandon this criterion would be tantamount to dismissing much of the existing anthropological knowledge. Moreover, abandoning the cephalic index in favour of new measuring techniques would have made it impossible to compare new results with old data sets.

A similar logic seems to have characterised the field of physical anthropology in general: new criteria of classification were introduced, but often as a supplement to previously established methods, for rejecting those would have meant abandoning huge amounts of data and starting the mapping of human variation from scratch. Unsurprisingly this measure was resisted.

When Bryn and Schreiner began their cooperation on the large survey of Norwegian military recruits, they had to decide which traits they wanted to map and the method by which they would do so. They discussed this question based on the premises that anthropology was a descriptive science. They emphasised that the data they recorded should be comparable with data from previous studies and that the collection and statistical treatment of the data should be feasible. The 'importance' of traits was emphasised as well, but without clarifying the criteria by which the data on such physical features was to be assessed. Troubles began when Bryn and Schreiner started analysing their 'descriptive' data. Basic theoretical issues were now on the agenda, disagreements arose and the two scientists ended up interpreting the data in very different ways. Although they analysed the same set of empirical data with the same discipline's stock of knowledge, the two scientists were unable to reach any agreement on the interpretation of their research results. This outcome was also due to the fact that anthropological knowledge was incoherent at the time, since theoretical and conceptual issues had been discussed within the discipline for decades but never settled.

Even granting that Halfdan Bryn was a sloppy scientist who was quick to jump to conclusions when confirming his own prejudices, his conflict with Schreiner cannot be understood solely as a story of false science being debunked by true science. By drawing on different anthropological research traditions, Bryn and Schreiner used the same set of data to construct conflicting scientific truths. Thus the results they produced helped confirm preconceived and conflicting perceptions of reality instead of leading to new insights. In that, the conflict between Bryn and Schreiner mirrored a tension within the anthropological research tradition itself, a discipline devoid of a coherent set of theories on how to interpret empirical data.

Initially their discussions about data interpretation was perceived as a debate between fellow-scientists. After they broke with Bryn, however, Alette and Kristian Emil Schreiner began to question the scientific credibility of Bryn and the ideas he represented. The Schreiners were thus instrumental in redefining Bryn's status—from 'scientist' to 'pseudo-scientist'—and in redrawing the boundary between science and non-science, which in turn helped to finally debunk the 'Nordic idea'.

We have examined the links between this conflict and reorientation within the tiny community of Norwegian anthropologists and the increasingly polarised and politicised debates on race in the international arena. From the mid-1920s onwards, German anthropologists increasingly turned their backs on the liberal legacy of Rudolf Virchow and his generation, instead embracing racial determinism, the Nordic idea and a racist form of eugenics. In the English-speaking world, however, an increasing number of scientists began to question some of the basic assumptions upon which the notion of the superior Nordic race was based. The debates became even more polarised after the Nazi takeover in Germany, when the majority of German anthropologists pledged loyalty to the new regime and its racial policy, while a number of non-German scholars began to engage in anti-racist campaigns.

While Bryn's increasingly strong advocacy of the Nordic idea accorded with the general trends in German anthropology, Alette and Kristian Emil Schreiner's dismissal of this concept was more in line with the overall development of anthropology within the English-speaking world. It is important to note, however, that both Kristian Emil Schreiner and Bryn had particularly strong relations to German anthropology from the outset. They read German textbooks and journals, travelled to Germany, had close contact with German colleagues and published their works in German. To an extent Norwegian anthropology in the interwar years could be regarded as a subdivision of German anthropology. Seen from this perspective, it was the two Schreiners, and not Bryn, who distanced themselves from the prevailing trends within their field of research. Schreiner's dismissal of the Nordic idea, nevertheless, did echo dominant attitudes among Norwegian academics around 1930, and this begs the question of why the concept of the Nordic master race followed such different trajectories in Norwegian and German academia. This question may have many answers, and the issue can be elucidated only partially with the help of the source material upon which this book is based. Nevertheless, it is possible to put forward some explanations.

Clearly the increasing scepticism towards the Nordic race idea in Norway was a direct response to the rise of Nazi Germany. During the 1930s, academic racism – in particular the notion of the Nordic master race – became increasingly tainted by its association with right-wing politics and Nazism. It thus became imperative that those who opposed right-wing ideologies renounced the Nordic idea. This is only a partial explanation, however, as it does not explain why right-wing racial ideas did not appeal to the vast majority of Norwegian academics who were engaged in studying the nation's history and culture. It is also important to note that Bryn had already begun to feel isolated in Norwegian academia by the end of the 1920s, at a time when his career flourished in Germany—academia in the two countries began to take different paths even before the Nazi movement was perceived as a real threat. An additional explanation lies in the changed relationship between the Norwegian and German academic worlds. While at the turn of the century Norwegian academia was closely related to the German academic world, politically Norway's neutrality had far stronger ties to Great Britain. Norway's neutrality during World War I did not prevent Germany from waging a submarine war against Norwegian merchant ships, killing thousands of Norwegian sailors and instilling anti-German sentiments among the people. This event led many Norwegian academics to reconsider their traditionally strong attachment to Germany.

These feelings were strengthened by a general decline in Germany's scientific prestige and the breakdown of international scientific cooperation caused by World War I. After the war many academic organisations boycotted Germany and Austria. German science thus lost its leading role and the international scientific world became more diverse, with German, French and English competing to be the dominant scientific language. Norwegian scholars kept many of their traditional ties with Germany while developing increasingly strong bonds with France, England and the U.S. This tendency was furthered by the Nazi takeover in Germany, although it must be emphasised that the interwar years never saw any definitive breakdown in academic relations between Norway and Germany.[1]

An even more important explanation for the varying success of the scientific concept of the Nordic master race in Germany and Norway lies in the different international roles and political situations the two countries faced during and after World War I. Andrew D. Evans has argued that the shift in German anthropology from 'racial liberalism' to racism occurred because members of the discipline accommodated their scientific goals and methods to the political and ideological context in which they worked. This process, Evans argues, started around the turn of the century when anthropologists increasingly began to adapt their science to the imperial aims of the German state. But the major shift occurred during World War I, when anthropologists put their discipline in the service of the war effort. Lacking access to the outside world, anthropologists began studying enemies in prison camps, portraying them as racial 'others'. This opened the way for a racist style of research, which began to dominate during the 1920s when a new generation strongly influenced by their wartime experiences obtained positions.[2] Robert Proctor has pointed

---

1   Jon Røyne Kyllingstad, *'Menneskeåndens universalitet' Instituttet for sammenlignende kulturforskning 1917-1940 Ideene, institusjonen og forskningen* (Ph.D. thesis, University of Oslo, 2008), pp. 11-222. Fredrik Thue, *In Quest of a Democratic Social Order. The Americanization of Norwegian Social Scholarship 1918-1970* (Ph.D. thesis, University of Oslo, 2005), pp. 33-75. Jorunn Sem Fure, *Universitetet i kamp: 1940-1945*, Vol. 4 (Oslo: Unipub, 2011), pp. 46-58.

2   Andrew D. Evans, *Anthropology at War: World War I and the Science of Race in Germany* (Chicago, IL: University of Chicago Press, 2012).

more specifically at Germany's situation in the aftermath of World War I when explaining the shift from liberal anthropology to *Rassenkunde*. After the defeat of Germany, the no less humiliating Treaty of Versailles and Germany's loss of her colonies, German anthropology adopted a certain 'therapeutic logic' aimed at rescuing the German people and the Germanic race from the perceived threats of external and internal enemies (such as the Jews and the Gypsies).[3]

The research by Norwegian anthropologists and their colleagues in related disciplines may also have been affected by the political and ideological context in which they worked. This context was quite different from the one faced by their German counterparts. In 1918, the Scandinavian countries were not great powers humiliated by victors and devastated by war; they were small and vulnerable nations that had managed to remain neutral, albeit while surrounded by aggressive and militaristic great powers. In the aftermath of the war, all three Scandinavian countries instituted policies of neutrality, peace and reconciliation, and in all three countries research was turned into a tool for promoting peace. This had a strong impact on the development of both the sciences and the humanities and influenced both academic and political notions of national identity.[4]

The link between the Scandinavian peace policy and research policy arose as a response to the breakdown of scientific internationalism during and after the war. The French-British post-war attempt to isolate German academia took place at the time of Germany's exclusion from the League of Nations, and was perceived by neutral countries as an unfair and politically dangerous containment policy. Numerous initiatives were taken to help reintegrate Germany into the international scientific world by the U.S. and others, including Scandinavia.[5] Denmark, Sweden and Norway conducted foreign policies of neutrality, peace, internationalism and

---

3   Robert Proctor, 'From *Anthropologie* to *Rassenkunde*', in George W. Stocking, Jr. (ed.), *Bones, Bodies, Behavior* (Madison, WI: University of Wisconsin Press, 1988), pp. 138-79.

4   Rebecka Lettevall, Geert Somsen and Sven Widmalm (eds.), *Neutrality in Twentieth-Century Europe: Intersections of Science, Culture, and Politics after the First World War* (New York: Routledge 2012).

5   Brigitte   Schroeder-Gudehus,   'Challenge   to   Transnational   Loyalties: International Scientific Organizations after the First World War', *Science Studies*, Vol. 3, no. 2 (1973), pp. 93-118. Robert Marc Friedman, *The Politics of Excellence. Behind the Nobel Prize in Science* (New York: W. H. Freeman & Co Ltd, 2002), pp. 75-81.

reconciliation with the aims of mitigating tensions between Scandinavia's powerful neighbours, promoting international law and branding the Nordic nations as highly civilised, modern and pacifist. The hope was that this would reduce the risk of invasion from militaristic neighbours. As part of the strategy, support was given to initiatives that could help to restore academic internationalism and rebuild amicable relations between academic elites in former enemy countries. Research directives became strongly linked to security concerns and foreign policy, a link which created new opportunities for legitimising and funding academic research.[6] It also led to the establishment of the Oslo Institute for Comparative Research in Human Culture. This publicly-funded research institution was informally linked to the Nobel Peace Prize Committee and had an entwined scientific and political agenda: to facilitate both comparative cultural research and peaceful international relations by serving as an international meeting place for scholars.

Even though it never managed to live up to its massive ambitions, the relatively well-funded Institute played a significant role in Norwegian academia during the 1920s and early 1930s and contributed to a cultural, political and ideological environment that was inhospitable to racism. A recurring idea of the political campaign that led to the founding of the Institute was that the historical sciences by nurturing nationalist attitudes had contributed to the political climate that had led to war. Comparative cultural research was presented as a cure for national chauvinism since it aimed at producing universal insight into the evolution of human culture. Because all humans are endowed with the same basic mental potentials, it was claimed, all human cultures develop according to the same set of 'laws' which could be revealed through the help of comparative research. Such research was to be based on international cooperation and was expected to produce the kind of knowledge that would serve as a counterweight to aggressive nationalism.[7]

---

6   Lettevall et al. (eds.), *Neutrality in Twentieth-Century Europe*.

7   Fredrik Stang, *Verdensakademier, Norden som sentralsted for internationalt videnskapelig arbeide* (Kristiania: Aschehoug, 1918); *De norske akademiplaner. Foredrag holdt i Bergen 30. januar 1918* (Kristiania: [n. pub.], 1918) and 'The Institute for Comparative Research in Human Culture: Its Origin and Aims', in Instituttet for sammenlignende kulturforskning, *Four Introductory Lectures/ Quatre conferénces d'inauguration/Vier Einleitungs- vorlesungen* (Oslo: ISKF and Cambridge, Mass: Harvard University Press, 1925), pp. 1-28.

The Institute's research programme was based on the notion that all humans were equally endowed and that cultural variation had to be explained not by racial differences and the struggle for survival, but by differences in the natural and social preconditions for cultural development. This research agenda and the ideas behind it had a significant impact on philological, ethnographic, historical and archaeological research in Norway and, as discussed in chapter 7, is likely to have had an effect on Kristian Emil Schreiner's attitudes towards race and national origins. The intellectual environment fostered by the Institute, however, not only promoted ideas of universalism and human unity, it also promoted a certain approach to Norwegian culture and history that was at odds with the Nordic idea.

The campaign that led to the founding of the Institute was based on a paradoxical mix of universalist and nationalist arguments. The nationalist argument was related to the political goal of framing Norway as a highly civilised, democratic and peace-loving nation, while at the same time helping to build a coherent national identity and culture. Traditional Norwegian rural culture was singled out as a particularly good empirical case for the comparative study of the evolution of human culture, and it was claimed that by turning the cultural history of the Norwegians into an object of international comparative research, Norway's international image as a highly cultured nation would be strengthened.[8]

In chapter 7 we saw that the study of 'Arctic cultures' was the first major undertaking of the Institute. From the late 1920s onwards, however, the Arctic programme was dwarfed by a new enterprise—the comparative study of the social and cultural history of peasant societies. This was probably the largest humanities research project ever undertaken in Norway. The research plans were developed in cooperation with the leading French and Austrian historians Marc Bloch and Alfons Dopsch, and, even if it ended up as a project of national scope, it was initially planned as an international comparative research in collaboration with European colleagues.[9]

However, in spite of being presented as a contribution to the universal history of humankind, the project was also the continuation of well-established national traditions in the writing of Norwegian history. We have seen how, due to the 'discontinuous' history of the Norwegian

---

8   Kyllingstad, *'Menneskeåndens universalitet'*, pp. 60-80.
9   Ibid., pp. 478-628.

state, nineteenth-century historians had turned their attention to peasant society in order to establish a coherent account of Norwegia's past. By making the social and cultural structure of Norwegian rural societies the object of their study, the Institute continued to support, and elaborate upon, this tradition. In contrast to the proponents of the Nordic idea who saw the Norwegian peasant as the epitome of the Nordic race, the Institute's research programme was based on the idea of a continuity in the social and material structure of peasant society. The latter was not considered to be determined by the racial qualities of the Nordic race, but by cultural, social and technological adaption to the specific natural environment of Norway.

The programme was launched and led by the leading socialist politician and historian, Edvard Bull, and it was partly based upon his Marxist-inspired materialist approach to history. Nonetheless, the programme included all the leading Norwegian historians, archaeologists, folklorists and experts on Germanic and Norse philology, representing a wide range of political and academic views. A key participant was the leader of the National Antiquities Collection, Anton Wilhelm Brøgger, who was the most influential archaeologist of his generation. He belonged to the urban and elitist wing of the *Venstre* movement and held that archaeology should foster the nation's unity by providing a coherent account of its history. In 1925, as part of an international conference at the Institute, he gave a series of lectures on 'The Antiquity of the Norwegian People' that attracted much public attention. In these lectures, he put forward a number of programmatic ideas that were typical of the Institute for Comparative Research in Human Culture and that later became important elements in its comparative rural history programme.

Brøgger saw the Norwegians as the descendants of different groups of people who had migrated to Norway over a long timespan. What had bound them together and turned them into one nation was the fact that they had adapted to the living conditions of the territory that later became Norway. Through their efforts at making a livelihood in this specific environment through hunting, fishing, livestock farming and agriculture, they had developed a common way of life, and with the advent of settled farming in the Early Iron Age, they were transformed into one unified people.[10] Brøgger's account implied that the nation arose through the

10 A. W. Brøgger, 'Viking', *Viking*, 1 (1937), p. 6; 'Nasjonen og fortiden', *Samtiden* (1928), pp. 490, 493-95; *Det norske folk i Oldtiden* (Oslo: ISKF, 1925), pp. 13-27,

merging of diverse peoples. This view did not necessarily rule out the relevance of race to the question of nationality, and even Brøgger may have believed that there was a limit to the degree of racial difference that could be combined into a nation. However, he remained critical of the use of racial explanations. Brøgger claimed that it was wrong for archaeologists to explain differences in material culture with the help of racial theories and declared that debates about prehistoric racial migrations and settlements in Scandinavia had became a caricature of science. He maintained that cultural progress was not driven by competition between races but by the slow and steady evolution of the methods for cultivating the land and utilising natural resources. It was the peaceful agricultural conquest of the Norwegian landscape—not the inhabitants' shared Nordic racial roots— that accounted for the 'Norwegianness' of the Norwegians.[11]

Brøgger's theories were influenced by ideas that had circulated among Norwegian historians since the 1870s, and by the intellectual environment of the Institute for Comparative Research in Human Culture. In its turn Brøgger had a significant impact on the Institute's plan to study peasant communities, and, most likely, on Kristian Emil Schreiner, the author of *Crania norvegica*. According to Schreiner, the term 'Nordic race' designated nothing more than a certain phenotype. This phenotype derived from the merging of different groups of people who had wandered into the territory during a long prehistoric timespan, before being moulded into a stable type.[12]

This conclusion, which implied that the Nordic race was not primordial but rather the product of racial mixing, was at odds with both the Nordic idea and with the racial ideology of the Nazis. However, it seemed to fit well with the vision of Norwegian prehistory advocated by Brøgger and with the Institute's notions of culture, ethnicity and race dominating the academic study of the country's past. Even if the concept of a Nordic race continued to be used into the post-war years as a tool for classifying ancient bones, it is clear that the idea of the master race had lost its scientific credibility, and that a notion of Norwegianness based on racial determinism and Nordic superiority was at odds with the leading scholarly trends established long before the outbreak of war.

156-76, 192.

11   Ibid., pp. 15-16, 27, 30, 156-77, 190-92.

12   K. E. Schreiner, *Crania norvegica II* (Oslo: Aschehoug/ISKF, 1946), pp. 62-63.

Selected Bibliography

Adriansen, Inge, '"Jyllands formodede tyskhed i oldtiden" — den dansk — tyske strid om Sønderjyllands urbefolkning', in E. Roesdahl and P. M. Sørensen (eds.), *The Waking of Angantyr: The Scandinavian Past in European Culture*, Acta Jutlandica, Humanities Series 70, Vol. 71, no. 1 (Aarhus: Aarhus University Press, 1996), pp. 120-46.

Alsvik, Ola T., *'Friskere, sterkere, større, renere': Om Carl Schiøtz og helsearbeidet for norske skolebarn* (Master's thesis, University of Oslo, 1991).

Ammon, Otto, *Die natürliche Auslese beim Menschen* (Jena: G. Fischer, 1893).

—, 'Zur Anthropologie Norwegens', *Zentralblatt für Anthropologie, Ethnologie und Uhrgeschichte*, Vol. 5, no. 3 (1900), pp. 129-37.

—, *Anthropologische Untersuchungen der Wehrpflichtigen in Baden* (Hamburg: Verlagsanstalt und Druckerei Actien-Gesellschaft, 1890).

Andersen, Per Sveaas, *Rudolf Keyser: embetsmann og historiker* (Oslo: Universitetsforlaget, 1960).

—, *Den blonde Brachycephal og dens sandsynlige udbredningsfelt* (Kristiania: Christiania Videnskabs-Selskab, 1906).

Arbo, C. O. E., 'Er der foregået nye invandringer i Norden? Foredrag på det skandinaviske naturforskermöde i Stockholm 1897', *Ymer*, Vol. 20, no. 1 (1900), pp. 25-49, http://runeberg.org/ymer/1900/0027.html

—, *Fortsatte Bidrag til Nordmændenes Anthropologi IV Lister og Mandals Amt*, Skr. Vidensk. Selsk. Christiania MN kl. 1897 (Kristiania: I Kommission hos Dybwad, 1897).

—, *Fortsatte Bidrag til Nordmændenes Anthropologi V. Nedenes amt*. Skr. Vidensk. Selsk. Christiania MN kl. 1898 (Kristiania: I Kommission hos Dybwad, 1898).

—, *Om Sessions-Undersøgelsernes og Recruterings-Statistikens Betydning for Videnskaben og Staten med et Udkast til en derpå grundet Statistik for de tre nordiske Riger* (Kristiania: Steenske bogtrykkeri, 1878).

—, 'Udsigt over der sydvestlige Norges anthropologiske forhold', *Ymer*, Vol. 14 (1894), pp. 165-86, http://runeberg.org/ymer/1894/0181.html

Arntzen, Jon Gunnar, et al. (eds.), *Norsk biografisk leksikon* (Oslo: Kunnskapsforlaget, 1999-2005).

Augstein, H. F., 'Aspects of Philology and Racial Theory in Nineteenth-Century Celticism: The Case of James Cowles Prichard', *Journal of European Studies*, Vol. 28, no. 4 (1998), pp. 355-71, http://dx.doi.org/10.1177/004724419802800402

Backman, Gaston, 'Den Europeiska rasfrågan ur antropologisk och sociala synspunkter', *Ymer*, Vol. 35, no. 4 (1915), pp. 330-50.

Barkan, Elazar, *The Retreat of Scientific Racism: Changing Concepts of Race in Britain and the United States between the World Wars* (Cambridge: Cambridge University Press, 1992).

—, 'Mobilizing Scientists against Nazi Racism 1933-1939', in George W. Stocking, Jr. (ed.), *Bones, Bodies, Behavior* (Madison, WI: University of Wisconsin Press, 1988), pp. 180-205.

Barth, Justus, 'Gustav A. Guldberg', *Forhandlinger i Videnskabs-selskabet i Christiania aar 1908* (Kristiania: I kommission hos Jacob Dybwad, 1909), pp. 11-24.

—, 'In Memoriam! Professor Dr. Med. G.A. Guldberg', *Internationale Monatsschrift für Anatomie und Physiologie* (1908), pp. 101-04.

—, *Norrønaskaller: crania antiqua in parte orientali Norvegiæ meridionalis inventa: En studie fra Universitetets Anatomiske Institut* (Kristiania: Aschehoug, 1896).

Bischoff, Christian Heinrich Ernst and Christoph Wilhelm Hufeland, *Some Account of Dr. Gall's New Theory of Physiognomy Founded upon the Anatomy and Physiology of the Brain* (London: Longman, Hurst, Rees, and Orme, 1807), http://bit.ly/1HSosvI

Blanckaert, Claude, 'On the Origins of French Ethnology: William Edwards and the Doctrine of Race', in George W. Stocking, Jr., ed., *Bones, Bodies, Behavior: Essays on Biological Anthropology* (Madison, WI: University of Wisconsin Press, 1988), pp. 18-55.

Bonde, Niels, 'Moderne systematik -fylogeni og klassifikation', in Niels Bonde et.al., ed., *Naturens historiefortællere* (København: Gad, 1996), pp. 126-81.

Bonnevie, Kristine, 'Papillarmuster und Psychische Eigenschaften', *Hereditas*, Vol. 9, nos. 1-3 (1927), pp. 180-92, http://dx.doi.org/10.1111/j.1601-5223.1927.tb03519.x

—, 'Studies on papillary patterns of human fingers', *Journal of Genetics*, Vol. 15, no. 1 (1924), pp. 1-111, http://dx.doi.org/10.1007/bf02983100

—, 'Was lehrt die Embryologie der Papillarmuster über ihre Bedeutung als Rassen- und Familiencharakter?', *Molecular and General Genetics MGG*, Vol. 50, no. 1 (1929), pp. 219-48, http://dx.doi.org/10.1007/bf01742055

—, 'Zur Mechanik der Papillarmusterbildung 1 & 2', *Development, Genes and Evolution*, Vol. 117, no. 1 (1929), pp. 384-420, http://dx.doi.org/10.1007/bf02110970 and Vol. 126, no. 2 (1932), pp. 348-72, http://dx.doi.org/10.1007/bf00576269

Brace, C. Loring, *Race Is a Four-Letter Word: The Genesis of the Concept* (New York: Oxford University Press, 2005).

Briggs, C. Stephen, 'C.C. Rafn, J.J.A. Worsaae, Archaeology, History and Danish National Identity in the Schleswig-Holstein Question', *Bulletin of the History of Archaelogy*, Vol. 15, no. 2 (2005), pp. 4-25, http://dx.doi.org/10.5334/bha.15202

Broberg, Gunnar, 'Eugenics in Sweden, Efficient Care', in his and Roll-Hansen (eds.), *Eugenics and the Welfare State*, pp. 77-150.

—, *Statlig rasforskning: en historik över Rasbiologiska Institutet* (Lund: Avdelningen för Idé- och lärdomshistoria vid Lunds Universitet, 1995).

—, 'Statens institut för rasbiologi—tilkomståren', in Gunnar Broberg, Gunnar Eriksson and Karin Johannisson, *Kunskapens trädgårdar: om institutioner och institutionaliseringar i vetenskapen och livet* (Stockholm: Atlantis, 1988).

— and Mattias Tydèn, *Oönskade i folkhemmet. Rashygien och Steriliseringar i Sverige* (Stockholm: Gidlund, 1991).

— and Nils Roll-Hansen (eds.), *Eugenics and the Welfare State, Sterilisation Policy in Denmark, Sweden, Norway, and Finland* (East Lansing, MI: Michigan State University Press, 1996).

—, Gunnar Eriksson and Karin Johannisson (eds.), *Kunskapens trädgårdar: om institutioner och institutionaliseringar i vetenskapen och livet* (Stockholm: Atlantis, 1988).

Broch, Hjalmar, 'Om noen av våre fremste zoologer', *Fauna*, Vol. 21 (1968), pp. 1-6.

Bryn Halfdan, 'Antropologiske Undersøgelser I. Trøndelagens rekrutteringsevne', *Norsk tidsskrift for Militærmedicin* (1914), pp. 1-31.

—, *Anthropologia Nidarosiensis* (Kristiania: Grøndahl, 1920).

—, 'Anthropologia Nidarosiensis', *Norsk Tidsskrift for Militærmedicin*, Vol. 24 (1920), pp. 1-10.

—, 'Arvelighetsundersøkelser. Om arv av øienfarven hos mennesker', *Tidsskrift for den Norske Lægeforening*, Vol. 40, no. 10 (1920), pp. 329-42.

—, 'Arvelighetsundersøkelser vedrørende index cephalicus', *Tidsskrift for den Norske Lægeforening*, Vol. 41, no. 10 (1921), pp. 431-52.

—, 'Den nordiske rases sjelelige trekk', *Ymer*, Vol. 49, no. 4 (1929), pp. 340-50.

—, *Der Nordische mensch* (München: J. F. Lehmann, 1929).

—, *Homo cæsius*, D. Kgl. no. Vid. Selsk. Skr. (Nidaros: F. Brun, 1930).

—, *Menneskerasene og deres utviklingshistorie* (Oslo: Det Norske studentersamfund, 1925).

—, *Møre fylkes antropologi*, Skr. D. n. Vidensk. Selsk. MN kl. (Kristiania: I kommission hos J. Dybwad, 1920).

—, *Norske folketyper*. D. Kgl. n. Videns. selsk. Skr. 6, 1933 (Trondheim: I kommission hos F. Bruns bokhandel, 1934).

—, 'Om vort folks kroniske og arvelige sykdomsbelastning', *Norsk Tidsskrift for Militærmedicin*, Vol. 25 (1921), pp. 138 46, Vol. 26 (1922), pp. 1-15.

—, 'Raceblandingen i Troms fylke', *Norsk Tidsskrift for Militærmedicin*, Vol. 26 (1922), pp. 121-35.

—, 'Researches into Anthropological Heredity. On the Inheritance of Eye Colour in Man. II. The Genetic of Index Cephalicus', *Hereditas*, Vol. 1, no. 2 (1920), pp. 186-212, http://dx.doi.org/10.1111/j.1601-5223.1920.tb02459.x

—, 'Seelische Unterschiede zweier Spielformen der nordischen Rasse', *Volk und Rasse*, Vol. 4 (1929), pp. 158-64.

—, *Selbu og Tydalen. En antropologisk undersøkelse av mænd, kvinder og barn i to norske indlandsbygder*, Skr. D. n. Vidensk. Selsk. MN kl 1921, no. 5 (Kristiania: I kommisjon hos Jacob Dybwad, 1921).

—, 'To grundracer i Norge', *Nyt Magazin for Naturvidenskaberne*, Vol. 57 (1920), pp. 29-64.

—, *Troms fylkes antropologi*, Skr. D. n. Vidensk. Selsk. MN kl 1921, no. 20 (Kristiania: I kommisjon hos J. Dybwad, 1922).

—, *Trøndelagens antropologi. Bidrag til belysning av det norske folks anthropologi i begyndelsen av det 20de aarhundrede*, Det kgl. n. Vid. selsk. Skr. 1917 (Trondheim: Aktietrykkeriet, 1918).

—, *Über die Augentypen in Norwegen und ihre Vererbungsverhältnisse*, Skr. D. n. Vidensk. Akad. MN kl. 1926, no. 9 (Oslo: I kommisjon hos Dybwad, 1926).

— and Ebenezer Howard, *Havebyer og jordbruksbyer i Norge* (Kristiania: Aschehoug, 1921).

— and Kristian E. Schreiner, *Die Somatologie der Norweger*, Skr. D. n. Vidensk. Akad. MN kl. (Oslo: I kommisjon hos Dybwad, 1929).

Brøgger, Anton W., *Den arktiske stenalder i Norge*, Skrifter, Videnskabselskapet i Kristiania, HF-kl. (Kristiania: I kommisjon hos Dybwad, 1909).

—, *Det norske folk i Oldtiden* (Oslo: ISKF, 1925).

—, 'Nasjonen og fortiden', *Samtiden*, Vol. 39 (1928), pp. 481-94.

—, *Norges Studier over Norges steinalder* (Kristiania: I kommission hos Jacob Dybwad, 1906).

—, 'Viking', *Viking*, Vol. 1 (1937), p. 6.

Brøgger, Waldemar C., *Strandliniens beliggenhed under stenalderen i det sydøstlige Norge* (Kristiania: Aschehoug, 1905).

Bull, Edvard, et al. (ed.), *Norsk biografisk leksikon* (Oslo: Aschehoug, 1923-1983).

Christiansen, Odd Haakon and Wilhelm K. Støren, *Trondheim i går og i dag: 1914-1964* (Trondheim: I kommisjon hos F. Bruns bokhandels forlag, 1973).

Closson, Carlos C., 'A Critic of Anthropo-Sociology', *Journal of Political Economy*, Vol. 8, no. 3 (1900), pp. 397-410, http://dx.doi.org/10.1086/250683

Cole, Simon A., 'Twins, Twain, Galton, and Gilman: Fingerprinting, Individualization, Brotherhood, and Race in Pudd'nhead Wilson', *Configurations*, Vol. 15, no. 3 (2007), pp. 227-65, http://dx.doi.org/10.1353/con.0.0036

Daa, Ludvig Kr., *Nationaliternes udvikling* (Kristiania: J. Chr. Abelsteds, 1869).

—, *Have germanerne invandret til Skandinavien fra nord eller fra syd?* Særtrykk av Forhandlinger ved de Skandinaviske Naturforskeres Møde (Kristiania: [n. pub.], 1869).

—, *Udsigt over Ethnologien: Indbydelseskrift til den offentlige Examen i Christiania Kathedralskole* (Kristiania: Steenske bogtrykkeri, 1855).

Daae, Hans, *Militærlægers bidrag til norsk anthropologi* (Kristiania: Grøndahl, 1907).

Dahl, Hans Fredrik, *En fører blir til* (Oslo: Aschehoug, 1991).

Dahl, Helge, *Språkpolitikk og skolestell i Finnmark 1814-1905* (Oslo: Universitetsforlaget, 1957).

Dahl, Ottar, 'Noen etnografisk synspunkter hos Ludv. Kr. Daa', *Norsk geografisk tidsskrift*, Vol. 16, nos. 1-8 (1957), pp. 46-58.

—, *Norsk historieforskning i det 19. og 20. århundre* (Oslo: Universitetsforlaget, 1990).

Dalhaug, Ole, *Mål og meninger. Målreisning og nasjonaldannelse 1877-1887* (Oslo: Norges forskningsråd, 1995).

Deniker, Joseph, *The Races of Man* (London: Walter Scott, 1900). English transl. of his *Les races et les peuples de la terre: elements d'anthropologie et d'ethnographie* (Paris: Schleicher, 1900).

Emberland, Terje and Matthew Kott, *Himmlers Norge. Nordmenn i det storgermanske prosjekt* (Oslo: Aschehoug, 2012).

Emberland, Terje, *Religion og rase, Nyhedenskap og nazisme i Norge 1933-1945* (Oslo: Humanist, 2003).

Eriksen, Knut Einar and Einar Niemi, *Den finske fare. Sikkerhetsproblemer og minoritetspolitikk i nord 1860-1940* (Oslo: Universitetsforlaget, 1981).

Esricht, Daniel Frederik, *Om Hovedskallerne: Beenradene i vore gamle Gravhöie* (Copenhagen: [n. pub.], 1837).

Evang, Karl, *Rasepolitikk og Reaksjon*, Socialistiske lægers forenings småskrifter no. 2 (Oslo: Fram, 1934).

Evans, Andrew D., *Anthropology at War: World War I and the Science of Race in Germany* (Chicago, IL: University of Chicago Press, 2012).

—, 'Race made Visible: The transformation of Museum Exhibits in Early-Twentieth-Century German Anthropology', *German Studies Review*, Vol. 31, no. 1 (Feb., 2008), pp. 87-108.

Bjørg Evjen, 'Kort- og langskaller: fysisk-antropologisk forskning på samer, kvener og nordmenn', *Heimen*, Vol. 37, no. 4 (2000), pp. 273-92.

—, 'Measuring Heads: Physical Anthropological Research in North Norway', *Acta Borealia*, Vol.14, no.2 (1997), pp. 3-30, http://dx.doi.org/10.1080/08003839708580465

Fabian, Ann, *The Skull Collectors. Race, Science and America's Unburied Dead* (Chicago, IL: University of Chicago Press, 2010), http://dx.doi.org/10.7208/chicago/9780226233499.001.0001

Fischer, Eugen, 'Der untergang der Kulturvölker im Lichte der Biologie', *Volkausartung, Erbkunde, Eheberatung* (Dec. 1928).

—, *Die Rehobother Bastards und das Bastardierungsproblem beim Menschen* (Jena: G. Fischer, 1913).

Fredrickson, George M., *Racism: A Short History* (Princeton, NJ: Princeton University Press 2002).

Friedman, Robert Marc, *The Politics of Excellence: Behind the Nobel Prize in Science* (New York: Times Books, 2001).

Fulsås, Narve, *Historie og nasjon. Ernst Sars og striden om norsk kultur* (Oslo: Universitetsforlaget, 1999).

Fure, Jorunn Sem, *Universitetet i kamp: 1940-1945* (Oslo: Vidarforlaget, 2007).

—, *1940-1945: Universitetet i kamp*, Universitetet i Oslo 1811-2011, Vol. 4 (Oslo: Unipub, 2011).

Furset, Ole Jacob, *Arktisk steinalder og etnisitet. En forskningshistorisk analyse* (Master's thesis, University of Tromsø, 1994).

Fürst, Carl M., 'Gustav Adolph Guldberg', *Anatomischer Anzeiger*, Vol. 32, nos. 19/20 (1908), pp. 506-12.

Gissis, Snait B., 'Visualizing "Race" in the Eighteenth Century', *Historical Studies in the Natural Sciences*, Vol. 41, no. 1 (2011) pp. 41-103, http://dx.doi.org/10.1525/hsns.2011.41.1.41

Gjessing, Gutorm and Marie Krekling Johannessen, *De hundre år: Universitetets etnografiske museums historie 1857-1957* (Oslo: Universitetets etnografiske museum, 1957).

Gjessing, Rolv R., *Die Kautokeinolappen: eine anthropologische Studie* (Oslo: ISKF/Aschehoug, 1934).

Gondermann, Thomas, 'Progression and Retrogression: Herbert Spencer's Explanations of Social Inequality', *History of the Human Sciences*, Vol. 20, no. 3 (2007), pp. 21-40, http://dx.doi.org/10.1177/0952695107079332

Gould, Stephen Jay, *The Mismeasure of Man* (London: Penguin, 1996).

Guldberg, Gustav A., *Anatomisk-anthropologiske Undersøgelser af de lange Extremitetknokler fra Norges Befolkning i Oldtid og Middelalder, 1, Undersøgelsesmethoderne, Laarbenene og Legemshøiden*, Skr. Vidensk. Selsk. Christiania MN kl. 1901 (Kristiania: Brøggers bogtrykkeri, 1901).

—, *Die Menschenknochen des Osebergschiffs aus dem jüngeren Eisenalter: eine anatomisch-anthropologische Untersuchung*, Skr. Vidensk. Selsk. Christiania MN kl. 1907 (Kristiania: I komission hos Dybwad, 1907).

—, 'Fra det anatomiske institut ved det kgl. Fredriks universitet', *Foreningen til norske fortidsmindesmærkers bevaring, Aarsberetning for 1900* (Kristiania: 1901).

—, *Om Darwinismen og dens rækkevidde: en almenfattelig fremstilling af nedstamningstheorien og Darwins lære om det naturlige udvalg samt udviklingstheorien: med kritiske bemærkninger* (Kristiania: Dybwad, 1890)

—, *Om det anatomiske studium: Tale tale ved tiltrædelsen af professoratet i anatomi ved Christiania universitet d. 7de septbr. 1888* (Kristiania: I kommission hos Dybwad, 1888).

—, *Om en samlet anthropologisk undersøgelse af Norges befolkning*, Christiania videnskabs-selskabs forhandlinger for 1904, no. 11 (Kristiania: I commission hos Dybwad, 1904).

—, 'Skeletfundet paa Rør i Ringsaker og Rør kirke', *Christiania videnskabs-selskabs forhandlinger*, no. 9 (1895).

—, 'Udsigt over en del fund af gammelnorske kranier', *Nordisk medicinsk arkiv*, Vol. 30, no. 13 (1897), pp. 1-6, http://dx.doi.org/10.1111/j.0954-6820.1897.tb00424.x

Günther, Hans F. K., *Rassenkunde Europas* (München: Lehmanns Verlag, 1929).

Gylseth, Christopher, Hals, 'Jon Alfred Mjøen', in *Norsk biografisk leksikon*, http://nbl.snl.no/Jon_Alfred_Mjøen

Haavardsholm, Jørgen, *Vikingtiden som 1800-tallskonstruksjon* (Oslo: University of Oslo, 2004).

Haave, Per, *Sterilisering av tatere 1934-1977: En historisk undersøkelse av lov og praksis* (Oslo: The Norwegian Research Council, 2000).

—, 'Sterilization Under the Swastika: The Case of Norway', *International Journal of Mental Health*, Vol. 36, no. 1 (2007), pp. 45-57, http://dx.doi.org/10.2753/imh0020-7411360104

—, 'Zwangssterilisierung in Norwegen—eine wohlfahrtsstaatliche Politik in sozialdemokratischer Regie?', *NORDEUROPA forum, Zeitschrift für Politik, Wirtschaft und Kultur,* Vol. 11, no. 2 (2001), pp. S55-78.

Hagemann, Gro, *Aschehougs Norgeshistorie,* Vol. 9 (Oslo: Aschehoug, 1997).

Hansen, Andreas M., *Landnåm i Norge. En udsigt over bosætningens historie* (Kristiania: Fabritius, 1904).

—, *Menneskeslektens ælde* (Kristiania: Jacob Dybwad, 1899).

—, *Norsk folkepsykologi: med politisk kart over Skandinavien* (Kristiania: Jakob Dybwad, 1899).

—, *Om determinisme og moral. Foredrag den 27. januar 1886. Den frisinnede studenterforenings foredrag og diskussioner I* (Kristiania: [n. pub.], 1886).

—, 'To grundraser i det danske folk', *Nyt magasin for naturvidenskaberne,* Vol. 53, no. 3 (1915), pp. 203-67.

Hansen, Lars Ivar and Einar Niemi, 'Samisk forskning ved et tidsskifte: Jens Andreas Friis og lappologien—vitenskap og politikk?', in Eli Seglen (ed.), *Vitenskap, teknologi og samfunn* (Oslo: Cappelen akademisk forlag, 2001), pp. 350-77.

Hansen, Søren 'Om Grundracer i Norden', *Forhandlinger ved De skandinaviske naturforskeres 16. møte i Kristiania den 10.-15. juli 1916* (Kristiania: A. W. Brøggers boktrykkeri, 1918), pp. 822-38.

Hansen, Tor Ivar, *Et skandinavistisk nasjonsbyggingsprosjekt: Skandinavisk selskab (1864-1971)* (Master's thesis, University of Oslo, 2008).

Harwood, Jonathan, *Styles of Scientific Thought: The German Genetics Community 1900-1933* (Chicago, IL: University of Chicago Press, 1993).

Hecht, Jennifer Michael, 'A Vigilant Anthropology: Léonce Manouvrier and the Disappearing Numbers', *Journal of the History of the Behavioral Sciences,* Vol. 33, no. 3 (1997), pp. 221-40, http://dx.doi.org/10.1002/(sici)1520-6696(199722)33:3<221::aid-jhbs2>3.3.co;2-x

—, 'The Solvency of Metaphysics: The Debate over Racial Science and Moral Philosophy in France, 1890-1919', *Isis,* Vol. 90, no. 1 (1999), pp. 1-24, http://dx.doi.org/10.1086/384239

Heiberg, Jacob, 'Om et biologisk laboratorium', *Norsk Magazin for lægevidenskaben,* no. 1 (1884), pp. 65-70.

Helliksen,Wenche, *Evolusjonisme i norsk arkeologi: Diskutert med utgangspunkt i A.W. Brøggers hovedverk 1909-25* (Oslo: Universitetets oldsaksamling, 1996).

Hestmark, Geir, 'En nasjonal-evolusjonær katekisme', *Norsk litteraturhistorie, sakprosa fra 1750 til 1995,* Vol. 1: 1750-1920 (Oslo: Universitetsforlaget, 1998), pp. 708-17.

Holck, Per, *Den fysiske antropologi i Norge. Fra anatomisk institutts historie 1815-1990* (Oslo: Anatomisk institutt, University of Oslo, 1990).

Hopstock, H., *Det anatomiske institutt 23. Januar 1815-23. Januar 1915* (Kristiania: I kommission hos Aschehoug, 1915).

Horsman, Reginald, 'Origins of Racial Anglo-Saxonism in Great Britain before 1850', *Journal of the History of Ideas,* Vol. 37, no. 3 (1976), pp. 387-410, http://dx.doi.org/10.2307/2708805

—, *Race and Manifest Destiny: The Origins of American Racial Anglo-Saxonism* (Cambridge, MA: Harvard University Press, 1981).

Hovdhaugen, Even, et al. (eds.), *The History of Linguistics in the Nordic Countries* (Helsinki: Societas Scientiarum Fennica, 2000).

Hudson, Nicholas, 'From "Nation" to "Race": The Origin of Racial Classification in Eighteenth-Century Thought', *Eighteenth-Century Studies*, Vol. 29, no. 3 (1996), pp. 247-64, http://dx.doi.org/10.1353/ecs.1996.0027

Hviid Nielsen, Torben, Arve Monsen and Tore Tennøe, *Livets tre og kodenes kode. Fra genetikk til bioteknologi Norge 1900-2000* (Oslo: Gyldendal akademisk, 2000).

Jansen, Jan, 'Minnetale over Alette Schreiner', *Årbok, Det Norske videnskaps-akademi* (Oslo: I kommisjon hos J. Dybwad, 1953), pp. 59-67.

—, 'Alette Schreiner', in *Norsk biografisk leksikon* (Oslo: Aschehoug, 1954), pp. 520-22.

Jernsletten, Regnor, *Samebevegelsen i Norge* (Tromsø: Senter for samiske studier, University of Tromsø, 1998).

Johannessen, Axel, 'Carl Oscar Eugen Arbo', *Tidsskrift for den norske lægeforening*, Vol. 26 (1906), pp. 516-19.

Jølle, Harald Dag, 'Nordpolens naboer', in Einar-Arne Drivenes and Harald Dag Jølle (ed.), *Norsk polarhistorie 2* (Oslo: Gyldendal, 2004), pp. 259-326.

Karcher, Nicola, 'Schirmorganisation der Nordischen Bewegung: Der Nordische Ring und seine Repräsentanten in Norwegen', *NORDEUROPA forum*, Vol. 19, no. 1 (2009), pp. 7-35.

Kevles, Daniel J., *In the Name of Eugenics: Genetics and the Uses of Human Heredity* (Berkeley, CA: University of California Press, 1986).

Keyser, Rudolf, *Norges Historie* (Kristiania: P. T. Malling, 1866-1870).

—, *Samlede afhandlinger* (Kristiania: P. T. Malling, 1868).

Kjeldstadli, Knut, 'Biologiens tid. Randbemerkninger om viten og venstrestat', in Erik Rudeng, ed., *Kunnskapsregimer* (Oslo: Pax, 1999), pp. 145-51.

Knut Kjeldstadli, 'Andreas M. Hansen', in *Norsk biografisk leksikon*, http://nbl.snl.no/Andreas_Hansen

Kr. Daa, Ludvig, *Udsigt over Ethnologien: Indbydelseskrift til den offentlige Examen i Christiania Kathedralskole* (Kristiania: Steenske bogtrykkeri, 1855).

Kühl, Stefan, *Die Internationale der Rassisten* (Frankfurt am Main: Campus, 1997).

Kyllingstad, Jon Røyne and Thor Inge Rørvik, *1870-1911: Vitenskapenes universitet*, Universitet i Oslo 1811-2011, Vol. 2 (Oslo: Unipub, 2011).

Kyllingstad, Jon Røyne, *Kortskaller og langskaller: Norsk fysisk antropologi i Norge og striden om det nordiske herremennesket* (Oslo: Spartacus, 2004).

—, *'Menneskeåndens universalitet' Instituttet for sammenlignende kulturforskning 1917-1940. Ideene, institusjonen og forskningen* (Ph.D. thesis, University of Oslo, 2008).

—, 'Norwegian Physical Anthropology and the Idea of a Nordic Master Race', *Current Anthropology*, Vol. 53, no. S5 (2012), pp. S46-S56, http://dx.doi.org/10.1086/662332

—, 'The Concept of a Lappish Race: Norwegian Research on Sami Skeletal Remains in the Interwar Year', in B. J. Sellevold (ed.), *Old Bones—Osteoarchaeology in Norway: Yesterday, Today and Tomorrow* (Oslo: Novus, 2014), pp. 287-304.

Larsen, C. F., *Nordlandsbefolkningen: antropologiske Undersøgelser 1904*, Skr. Viden. selsk. Christiania MN kl.1905 (Kristiania: I kommission hos Dybwad, 1905).

—, *Norske kranietyper: efter Studier i Universitetets anatomiske Instituts Kraniesamling*. Skr. Vidensk. Selsk. Christiania MN kl., 1901, no. 5 (Kristiania: Videnskabsselskabet, 1901).

Larsen, C. F., *Trønderkranier og trøndertyper*, Skr. Viden. selsk. Christiania MN kl. 1903 (Kristiania: I kommission hos Dybwad, 1903).

Larsen, Stian, *Med dragning mot nord. Gerhard Schøning som historiker* (Master's thesis, University of Tromsø, 1999).

Latham, Robert G., *Norway and the Norwegians* (London: Bentley, 1840).

Lenoir, Timothy, 'Kant, Blumenbach, and Vital Materialism in German Biology', *Isis*, Vol. 71, no. 1 (1980), pp. 77-108, http://dx.doi.org/10.1086/352408

Lettevall, Rebecka, Geert Somsen and Sven Widmalm (eds.), *Neutrality in Twentieth-Century Europe: Intersections of Science, Culture, and Politics after the First World War* (New York: Routledge, 2012).

Liestøl, Knut, *Moltke Moe* (Oslo: Aschehoug, 1949).

Lipphardt, Veronika, 'Isolates and Crosses in Human Population Genetics; or: A Contextualization of German Race Science', *Current Anthropology*, Vol. 53, no. S5 (2012). pp. S69-S82, http://dx.doi.org/10.1086/662574

Livi, Ridolfo, *Antropometria Militare* (Roma, Presso il Giornale medico del Regio Esercito, 1896-1905).

Ljungström, Olof, *Oscariansk antropologi. Etnografi, förhistoria och rasforskning under sent 1800-tal* (Hedemora: Gidlund, 2004).

Llobera, Josep R., 'The Fate of Anthroposociology in L'année Sociologique', *Jaso*, Vol. 27, no. 3 (1996), pp. 235-51.

Lundborg, Herman, 'Rassen- und Gesellschafts-probleme in Genetischer und Medizinischer Beleuchtung', *Hereditas*, Vol. 1, no. 2 (1920), pp. 135-77, http://dx.doi.org/10.1111/j.1601-5223.1920.tb02457.x

—, *Medizinisch-biologische Familienforschungen innerhalb eines 2232-köpfigen Bauerngeschlechtes in Schweden (Provinz Blekinge)* (Jena: Fischer, 1913).

Lunden, Kåre, 'History and Society', in William Hubbard, et al. (eds.), *Making a Historical Culture: Historiography in Norway* (Oslo: Scandinavian University Press, 1995), pp. 15-51.

Manias, Chris, 'The *Race prussienne* Controversy: Scientific Internationalism and the Nation', *Isis*, Vol. 100, no. 4 (2009), pp. 733-57, http://dx.doi.org/10.1086/652017

Martin, Rudolf, *Lehrbuch der Anthropologie in systematischer Darstellung mit besonderer Berücksichtigung der anthropologischen Methoden* (Jena: Gustav Fischer, 1914; 2nd ed. 1928).

Massin, Benoit 'From Virchow to Fischer: Physical Anthropology and "Modern Race Theories" in Wilhelmine Germany', in George W. Stocking, Jr., (ed.), *Volksgeist as Method and Ethic* (Madison, WI: University of Wisconsin, 1996).

McMahon, Richard, 'Anthropological Race Psychology 1820-1945: A Common European System of Ethnic Identity Narratives', *Nations and Nationalism*, Vol. 15, no. 4 (2009), pp. 575-96, http://dx.doi.org/10.1111/j.1469-8129.2009.00393.x

—, *The Races of Europe: Anthropological Race Classification of Europeans 1839-1939* (Ph.D. thesis, European University Institute, 2007).

Mjøen, Jon Alfred, *Racehygiene* (Oslo: Dybwad, 1914; 2nd ed. 1938).

Mohr, Otto Lous, 'Kristian Emil Schreiner', in Jan Jansen and Alf Brodal (eds.), *Aspects of Cerebellar Anatomy* (Oslo: Johan Grundt Tanum, 1954).

Monsen, Arve, *Politisk biologi. Opprettelsen av Institutt for arvelighetsforskning i 1916* (Oslo: TMV, 1997).

Mosse, George L., *The Crisis of German Ideology: Intellectual Origins of the Third Reich* (London: Weidenfeld and Nicolson, 1964).

—, *Toward the Final Solution: A History of European Racism* (New York: Howard Fertig, 1997).

Munch, P. A., *Om den saakaldte nyere historiske Skole i Norge* (Kristiania: Tønsberg, 1853).

—, *Skandinavismen nærmere undersøgt med Hensyn til Nordens Ældre national og litteraire Forhold* (Kristiania: Johan Dahls, 1849).

—, *Verdenshistoriens vigtigste Begivenheder: fra de ældste Tider indtil den franske Revolution i kortfattet Fremstilling* (Kristiania: Cappelen, 1840).

Mühlmann, Wilhelm E., *Geschichte der Anthropologie* (Frankfurt am Main: Athenäum Verlag, 1968).

Myhre, Jan Eivind (ed.), *Historie, etnisitet og politikk* (Tromsø: Institutt for historie, University of Tromsø, 2000).

Nielsen, Yngvar, *Universitetets ethnografiske samlinger 1857-1907* (Kristiania: Fabritius og sønner, 1907).

Nilsson, Sven, *Skandinaviska Nordens Ur-Invånare. Ett försök i komparativa Ethnografien och ett Bidrag til Menniskoslägtets utvecklings historia* (Lund: Berlingska Boktryckeriet, 1838-1843).

—, *Skandinaviska Nordens Ur-Invånare, ett forsök i komparativa Ethnografien och ett bidrag til menniskoslägtets utvecklings historia*, Vol. 1 (Stockholm: P. A. Norstedt & Söner, 1866).

Nordal, Inger, Dag O. Hessen and Thore Lie, *Kristine Bonnevie: Et forskerliv* (Oslo: Cappelen Damm, 2012).

Norsk tidsskrift for militærmedicin. Kristiania. First issue: 1897.

Nyhart, Lynn K., *Biology Takes Form: Animal Morphology and the German Universities, 1800-1900* (Chicago, IL: University of Chicago Press, 1995).

Olsen, Bjørnar, 'Kjelmøyfunnenes (virknings) historie og arkeologi', *Viking*, Vol. 54 (1991), pp. 65-88.

Om pressefrihedens grænser i tilknytning til diskussionen om justitsforfølgningen mod Hans Jæger. Den frisinnede studenterforenings foredrag og diskussioner II (Kristiania: I kommissjon hos Huseby & Co., 1886).

Pedersen, Helge, '*Gud har skapat svarta och vita människor, jäfvulen derimot halfnegeren'. En komparativ analyse av Jon Alfred Mjøen og Herman Lundborgs rasehygieniske ideer i Norge og Sverige. Ca. 1900-1935* (Master's thesis, University of Oslo, 2003).

Peel, J. D. Y., *Herbert Spencer: The Evolution of a Sociologist* (Aldershot: Gregg Revivals, 1992).

Penka, Karl, *Die Herkunft der Arier. Neue Beiträge zur historischen Anthropologie der europäischen Völker* (Vienna: K. Prochaska, 1886).

Pettersen, Trond Werner, *Fra dannelse til forskning: filologien ved Det kgl. Fredriks Universitet 1811-1864* (Master's thesis, University of Oslo, 2007).

Pickering, Mary, *Auguste Comte: An Intellectual Biography* (Cambridge: Cambridge University Press, 1993).

Prichard, James Cowles, *Researches into the Physical History of Mankind*. Vol. 2 (London: Sherwood, Gilbert, and Piper, 1837).

Proctor, Robert, 'From *Anthropologie* to *Rassenkunde* in the German Anthropological Tradition', in George W. Stocking, Jr. (ed.), *Bones, Bodies, Behavior* (Madison, WI: University of Wisconsin Press, 1988), pp. 138-79.

Retzius, Anders, *Ethnologische Schriften von Anders Retzius. Nach dem Tode des Verfassers gesammelt* (Stockholm: P. A. Norstedt & Söner, 1864).

—, *Om formen af nordboernes cranier. Aftryckt ur Förhandl. vid Naturforskarnes Möte i Stockholm år 1842* (Stockholm: P. A. Norstedt, 1843).

—, *Phrénologien bedömd från en anatomisk ståndpunkt. Föredrag hållet vid Skandinaviska Naturforskare-Sällskapets möte i Köpenhamn i Juli 1847* (Copenhagen: Trier, 1848).

Retzius, Gustav, 'Blick på den fysiska antropologiens historia', *Ymer*, Vol. 16, no. 4 (1896), pp. 221-45, http://runeberg.org/ymer/1896/0230.html

—, 'Crania Suecica Antigua', *Ymer*, Vol. 20, no. 76 (1900), pp. 76-87.

— and Carl M. Fürst, *Anthropologia suecica: beiträge zur Anthropologie der Schweden nach den auf Veranstaltung der schwedischen Gesellschaft für Anthropologie und Geographie in den Jahren 1897 und 1898 ausgeführten Erhebungen* (Stockholm: [n. pub.], 1902).

Rian, Øystein, 'Norway in Union with Denmark', in William H. Hubbard, et al. (eds.), *Making a Historical Culture: Historiography in Norway* (Oslo: Scandinavian University Press, 1995), pp. 132-55.

Ripley, William Z., *The Races of Europe. A Sociological Study* (London: Kegan Paul, Trench, Trübner & Co., 1899).

Rolfsen, Nordahl, et al. (eds.), *Norge i det nittende aarhundrede*, 2 Vols. (Kristiania: Cammermeyer, 1900).

Roll-Hansen, Nils, 'Den norske debatten om rasehygiene', *Historisk tidsskrift*, Vol. 59 (1980), pp. 259-83.

—, 'Eugenics before World War II: The Case of Norway', *History and Philosophy of the Life Sciences*, Vol. 2, no. 2 (1980), pp. 269-98.

—, 'Eugenics in Scandinavia after 1945: Change of Values and Growth in Knowledge', *Scandinavian Journal of History*, Vol. 24, no. 2 (1999), pp. 199-13, http://dx.doi.org/10.1080/03468759950115809

—, 'Geneticists and the Eugenics Movement in Scandinavia', *The British Journal for the History of Science*, Vol. 22, no. 3 (1989), pp. 335-46.

—, 'Norwegian Eugenics: Sterilization as social reform', in Broberg and Roll-Hansen (eds.), *Eugenics and the Welfare State*, pp. 151-94.

Rowley-Conwy, Peter, *From Genesis to Prehistory: The Archaeological Three Age System and its Contested Reception in Denmark, Britain, and Ireland* (Oxford: Oxford University Press, 2007).

—, 'The Concept of Prehistory and the Invention of the Terms "Prehistoric" and "Prehistorian":TheScandinavianOrigin,1833-1850',*EuropeanJournalofArchaeology*, Vol. 9, no. 1 (2006), pp. 103-30, http://dx.doi.org/10.1177/1461957107077709

Saller, Karl, 'Die entstehung der "nordischen Rasse"', *Zeitschrift für die gesamte anatomie/Zeitschrift für anatomie und entwicklungsgeschichte*, Vol. 83, no. 4 (1927), pp. 411-590, http://dx.doi.org/10.1007/bf02117869

Sanness, John, *Patrioter, Intelligens og Skandinaver* (Oslo: Universitetsforlaget, 1959).

Saxlund, Sigurd, *Rase og kultur. Raseblandingens følger* (Oslo: Stenersen, 1940).

Schanche, Audhild, *Graver i ur og berg. Samisk gravskikk og religion 1000 f.kr. til 1700 e. Kr.* (Ph.D. thesis, University of Tromsø, 1997).

—, *Graver i Ur og Berg. Samisk gravskikk og religion fra forhistorisk til nyere tid* (Karasjok: Davvi girji, 2000).

—, 'Rase, etnisitet og samisk forhistorie: et forskningshistorisk tilbakeblikk', in Jan Eivind Myhre (ed.), *Historie, etnisitet og politikk*, pp. 3-18.

—, 'Saami Skulls, Anthropological Race Research and the Repatriation Question in Norway', in Cressida Fforde, Jane Hubert and Paul Tumbull (eds.), *The Dead and their Possessions. The Repatriation in Principle, Policy and Practice* (London: Routledge, 2002), pp. 47-58, http://dx.doi.org/10.4324/9780203165775

—, 'Samiske hodeskaller og den antropologiske raseforskningen i Norge', appendix to I. Lønnig, M. Guttor, J. Holme, et al. (eds.), *Innstilling fra Utvalg for vurdering av retningslinjer for bruk og forvalting av skjelettmateriale ved Anatomisk institutt* (Oslo: University of Oslo, 1998).

Scheidt, Walter, 'Die rassischen Verhältnisse in Nordeuropa nach dem gegenwärtigen Stand der Forschung', *Zeitschrift für Morphologie und Anthropologie*, Vol. 28, nos. 1/2 (1930), pp. 1-197.

—, *Die rassischen Verhältnisse in Nordeuropa* (Stuttgart: Schweizerbart, 1930).

Schmidt-Nielsen, S., 'Halfdan Bryn: Minnetale i Fellesmøtet 10 de april 1933', *Det kgl. n. Vid. Selsk. Forhandlinger*, Vol. 6, no. 16 (Trondheim: I kommisjon hos F. Bruns bokhandel, 1933), pp. 56-65.

Schreiner, Alette, *Anthropologische Lokaluntersuchungen in Norge, Hellemo (Tysfjordlappen)*, Skr. D. n. Vidensk. Akad. MN kl. Oslo 1932 (Oslo: I kommission hos Dybwad, 1932).

—, *Anthropologische Lokaluntersuchungen in Norge. Hellemo (Tysfjordlappen)* (Oslo: ISKF/Aschehoug, 1932).

—, *Anthropologische Lokaluntersuchungen in Norge. Valle, Hålandsdal und Eidfjord*, Skr. D. n. Vidensk. Akad. MN kl.1929 (Oslo: I kommisjon hos Dybwad, 1930).

—, *Anthropologische studien an Norwegische Frauen*, Skr D. n. Vidensk. Selsk. MN kl 1924 (Kristiania: I Kommisjon bei Jacob Dybwad, 1924).

—, *Die Nord-norweger*, Skr. D. n. Vidensk. Akad. MN kl. (Oslo: I kommisjon hos Dybwad, 1929).

—, 'Livsutvikling og livsanskuelse', *Kirke og kultur*, Vol. 36 (1929), pp. 453-74.

—, *Skapende kræfter i livsformenes historie; utsyn over et centralt omraade av den almindelige biologi med særlig blik paa dyreriket* (Kristiania: Aschehoug, 1912).

—, *Slegtslivet hos menneskene* (Kristiania: Aschehoug, 1914).

—, 'Zur erblichkeit der Kopfform', *Genetica* (1923), Vol. 5, nos. 5-6 (1923), pp. 385-454, http://dx.doi.org/10.1007/bf01507854

Schreiner, Kristian E. *Anthropological Studies in Sogn*, Skr. D. n. Vidensk. Akad. MN kl.19 (Oslo: I kommisjon hos Jacob Dybwad, 1951).

Schreiner, Kristian E., *Crania norvegica I* (Oslo: ISKF/Aschehoug 1939).

—, *Crania norvegica II* (Oslo: ISKF/Aschehoug 1946).

—, 'Europas menneskeraser', *Universitetets radioforedrag: Mennesket som ledd i naturen* (Oslo: [n. pub.], 1932), pp. 127-45.

—, 'Hva er nordisk rase?' *Forhandlinger*, Det norske vitenskapsakademi (Oslo: [n. pub.], 1946), pp. 23-24.

—, 'Minnetale over divisjonslæge Halfdan Bryn', *Årbok, Det Norske videnskaps-akademi. I MN kl.* (1933) (Oslo: Videnskaps-akademiet, 1934), pp. 55-59.

—, *Zur Osteologie der Lappen II* (Oslo: ISKF/Aschehoug, 1935).

Schroeder-Gudehus, Brigitte, 'Challenge to Transnational Loyalties: International Scientific Organizations after the First World War', *Science Studies*, Vol. 3, no. 2 (1973), http://dx.doi.org/10.1177/030631277300300201

Shetelig, Haakon, *Norske museers historie* (Oslo: J. W. Cappelens, 1944).

Simpson, Donald, 'Phrenology and the Neurosciences: Contributions of F. J. Gall and J. G. Spurzheim', *ANZ Journal of Surgery*, Vol. 75, no. 6 (2005), pp. 475-82, http://dx.doi.org/10.1111/j.1445-2197.2005.03426.x

Skorgen, Torgeir, *Rasenes oppfinnelse: rasetenkningens historie* (Oslo: Spartacus, 2002).

Smith, P., Lorenz, *Kautokeino og Kautokeino-lappene: en historisk og ergologisk regionalstudie.* (Oslo: ISKF/Aschehoug, 1938).

Solberg, Ole M., *Eisenzeitfunde aus Ostfinmarken* (Kristiania: I Kommission bei Dybwad, 1909).

Stang, Fredrik, *De norske akademiplaner. Foredrag holdt i Bergen 30. januar 1918* (Kristiania: [n. pub.], 1918).

—, 'The Institute for Comparative Research in Human Culture: Its Origin and Aims', in Instituttet for sammenlignende kulturforskning, *Four Introductory Lectures/ Quatre conferénces d'inauguration/Vier Einleitungs- vorlesungen* (Oslo: ISKF and Cambridge, MA: Harvard University Press, 1925), pp. 1-28.

—, *Verdensakademier, Norden som sentralsted for internationalt videnskapelig arbeide* (Kristiania. Aschehoug, 1918).

Staum, Martin, 'Nature and Nurture in French Ethnography and Anthropology, 1859-1914', *Journal of the History of Ideas*, Vol. 65, no. 3 (2004), pp. 475-95, http://dx.doi.org/10.1353/jhi.2005.0009

Stenseth, Bodil, *En norsk elite: nasjonsbyggerne på Lysaker 1890-1940* (Oslo: Aschehoug, 1983).

Stocking, Jr., George W., 'What's in a Name? The Origins of the Royal Anthropological Institute (1837-71)', *Man*, New Series, Vol. 6, no. 3 (1971), pp. 369-90, http://dx.doi.org/10.2307/2799027

Storli, Inger, 'Fra "kultur" til "natur". Om konstitueringa av den "arktiske" steinalderen', *Viking*, Vol. 56 (1993), pp. 7-22.

246   *Measuring the Master Race*

Studentene fra 1882 (Kristiania: [n. pub.], 1907).

Studentene fra 1882 (Kristiania: [n. pub.], 1932).

Thomsen, Ann, 'Issues at Stake in Eighteenth-Century Racial Classification', *Cromohs*, no. 8 (2003), pp. 1-20.

Thue, Fredrik, *In Quest of a Democratic Social Order. The Americanization of Norwegian Social Scholarship 1918-1970* (Ph.D. thesis, University of Oslo, 2005).

Torgersen, Johan, *Mennesket: Vidunder og problembarn i livets historie* (Oslo: Aschehoug, 1956).

—, 'Minnetale over Kristian Emil Schreiner', Årbok, Det Norske videnskaps-akademi (Oslo: I kommisjon hos J. Dybwad, 1958), pp. 59-71.

Trigger, Bruce, *A History of Archaeological Thought* (Cambridge: Cambridge University Press, 2006), http://dx.doi.org/10.1017/cbo9780511813016

Undseth, Ingvald, *Om et norsk National-Museum* (Kristiania: Cammermeyer, 1885).

UNESCO, *Statement on the Nature of Race and Race Differences* (Paris: UNESCO, 1951), http://unesdoc.unesco.org/images/0015/001577/157730eb.pdf

Vogt, Ragnar, *Arvelighetslære og racehygiene* (Kristiania: Cammermeyer, 1913).

Voldgiftssag mellem Norge og Sverige angaaende renbeite. Første afdeling angaaende tilveiebringelse af oplysninger og bevisligheder. Forhandlinger og beslutninger i Kjøbenhavn 1909-1910 (Kristiania: S. M. Brydes boktrykkeri, 1910).

Walløe, Lars, 'Carl Arbo', in *Norsk biografisk leksikon*, https://nbl.snl.no/Carl_Arbo

—, 'Otto Lous Mohr', in *Norsk biografisk leksikon*, http://nbl.snl.no/Otto_Lous_Mohr

Weikart, Richard, 'The Origins of Social Darwinism in Germany, 1859-1895', *Journal of the History of Ideas*, Vol. 54, no. 3 (1993), pp. 469-88, http://dx.doi.org/10.2307/2710024

Weindling, Paul, 'Weimar Eugenics: The Kaiser Wilhelm Institute for Anthropology, Human Heredity and Eugenics in Social Context', *Annals of Science*, Vol. 42, no. 3 (1985), pp. 303-18, http://dx.doi.org/10.1080/00033798500200221

Weiss, Sheila Faith, 'The Race Hygiene Movement in Germany', *Osiris*, 2nd series, Vol. 3 (1987), pp. 193-236, http://dx.doi.org/10.1086/368666

Werenskiold, Werner, 'Andreas M. Hansen', in *Norsk biografisk leksikon*, Vol. 5 (Oslo: Aschehoug, 1931), pp. 358-63.

Williams, Elisabeth A., 'Anthropological Institutions in Nineteenth-Century France', *Isis*, Vol. 76, no. 3 (1985), pp. 331-48, http://dx.doi.org/10.1086/353877

Worsaae, J. J. A., *Om en forhistorisk, saakaldet 'tydsk' Befolkning i Danmark: med Hensyn til Nutidens politiske Bevægelser* (Kjøbenhavn: Reitzel, 1849).

Zola-Morgan, S., 'Localization of Brain Function: The Legacy of Franz Joseph Gall (1758-1828)', *Annual Review of Neuroscience*, Vol. 18, no. 1 (1995), pp. 359-83, http://dx.doi.org/10.1146/annurev.neuro.18.1.359

Unpublished Sources and Abbreviations

American Philosophical Society Library, B: D27 Charles Davenport Papers.

Bryn's archive: NTNU University Library/Universitetsbiblioteket i Trondheim: Halfdan Bryn's private archive.

C. M. Fürst's archive: Lund University Libraries/Lunds universitetsbibliotek: Carl M. Fürst's correspondence with Kristian Emil Schreiner and Halfdan Bryn.

ISKF-archive: The National Archives in Oslo/Riksarkivet, Private archive 424; Institute for Comparative Research in Human Culture.

Norwegian Geographical Society/ Norsk Geografisk Selskap, archive: Andreas M. Hansen's papers.

RA, S-2536 UiO Medfak: The National Archives in Oslo/Riksarkivet, The archive of the Medical Faculty at the University of Kristiania .

Stort. Forh.: Norwegian Parliamentary proceedings/ Stortingsforhandlinger.

The University of Oslo/Universitetet i Oslo, Institute of Basic Medical Sciences/ Institutt for medisinske basalfag, Anatomy Department/avdeling for anatomi, archive of the Schreiner collections/De schreinerske samlinger.

University of Kristiania, annual reports /Det kongelige norske Frederiks Universitets Aarsberetninger 1889-1930s (Kristiania: Universitetet, 1889-1894).

Uppsala University Library, Manuscript Collections/Uppsala universitetsbibliotek, handskriftsavdelningen: Herman Lundborg's correspondence with Halfdan Bryn and Kristian Emil Schreiner.

Vitak: The National Archives in Oslo/Riksarkivet, Private archive RA/PA-0682; Det Norske Videnskaps-Akademi/The Norwegian Academy of Science and Letters, board minutes/styreprotokoll 1910-1920, records/journal nr. 218, outgoing letters/kopibok 1919.

Index

This book need not end here...

At Open Book Publishers, we are changing the nature of the traditional academic book. The title you have just read will not be left on a library shelf, but will be accessed online by hundreds of readers each month across the globe. We make all our books free to read online so that students, researchers and members of the public who can't afford a printed edition can still have access to the same ideas as you.

Our digital publishing model also allows us to produce online supplementary material, including extra chapters, reviews, links and other digital resources. Find *Measuring the Master Race* on our website to access its online extras. Please check this page regularly for ongoing updates, and join the conversation by leaving your own comments:

http://www.openbookpublishers.com/isbn/9781909254541

If you enjoyed this book and feel that research like this should be available to all readers, regardless of their income, please think about donating to us. Our company is run entirely by academics, and our publishing decisions are based on intellectual merit and public value rather than on commercial viability. We do not operate for profit and all donations, as with all other revenue we generate, will be used to finance new Open Access publications.

For further information about what we do, to donate to OBP, to access additional digital material related to our titles or to order our books, please visit our website: http://www.openbookpublishers.com

Knowledge is for sharing

OpenBook
Publishers

www.ingramcontent.com/pod-product-compliance
Lightning Source LLC
Chambersburg PA
CBHW061005280326
41935CB00009B/845